Lecture Notes of the Institute for Computer Sciences, Social Informatics and Telecommunications Engineering

669

The LNICST series publishes ICST's conferences, symposia and workshops.
LNICST reports state-of-the-art results in areas related to the scope of the Institute.
The type of material published includes

- Proceedings (published in time for the respective event)
- Other edited monographs (such as project reports or invited volumes)

LNICST topics span the following areas:

- General Computer Science
- E-Economy
- E-Medicine
- Knowledge Management
- Multimedia
- Operations, Management and Policy
- Social Informatics
- Systems

William Knottenbelt · Dalila Ressi ·
Sabina Rossi · Francesco Tiezzi
Editors

Blockchain Technology and Emerging Applications

4th EAI International Conference, BlockTEA 2025
Venice, Italy, September 18–19, 2025
Proceedings

 Springer

Editors
William Knottenbelt (ID)
Imperial College London
London, UK

Dalila Ressi (ID)
Ca' Foscari University of Venice
Venice, Italy

Sabina Rossi (ID)
Ca' Foscari University of Venice
Venice, Italy

Francesco Tiezzi (ID)
University of Florence
Florence, Italy

ISSN 1867-8211   ISSN 1867-822X (electronic)
Lecture Notes of the Institute for Computer Sciences, Social Informatics
and Telecommunications Engineering
ISBN 978-3-032-12334-3   ISBN 978-3-032-12335-0 (eBook)
https://doi.org/10.1007/978-3-032-12335-0

This Springer imprint is published by the registered company Springer Nature Switzerland AG
The registered company address is: Gewerbestrasse 11, 6330 Cham, Switzerland

If disposing of this product, please recycle the paper.

Preface

This volume contains the proceedings of the 4th EAI International Conference on Blockchain Technology and Emerging Applications (BlockTEA 2025), held on September 18–19, 2025, in Venice, Italy. It was organized by the Ca' Foscari University of Venice and the University of Florence.

Motivated by the success of cryptocurrency, blockchain technology has been emerging as a technology with potential applications in various domains, including finance, computer science, electronic engineering, agriculture, healthcare and more. Blockchain-based emerging applications are able to aid the current systems and networks by leveraging the benefits provided by blockchain technology, such as a decentralized, immutable, and cryptographically secured ledger. The aim of BlockTEA is to bring together researchers and practitioners from different disciplines and discuss recent advancements in blockchain and its emerging applications.

BlockTEA 2025 solicited contributions in six different categories: (1) regular research papers; (2) short papers describing, e.g., case studies, calls for action, opinions, and visions; (3) systemization of knowledge papers; (4) tool papers describing technological artefacts; (5) oral presentations describing research in progress or already published works; and (6) posters. The contributions pertaining to the latter two categories are not included in the conference proceedings.

There were 45 submissions distributed over the different categories: 35 regular research papers, 5 short papers, 2 systemization of knowledge papers, 1 oral presentation, and 2 posters. The selection of the papers was entrusted to the Technical Program Committee (TPC), consisting of 26 members from 13 different countries.

The selection of the papers was done electronically, in two phases. In the first phase, which lasted four weeks, each submission was single-blind reviewed by at least three PC members. During the second phase, which lasted slightly less than one week, the papers were thoroughly discussed. The decision to accept or reject a paper was based not only on the reviews and scores but also on these in-depth discussions. In the end, 19 contributions were selected to be presented at the conference: 11 regular papers, 2 short papers, 1 systemization of knowledge paper, 2 oral presentations, and 3 posters.

In addition to the conference sessions dedicated to the accepted contributions, the event included two keynote talks. The two keynote speakers and the titles of their talks (whose abstracts are included in this volume) are listed below:

- Carlo Campajola (University College London, UK) – *The Economics of Transparency and Centralization in Blockchains: From Mining Cartels to Market Crises*;
- Andrea Vitaletti (Sapienza University of Rome, Italy) – *Beyond the chain: synergies between on-chain and off-chain worlds*.

As General and Program chairs, we also selected the best paper of BlockTEA 2025:

- *Optimizing Smart Contract Testing via Neural-MCTS Test Prioritization* by Morena Barboni, Filippo Lampa, Andrea Morichetta, and Andrea Polini.

We are grateful to all the people involved in BlockTEA 2025. In particular, we thank the authors for their submissions, the keynote speakers for accepting our invitation, the attendees of the conference for their participation, the TPC members and external reviewers for their work in reviewing submissions and participating in the discussions, the Web chairs Lorenzo Benetollo and Luca Olivieri for taking care of the conference's website, the Publicity and Social Media chairs Ivan Mercanti and Jessica Piccioni for taking care of the announcements, the Sponsorship and Exhibits chair Claudio Schifanella for managing sponsorships, the Publications chair Alessandro Marcelletti for support in finalizing the proceedings, the Local chairs Diletta Olliaro, Alvise Spanò, and Daria Smuseva for their excellent job, and the colleagues and students who volunteered their time to help. We also thank the providers of the EasyChair and Confy+ conference management systems, which were of great help in the submission and reviewing process, and in the preparation of the proceedings. We would also like to acknowledge the prompt and professional support from Springer, which published these proceedings in printed and electronic volumes as part of their LNICST book series.

Finally, we would like to thank the Dipartimento di Statistica, Informatica, Applicazioni "Giuseppe Parenti" of the Università degli Studi di Firenze for financial support, and the Dipartimento di Scienze Ambientali, Informatica e Statistica of Università Ca'Foscari di Venezia for providing administrative support.

September 2025

Sabina Rossi
General Chairs, BlockTEA 2025

Francesco Tiezzi
William Knottenbelt
Dalila Ressi
Program Chairs, BlockTEA 2025

Organization

Steering Committee

Sabina Rossi	Ca'Foscari University of Venice, Italy
Francesco Tiezzi	University of Florence, Italy
William Knottenbelt	Imperial College London, UK
Dalila Ressi	Ca'Foscari University of Venice, Italy

Organizing Committee

General Chairs

Sabina Rossi	Ca'Foscari University of Venice, Italy
Francesco Tiezzi	University of Florence, Italy

TPC Chairs

William Knottenbelt	Imperial College London, UK
Dalila Ressi	Ca'Foscari University of Venice, Italy

Sponsorship and Exhibit Chair

Claudio Schifanella	University of Turin, Italy

Local Chairs

Diletta Olliaro	Ca'Foscari University of Venice, Italy
Alvise Spanò	Ca'Foscari University of Venice, Italy
Daria Smuseva	Ca'Foscari University of Venice, Italy

Publicity & Social Media Chairs

Ivan Mercanti	University of Perugia, Italy
Jessica Piccioni	University of Camerino, Italy

Publications Chair

Alessandro Marcelletti   University of Camerino, Italy

Web Chairs

Lorenzo Benetollo   Ca'Foscari University of Venice, Italy
Luca Olivieri   Ca'Foscari University of Venice, Italy

Technical Program Committee

Massimo Bartoletti   Università degli Studi di Cagliari, Italy
Stefano Bistarelli   Università di Perugia, Italy
Andrea Bracciali   University of Turin, Italy
Michele Ciampi   University of Edinburgh, UK
Arlindo Conceicao   Federal University of São Paulo, Brazil
Claudio Di Ciccio   Utrecht University, The Netherlands
Michele Fabi   ENSAE CREST IP-PARIS, France
Jan Gorzny   Zircuit, Canada
Felix Härer   University of Applied Sciences Northwestern
                Switzerland, Switzerland
Dimitris Karakostas   University of Edinburgh, UK
Mario Larangeira   Tokyo Institute of Technology/IOHK, Japan
Alessandro Marcelletti   Università di Camerino, Italy
Somnath Mazumdar   Copenhagen Business School, Denmark
Weizhi Meng   Lancaster University, UK
Giovanni Meroni   Technical University of Denmark, Denmark
Jose L. Muñoz   Universitat Politècnica de Catalunya, Spain
Luca Olivieri   Ca' Foscari University of Venice, Italy
Cristina Pérez-Solà   Universitat Autònoma de Barcelona, Spain
Laura Ricci   Università di Pisa, Italy
Claudio Schifanella   Università di Torino, Italy
Stefan Schulte   TU Hamburg, Germany
Matteo Signorini   Nokia Bell Labs, USA
Alvise Spanò   Ca' Foscari University of Venice, Italy
Stefan Tai   TU Berlin, Germany
Edgar Weippl   University of Vienna, Austria
Katinka Wolter   Freie Universität Berlin, Germany

Additional Reviewers

Davide Basile
Fernando Castillo
Oscar Esparza
Tarek Galal
Marc Guzmán Albiol
Filippo Lampa
Chiara Luchini
Edoardo Marangone
Lorenzo Martinico
Ivan Mercanti
Jessica Piccioni
Jingxin Qiao
Luca Maria Tutino
Giannis Tzannetos

Kaynote Talks

The Economics of Transparency and Centralization in Blockchains: From Mining Cartels to Market Crises

Carlo Campajola

University College London, UK
`c.campajola@ucl.ac.uk`

In this talk, I will present our recent works studying the effects of centralization and transparency across multiple layers of blockchain-based systems. Centralization in blockchains can manifest differently across consensus, protocol, and application layers, challenging the simplistic view of decentralized versus centralized systems [1–2]. I will start by presenting our mathematical model of centralization effects in proof-of-work mining, which quantifies how hash rate concentration and block propagation dynamics affect fork rates and resource efficiency in distributed ledgers [3]. I will also discuss our method for the statistical detection of selfish mining in several proof-of-work blockchains, which offered the first empirical evidence of coordinated strategic behaviour in mining [4]. I will then move to the application layer to present our study on DEX liquidity dynamics during the Silicon Valley Bank collapse, where we focus on the counterintuitive effects of transparency during market stress [5]. We show how USDC's frequent disclosures led to swift market reactions and reduced dominance, while USDT's opacity provided relative stability through delayed information propagation. Our empirical analysis builds on a successful stream of financial economics literature about how transparency regimes affect market dynamics. Our work encourages a more critical assessment of the economics of blockchain-based systems. I will conclude by discussing my views on where we should look in the coming years to design appropriate risk management practices for users, developers and regulators, particularly in the context of the growing DeFi-TradFi integration.

References

1. Campajola, C., Cristodaro, R., De Collibus, F. M., Yan, T., Vallarano, N., Tessone, C. J.: The evolution of centralisation on cryptocurrency platforms. arXiv preprint arXiv:2206.05081 (2022)
2. De Collibus, F. M., Campajola, C., Tessone, C. J.: The microvelocity of money in Ethereum. EPJ Data Sci.**14**(1), 11 (2025)
3. Barucca, P., Campajola, C., Xu, J.: How the interplay between power concentration, competition, and propagation affects the resource efficiency of distributed ledgers. arXiv preprint arXiv:2411.10249 (2024)

4. Li, S. N., Campajola, C., Tessone, C. J.: Statistical detection of selfish mining in proof-of-work blockchain systems. Sci. Rep.**14**(1), 6251 (2024)
5. Cruz, W. H., Xu, J., Tasca, P., Campajola, C.: No Questions Asked: Effects of Transparency on Stablecoin Liquidity During the Collapse of Silicon Valley Bank. arXiv preprint arXiv:2407.11716 (2024)

Beyond the Chain: Synergies Between On-chain and Off-chain Worlds

Andrea Vitaletti

Sapienza University of Rome, Italy
`andrea.vitaletti@uniroma1.it`

As blockchain technology matures, the divide between on-chain and off-chain systems is evolving into a dynamic space of collaboration and innovation. The keynote explores the growing synergies between decentralized, trustless environments and the rich, data-intensive off-chain world. We will examine how hybrid architectures are enabling new use cases by bridging smart contracts with real-world data and processes. Topics include oracle networks and succinct zeroknowledge proofs (zk-proofs) for off-chain computation. While these technologies hold great promise real-world adoption, particularly of zk systems, still faces challenges in performance, tooling, and developer accessibility. By highlighting practical examples and emerging patterns, this talk offers a forward-looking perspective on how combining on-chain integrity, transparency, and incentive mechanisms with off-chain flexibility and computational power can reshape digital trust and enable scalable, real-world blockchain applications.

Contents

Applications

Smart Contract Verification

Blockchain and AI

Towards Automating Blockchain Consensus Verification with IsabeLLM

Elliot Jones[✉] and William Knottenbelt

Department of Computing, Imperial College London, London, UK
`e.jones24@imperial.ac.uk`

Abstract. Consensus protocols are crucial for a blockchain system as they are what allow agreement between the system's nodes in a potentially adversarial environment. For this reason, it is paramount to ensure their correct design and implementation to prevent such adversaries from carrying out malicious behaviour. Formal verification allows us to ensure the correctness of such protocols, but requires high levels of effort and expertise to carry out and thus is often omitted in the development process. In this paper, we present IsabeLLM, a tool that integrates the proof assistant Isabelle with a Large Language Model to assist and automate proofs. We demonstrate the effectiveness of IsabeLLM by using it to develop a novel model of Bitcoin's Proof of Work consensus protocol and verify its correctness. We use the DeepSeek R1 API for this demonstration and found that we were able to generate correct proofs for each of the non-trivial lemmas present in the verification.

Keywords: Blockchain · Consensus · Formal Verification · Theorem Proving · Artificial Intelligence

1 Introduction

A blockchain enables peer-to-peer digital transactions without the need for a trusted intermediary. This is only possible because of its consensus protocol, which allows nodes within the system to agree on the state of the blockchain, even in the presence of adversaries. For this reason, it is paramount that consensus is designed and implemented correctly to prevent the system from reaching unwanted states that can be exploited by adversaries. The most famous example of this is Bitcoin's Proof of Work (PoW) consensus protocol and its susceptibility to a 51% attack, where adversaries control the majority of the compute power in the system, which gives them the potential to double spend. Infamous examples of such attacks include Ethereum Classic [16], Bitcoin Gold [15], and Vertcoin [14], totalling losses of over \$30 million.

Other key components of modern blockchain systems are bridging protocols for cross-chain data transfer and smart contracts for automated agreement

W. Knottenbelt et al. (Eds.): Blocktea 2025, LNICST 669, pp. 3–18, 2026.
https://doi.org/10.1007/978-3-032-12335-0_1

execution. These components are also not without their exploits, with infamous examples such as the Poly Network [43], Wormhole Bridge [25], Binance Smart Chain [19], and Qubit Finance [12], totalling losses of over \$1.5 Billion. These failures further underscore the need to ensure correctness across the domain.

Formal verification is the process of formalising a system and then mathematically proving its correctness. However, it is often underutilised in the software development process because of the large amount of effort and expertise it requires. The blockchain domain is no exception to this, resulting in the huge financial losses discussed previously. Furthermore, blockchain systems cannot rely on the traditional 'test and patch' model for their consensus protocols as patching would require a hard fork, such as the Ethereum/Ethereum Classic split [13]. Hard Forks are extremely disruptive and controversial as they challenge blockchain's core principle of immutability. Furthermore, patching smart contracts is often impossible once they have been deployed on a blockchain as they are usually immutable [26] with the exception of some upgradeable contracts [1]. This further amplifies the need for formal verification, as it can be used for correctness-by-construction [10] and minimise the need for costly post-deployment fixes.

In recent years, the field of Artificial Intelligence has made incredible progress, particularly within the realm of Large Language Models (LLMs) like OpenAI's ChatGPT and High-Flyer's DeepSeek. This advancement has opened up new opportunities across all domains, including the formal verification space. In particular, AI for theorem proving has gained traction and has started to see applications outside of purely mathematical statements and instead for program verification. An example of this is FVEL [34], which is used to assist in automated verification of C/C++ programs in the Isabelle proof assistant. This reduces the entry barrier for the formal verification of such programs, making it more accessible and less time-consuming.

In this paper, we present IsabeLLM, a tool that integrates the proof assistant Isabelle with a Large Language Model to assist and automate proofs. We demonstrate the effectiveness of IsabeLLM by using it to prove the correctness of a novel model for Bitcoin's Proof-of-Work consensus protocol. The contributions of this paper are as follows:

1. The IsabeLLM tool, which can be used with any LLM API and is general purpose, allowing it to be used for theorem proving within any domain. In this paper, we focus on verifying blockchain consensus. We describe IsabeLLM's architecture (Sect. 5.1) and implementation (Sect. 5.2).
2. A novel mechanised model of Bitcoin's Proof of Work consensus protocol in Isabelle, with correctness proven using IsabeLLM. The model is an extension of the work done in [30], which we describe in Sect. 4. We use DeepSeek R1 as our chosen LLM to integrate with IsabeLLM.
3. Analysis of the performance of IsabeLLM, looking at success rate, number of iterations, and any emerging pain points. We describe the results in Sect. 6.

2   Background

2.1   Blockchain

A blockchain is a decentralised ledger that allows two parties to carry out transactions without the need of a trusted intermediary, eliminating the need for trust. This is only possible through a blockchain's consensus protocol, which allows all parties to agree on the current state of the blockchain and the transactions recorded on it. The most popular consensus protocol is Proof of Work (PoW) used by Bitcoin's blockchain, which has around 1.2 billion recorded transactions [9] with Bitcoin's market capitalisation sitting around $1.8 trillion [17]. The core idea of PoW is that the longest blockchain is correct since it assumes the majority of computing power within the system is honest and therefore should be able to solve hashes and add blocks faster than adversaries [37].

2.2   Isabelle

Isabelle is a proof assistant written in Scala and ML that uses Higher-Order Logic (HOL). It is used to write and verify formal proofs with high assurance due to the mechanisation of these proofs [39]. Isabelle's Isar proof language allows these proofs to be more readable than the traditional approach to theorem proving by repeatedly applying tactics. Isabelle also makes use of automation tools like Sledgehammer, which uses external automated theorem provers (ATPs) to help you complete proofs. Outside of the proof assistant itself, the Scala library Scala-Isabelle provides the functionality to interact with an Isabelle process inside of a Scala application [47].

3   Related Work

Isabelle has been used extensively in the last 20 years to carry out numerous verifications. Some of the most notable verifications include the seL4 Microkernel [31], the ML compiler [24], and numerous protocol and program verifications [20,22,35]. Outside of verification, Isabelle has been used to formalise a large amount of mathematics that can be found in the Archive of Formal Proofs (AFP) [27]. Some of the most notable formalisms in the AFP include Gödel's incompleteness theorems [41], Jordan curve theorem [46], and Ramsey's Theorem [40]. In recent years, Isabelle has been used for verifications and formalisms of blockchain systems, including the Ethereum Virtual Machine [5] and a framework to verify solidity smart contracts [36].

Outside of Isabelle, various other theorem provers have been used to carry out verifications in the blockchain domain. To name a few, Agda [2,3,44], Coq [4, 45,52], and Lean [38,42] have been used for the formalisms of blockchain. The field has also started to see formalisms of Decentralised Finance (DeFi) specific components [6–8] but are yet to be mechanised. Other major works within the space include KEVM [23], Certora Prover [11], and Mythril [18].

The field of AI for theorem proving has seen the development of major data sets for proof assistants in recent years, including IsarStep and PISA for Isabelle [28,33], LeanDojo for Lean [51], and GamePad and CoqGym for Coq [50]. Using these datasets has allowed for the development of various theorem proving models, including LEGO-Prover [48], LISA [28] and DeepSeek-Prover [49]. Artificial Intelligence for formal verification has seen limited use, with the aforementioned FVEL [34] being the major work in this area. As for AI for formal verification of blockchain, the literature is sparse and has only seen research into extracting smart contract specifications from natural language [32] to the best of our knowledge.

4 Model

Table 1. Lines of Proof (LoP) for each tree model.

Lemma Name	Binary Tree	N-ary Tree
subtree_height	N/A	15
height_mono	1+1	23
obtain_max	N/A	23
foldr_max_eq	N/A	37
branch_height	N/A	30
sub_longest	N/A	28
sub_branch	N/A	41
weaken_distance	1	18
weaken_depth	1	15
common_prefix	25+12	38
height_add (mining)	10+5	36
check_add (mining)	49+158	1
height_add (honest)	10+5	32
check_add (honest)	22+13	36
bounded_check	56	17
consensus	1	5
Total	**175+193**	**395**

Our consensus model builds on previous work [30] by generalizing the blockchain structure from a binary tree to an n-ary tree. This extension enables the model to account for an arbitrary number of forks in any given block, reflecting a more realistic view of a blockchain. We prove that consensus holds in a majority honest network using the common prefix and chain quality properties outlined in the Bitcoin Backbone Protocol [21], where they are discussed in more detail.

We make the same assumptions of majority honesty and synchronisation in the network, meaning that the majority of the computing power in the network is honest and that everyone shares the same view of the blockchain. As in the previous work, we can omit the chain quality property under our majority honesty assumption, leaving us with the common prefix property which states that all honest parties agree on a common chain up to the last k blocks in a chain. This is a safety property, showing honest nodes do not diverge except near the tip of the chain. Its implementation in our Isabelle model can be seen in Fig. 1.

```
1   theorem consensus:
2     fixes t assumes "t ∈ traces"
3     and "p ∈ longest (State (hd t))"
4     and "p' ∈ longest (State (hd t))"
5   shows "take k p = take k p'"
```

Fig. 1. Consensus theorem in Isabelle

This statement is identical to the consensus statement for the binary tree model. However, the generalisation to an n-ary tree significantly increases the complexity of the proof. In the binary tree case, inductive arguments typically require only two cases (e.g., left and right subtrees), whereas the n-ary setting necessitates reasoning over an arbitrary number of branches, complicating case distinctions and inductive reasoning. To show this, Table 1 shows the Lines of Proof (LoP) required to complete the verification of each model. We only list the lemmas that were more than one LoP in at least one of the models. In the binary tree column, "N/A" means that the lemma was not required for the verification. For the rows with $x + y$, x is the LoP that are 'original' and y is the LoP that are symmetric to x and are just repeated for the different cases. With this in mind, it is clear that the n-ary tree model has more than double the original LoP when compared to the binary tree model.

5   IsabeLLM

IsabeLLM is an interface between the Isabelle proof assistant and an LLM. It is designed for general purpose and so can be used to prove any kind of statements within Isabelle. It should be noted that if you are using bespoke imports for your theory file, then they should be given to the LLM as context for it to understand. In our models, we are only importing Isabelle's Main library, and everything is contained within the single theory file, meaning we do not need to provide extra context.

5.1   Architecture

The high-level architecture for IsabeLLM can be seen in Fig. 2. The main idea is that we use an LLM to understand the high-level structure of a proof and then

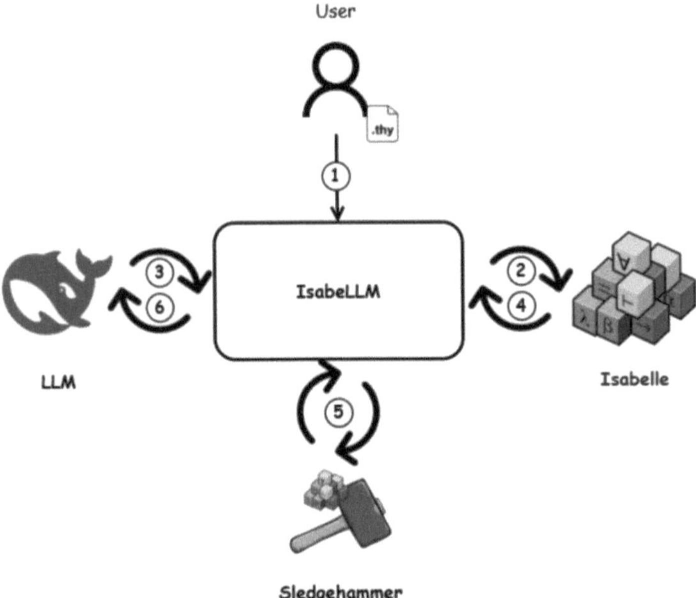

Fig. 2. IsabeLLM Architecture.

use Isabelle's Sledgehammer tool to solve the intermediate steps that the LLM failed (if any). The general workflow for IsabeLLM is as follows:

1. The user uploads their Isabelle theory file (.thy) to their working directory, along with a ROOT file so that the Isabelle server knows which files to look at. The user starts IsabeLLM.

2. IsabeLLM first uses the Isabelle server to try and build the theory file. If there are no issues with the file and all statements have been proven, then the build completes, and we are done. If not, then IsabeLLM captures the errors raised to identify the unproven statements and extracts them.

3. IsabeLLM sends the context of the theory file and the unproven lemma to the LLM via its API. The LLM tries to prove the lemma and returns a proof of the statement.

4. IsabeLLM injects the new proof into the theory file and tries to build it again. If this fails, we send the file to Isabelle's Sledgehammer tool.

5. Sledgehammer tries to solve each unproven line within the proof. If some are left unproven, then IsabeLLM extracts these lines and their errors, along with the rest of the updated theory file.

6. IsabeLLM returns the current proof state to the LLM and asks it to resolve the remaining errors. The LLM returns a proof of the statement.

7. Steps 4–6 are repeated until the theory file is successfully built or IsabeLLM reaches a set number of iterations.

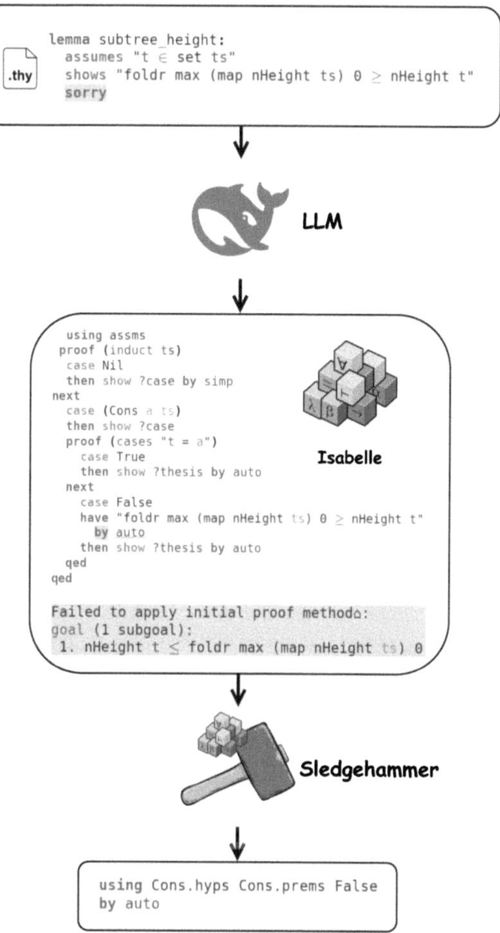

Fig. 3. IsabeLLM example workflow.

Figure 3 shows an example workflow in IsabeLLM. In this example, we prove the lemma subtree_height which states that the height of a tree in a set of trees is always greater than or equal to the maximum height of the set of trees. The LLM generates a proof that fails a proof step, which we then correct with Sledgehammer. The proof is by induction over the list of trees and splitting the inductive step into the cases of whether the tree is at the head of the list or not. For this paper, we opted to use DeepSeek R1 as our LLM due to its strong coding benchmarks and free access to its API. Claude Sonnet was also considered, but was ultimately decided to be too expensive. Other models like OpenAI's GPT-4 and Mistral's Le Chat were also considered but showed poor performance during manual testing. As for our choice of proof assistant, we chose Isabelle due to its existing automation tool Sledgehammer and integration library Scala-Isabelle.

Although not integral, the Isar language also helps to understand the logic of the proofs and the dialogue between IsabeLLM and DeepSeek. We also note that we use Isabelle2022 as it is compatible with Scala-Isabelle.

Table 2. Isabelle build errors.

Error	Description
"Sorry" Detected in Proof	The sorry keyword is used to mark incomplete proofs. IsabeLLM uses sorry to detect on which part of the theory file to call the LLM.
Failed Proof	The proof method/tactic failed to complete the goal. This means the generated proof was incorrect. We first attempt to Sledgehammer the proof before returning to the LLM.
Undefined Fact/Method	Usually means the LLM has hallucinated a fact, method, or attribute of either that does not exist. We simply remove these hallucinations and try to rebuild.
Lexical/Syntax Error	Bad syntax injected into the theory file. IsabeLLM has various methods for trying to detect these issues and resolving them. If IsabeLLM fails to resolve the issue, it will either return the proof back to the LLM or cancel the computation and ask the user to make amends. The latter is usually reserved for when the LLM gives a very incoherent answer, such as DeepSeek responding in Mandarin or looping, which is uncommon.
Timeout	The theory file does not build in the allotted time. This usually means there is a hanging proof step that is not evaluating correctly. The metis and blast tactics are common culprits for this. IsabeLLM searches through the modified proofs for occurrences of these tactics and calls Sledgehammer on each of them to check if they are being evaluated correctly.

5.2   Implementation

Almost all of IsabeLLM is written in Scala, with some Python to access the LLM API using the openai library. The main reason for choosing Scala is to be able to use the Scala-Isabelle library, which offers the functionality to control an Isabelle process from a Scala application. In particular, we make use of Scala-Isabelle for calling Sledgehammer in our theory file. Our approach to using Scala-Isabelle was inspired by the work done on PISA [28]. All of our code, including the IsabeLLM source code and theory files, can be found at [29]. We list IsabeLLM's features below:

1. Interface between Isabelle and a LLM API.
2. Code extraction from a theory file, including lemmas, definitions, and proofs.
3. Injection of code into a theory file, including lemmas, definitions, and proofs.

4. Sledgehammer functionality with a timeout control and option to select which provers it uses. In this paper, we set this timeout to 60 s and use the default provers.
5. Handling of errors in the build process.
6. Records and updates to the LLM chat history.
7. LLM Prompt Generation.
8. Workflow for automated theorem proving using all of the above. The workflow has a control for the maximum number of LLM iterations before timing out to prevent endless loops.

Due to the stochastic nature of LLMs, the most challenging part of automating proof with IsabeLLM is ensuring the output from the LLM has the correct syntax to be injected into Isabelle. Generally speaking, most models understand the syntax well enough to give a coherent response. However, most outputs will trigger at least one error in the build process and must be handled accordingly. Table 2 highlights the general types of error that are encountered when trying to build the theory file after injecting a generated proof.

When sending requests to the LLM, IsabeLLM automatically builds the required prompts to make the context clearer. When we first initialise a proof, we send a prompt that includes the context of the lemma we are trying to prove and everything in the theory file before it. After the initialisation prompt, we send prompts that include only the current proof state of the lemma. The templates for these prompts can be seen in Table 3. IsabeLLM also maintains the chat history with the LLM. To minimise the size of our context, we reset the history after successfully proving a lemma, then update the initial context to the theory file with the updated lemma. A JSON file containing the chat history for each lemma is stored.

Table 3. IsabeLLM prompts.

Prompt	Text
Initialisation	I am trying to complete a proof in Isabelle. Here is my theory file so far: (.thy file). I am trying to prove the following lemma: (lemma). Please prove this lemma. Return only the raw code without any additional text, explanations, formatting, or commentary. Do not include " or language tags. Just the pure code.
Error	Your proof is incorrect. The current proof state is: (proof state). The line: (error line) produced the following error message: (error). Please amend the proof to deal with this error. Return only the raw code without any additional text, explanations, formatting, or commentary. Do not include " or language tags. Just the pure code.

6 Results

To test the effectiveness of IsabeLLM, we try to prove each of the 16 lemmas listed in Table 1 10 times with a maximum of 5 iterations per attempt, not counting instances when the LLM would return an empty response. It should be noted that the LoP specified for each lemma can vary as the LLM can generate different proofs for the same thing. As mentioned previously, we used the DeepSeek R1 API for this experiment. We consider an attempt to be a failure if it exceeds the maximum number of iterations or exits prematurely (often due to syntax issues). Table 4 shows the results of using IsabeLLM for each lemma.

Generally speaking, IsabeLLM was able to prove each lemma multiple times, often with a varying number of iterations required to do so. Some lemmas, like subtree_height, were repeatedly solved with one iteration but almost always required intervention to amend either incorrect syntax or Sledgehammer incorrect proof steps. The general approach of the proofs generated for these lemmas was always very similar and showed little variation. This probably stems from the fact that these lemmas usually had shorter proofs on average, leaving less room for variety.

As expected, we tended to see fewer successful attempts for the larger proofs, which left more room for variety. The lemmas with which it seemed to struggle most was branch_height and bounded_check. We found that Sledgehammer struggled to resolve the intermediate steps provided by the LLM despite the fact

Table 4. Number of successful proof attempts

Lemma Name	Successful Attempts	Avg. Iterations (Success)	Lines of Proof
subtree_height	10	1	15
height_mono	10	1	23
obtain_max	9	1.4	23
foldr_max_eq	5	2	37
branch_height	3*	2	30
sub_longest	7	1.1	28
sub_branch	5	1.8	41
weaken_distance	10	1	18
weaken_depth	10	1	15
common_prefix	6	1.5	38
height_add (mining)	6	2	36
check_add (mining)	10	1	1
height_add (honest)	8	1.7	32
check_add (honest)	9	1.2	36
bounded_check	7*	1	17
consensus	10	1	5

* Indicates these proofs were completed using Sledgehammer from Isabelle2025.

that the high-level was sound. Interestingly, we repeated Sledgehammer on these steps in Isabelle2025 and they were solved every time, highlighting IsabeLLM's potential to evolve with Isabelle.

As for the failed attempts, we saw a recurring pattern in which the LLM would fixate on a proof step and disregard the proof as a whole. In particular, when a proof step would fail and IsabeLLM was unable to find a proof with Sledgehammer, we would send this error back to LLM. The LLM would often just repeat the same proof back to us with a slightly modified proof of the step, which would very rarely succeed if Sledgehammer had already failed to find one. This would create a loop of tweaking and failing the same step without progress. IsabeLLM was most successful when the LLM broke the proof step down into more manageable parts, which Sledgehammer could then solve itself.

7   Discussion

One limitation we faced was the speed and occasionally unreliable API for DeepSeek R1. We used the free OpenRouter API for this work and found it to be considerably slow at times. This was to be expected with the free API, as OpenRouter also offers a paid version with improved latency and tokens per second. An unexpected issue was that the API would occasionally return an empty output, forcing us to add a condition to handle this and repeat the iteration. We expect these limitations to be mitigated with an improved API or by running the LLM locally. Another expected issue was hallucinations of the LLM. It is common for the LLM to get Isabelle's syntax wrong, use a non-existent theorem, or try to prove something that was impossible. Many of these issues were handled in the workflow, as discussed in Sect. 5.2, but sometimes manual intervention was required to sort out the issues before resuming the computation. Unfortunately, there is not much that can be done here, but we expect this issue to minimise with time as LLMs and Sledgehammer improve.

A key area of improvement would be to improve the efficiency of Sledgehammer. As mentioned previously, IsabeLLM runs on Isabelle2022 and so does not benefit from the improved Sledgehammer in later releases. This highlights the need to make IsabeLLM compatible with later Isabelle releases. We also found that calling Sledgehammer remotely for IsabeLLM does not generate counterexamples for impossible proofs. These are usually detected by nitpick, an internal Sledgehammer tool, before running the provers on the step. This would save us from wasting computation time on impossible proofs and also allow us to give more context to the LLM. Furthermore, we found that Sledgehammer would be repeatedly called on the same proof steps between iterations as the LLM would ignore our new proof step and go back to using the incorrect step it gave us from a previous iteration. With this in mind, it would be effective to incorporate functionality that detects repeated steps and stores the correct proof so that it can be injected quickly without having to run again. The final issue with Sledgehammer was its high memory use, particularly when there were back-to-back calls, usually when consecutive generated proof steps are incorrect. We would find that the first call would still use significant memory when the next Sledgehammer was called, causing our machine to run out of memory and killing the process. This issue is largely internal for Sledgehammer and is out of IsabeLLM's control, but again this should improve with later Isabelle releases.

IsabeLLM's main limitation as a proof automation tool is that it only automates the proof of statements, not the generation of the statements themselves. This means that the user must specify a statement before it can be proven, including other key parts of the theory, such as functions, locales, and sets. However, this issue will be largely mitigated if IsabeLLM is used in conjunction with existing blockchain verification frameworks, rather than building from the ground up like our model. For example, Isabelle/Solidity [36] builds most of the model automatically, and you only have to specify the invariant property you are trying to verify for a given smart contract. A challenge that comes with this is for the LLM to understand the bespoke calculus that comes with such frameworks, as there will be far fewer proof corpora to learn from.

8   Conclusion

In this paper, we introduce the proof automation tool IsabeLLM for Isabelle proof assistant. We then used IsabeLLM to complete a novel verification of PoW consensus and analysed its effectiveness.

An area of future work would be to modify IsabeLLM so that it constructs a proof tree by querying the LLM in parallel and branching the proof in different directions for each different proof the LLM gives. This is the standard method used in the field for AI for theorem proving [28,49] and would help prevent IsabeLLM from getting stuck in a loop of repeatedly trying to prove the same step. This could be taken further by using different LLMs, which would likely generate different approaches to the proof. As the field progresses, more advanced models like Claude Opus 4 are likely to replace our choice of DeepSeek.

Another area of work is using IsabeLLM for more complex proofs that are not necessarily within the blockchain domain and split across multiple theory files. As mentioned previously, IsabeLLM is designed for general purpose and so can be used for proofs in any domain. Furthermore, LLMs could also be fine-tuned on proof corpora datasets like the Archive of Formal Proofs to see how it improves performance. Alternatively, instead of an LLM, bespoke language models could be created and used for Isabelle, such as the work done on LISA [28] that used AFP as a training set.

Lastly, auxiliary techniques like Retrieval-Augmented Generation (RAG) or Static Prompt Templating could be employed to mitigate our issue of the LLM re-attempting failed proof steps with minimal variation and hallucinations as a whole. Doing so could make IsabeLLM more robust and less dependent on the quality of the LLM itself.

IsabeLLM shows great promise towards automated verification and will only improve in ability as LLMs and Sledgehammer continue to evolve. Further work on IsabeLLM's functionality to handle different syntax errors from generated proofs could also help to improve the speed and reliability of the automation process.

Appendix

All relevant code for IsabeLLM can be found at:

$$\text{https://github.com/EllbellCode/IsabeLLM}$$

The repository includes:

- Source code for IsabeLLM.
- Isabelle theory files for the n-ary tree PoW model.
- Setup instructions.

References

1. Alchemy: What are upgradeable smart contracts? (2024). https://docs.alchemy. com/docs/upgradeable-smart-contracts. Accessed Apr 2025
2. Alhabardi, F., Setzer, A.: A simulator of Solidity-style smart contracts in the theorem prover Agda. In: Proceedings of the 2023 6th International Conference on Blockchain Technology and Applications, pp. 1–11 (2023)
3. Alhabardi, F.F., Beckmann, A., Lazar, B., Setzer, A.: Verification of bitcoin script in Agda using weakest preconditions for access control. arXiv preprint arXiv:2203.03054 (2022)
4. Alturki, M.A., et al.: Towards a verified model of the Algorand consensus protocol in coq. In: International Symposium on Formal Methods, pp. 362–367. Springer (2019)
5. Amani, S., Bégel, M., Bortin, M., Staples, M.: Towards verifying Ethereum smart contract bytecode in Isabelle/HOL. In: Proceedings of the 7th ACM SIGPLAN International Conference on Certified Programs and Proofs, pp. 66–77 (2018)
6. Bartoletti, M., Chiang, J.H.y., Lafuente, A.L.: Towards a theory of decentralized finance. In: Financial Cryptography and Data Security. FC 2021 International Workshops: CoDecFin, DeFi, VOTING, and WTSC, Virtual Event, March 5, 2021, Revised Selected Papers 25, pp. 227–232. Springer (2021)
7. Bartoletti, M., Chiang, J.H.y., Lluch-Lafuente, A.: A theory of automated market makers in DeFi. Logical Methods Comput. Sci. **18** (2022)
8. Bartoletti, M., Zunino, R.: A theoretical basis for blockchain extractable value. arXiv preprint arXiv:2302.02154 (2023)
9. Blockchain.com: BTC total number of transactions (2025). https://www. blockchain.com/explorer/charts/n-transactions-total. Accessed Apr 2025
10. Bordis, T., Runge, T., Kittelmann, A., Schaefer, I.: Correctness-by-construction: an overview of the corc ecosystem. Ada Lett. **42**(2), 75–78 (2023)
11. Certora: Certora prover. https://www.certora.com/prover

12. Chainalysis: The \$80 million qubit hack likely the work of north Korea-linked cybercriminals (2023). https://www.chainalysis.com/blog/qubit-hack-north-korea/. Accessed Apr 2025
13. CoinBase: Ethereum classic and the Ethereum hard fork (2016). https://help.coinbase.com/en/coinbase/getting-started/crypto-education/eth-hard-fork. Accessed Apr 2025
14. CoinDesk: The Vertcoin cryptocurrency just got 51% attacked – again (2019). https://www.coindesk.com/tech/2019/12/02/the-vertcoin-cryptocurrency-just-got-51-attacked-again. Accessed Apr 2025
15. CoinDesk: Bad actors rent hashing power to hit bitcoin gold with new 51% attacks (2020), https://www.coindesk.com/tech/2020/01/27/bad-actors-rent-hashing-power-to-hit-bitcoin-gold-with-new-51-attacks. Accessed Apr 2025
16. CoinDesk: Ethereum classic hit by third 51% attack in a month (2021). https://www.coindesk.com/markets/2020/08/29/ethereum-classic-hit-by-third-51-attack-in-a-month. Accessed Apr 2025
17. CoinMarketCap: BTC market capitalisation (2025). https://coinmarketcap.com/currencies/bitcoin/. Accessed Apr 2025
18. Consensys: Mythril. https://mythx.io/
19. Decrypt: BNB chain hits record-high sandwich attacks exposing \$1.5 billion in trades (2024). https://decrypt.co/294648/bnb-smart-chain-blocks-hits-record-high-sandwich-attacks. Accessed Apr 2025
20. Foster, S., Huerta y Munive, J.J., Gleirscher, M., Struth, G.: Hybrid systems verification with Isabelle/HOL: Simpler syntax, better models, faster proofs. In: Formal Methods: 24th International Symposium, FM 2021, Virtual Event, November 20–26, 2021, Proceedings 24, pp. 367–386. Springer (2021)
21. Garay, J., Kiayias, A., Leonardos, N.: The bitcoin backbone protocol: analysis and applications. In: Annual International Conference on the Theory and Applications of Cryptographic Techniques, pp. 281–310. Springer (2015)
22. Gomes, V.B., Kleppmann, M., Mulligan, D.P., Beresford, A.R.: Verifying strong eventual consistency in distributed systems. Proc. ACM Programm. Lang. 1(OOPSLA), 1–28 (2017)
23. Hildenbrandt, E., et al.: Kevm: A complete formal semantics of the Ethereum virtual machine. In: 2018 IEEE 31st Computer Security Foundations Symposium (CSF), pp. 204–217. IEEE (2018)
24. Hupel, L., Nipkow, T.: A verified compiler from isabelle/HOL to CakeML. In: European Symposium on Programming, pp. 999–1026. Springer (2018)
25. Investopedia: Crypto worth over \$320 million taken in wormhole hack (2022). https://www.investopedia.com/crypto-theft-of-usd320-million-wormhole-hack-5218062. Accessed Apr 2025
26. Investopedia: What are smart contracts on the blockchain and how do they work? (2024). https://www.investopedia.com/terms/s/smart-contracts.asp#:~:text=Smart%20Contract%20Pros%20and%20Cons&text=Accuracy%3A%20There%20can%20be%20no,The%20programming%20cannot%20be%20altered. Accessed Apr 2025
27. Isabelle/HOL: Archive of formal proofs (2004), https://www.isa-afp.org/, [Accessed April 2025]
28. Jiang, A.Q., Li, W., Han, J.M., Wu, Y.: Lisa: Language models of isabelle proofs. In: 6th Conference on Artificial Intelligence and Theorem Proving (AITP) (2021)
29. Jones, E.: IsabeLLM. https://github.com/EllbellCode/IsabeLLM (2025)

30. Jones, E., Marmsoler, D.: Towards mechanised consensus in isabelle. In: 5th International Workshop on Formal Methods for Blockchains (FMBC 2024). Schloss Dagstuhl–Leibniz-Zentrum für Informatik (2024)
31. Klein, G., Sewell, T., Winwood, S.: Refinement in the formal verification of the seL4 microkernel. In: Design and Verification of Microprocessor Systems for High-Assurance Applications, pp. 323–339. Springer (2010)
32. Leite, G., Arruda, F., Antonino, P., Sampaio, A., Roscoe, A.: Extracting formal smart-contract specifications from natural language with LLMs. In: International Conference on Formal Aspects of Component Software, pp. 109–126. Springer (2024)
33. Li, W., Yu, L., Wu, Y., Paulson, L.C.: Isarstep: a benchmark for high-level mathematical reasoning. arXiv preprint arXiv:2006.09265 (2020)
34. Lin, X., et al.: FVEL: Interactive formal verification environment with large language models via theorem proving (2024). https://arxiv.org/abs/2406.14408
35. Marić, F.: Formal verification of a modern SAT solver by shallow embedding into Isabelle/HOL. Theoret. Comput. Sci. **411**(50), 4333–4356 (2010)
36. Marmsoler, D., Brucker, A.D.: A denotational semantics of solidity in Isabelle/HOL. In: International Conference on Software Engineering and Formal Methods, pp. 403–422. Springer (2021)
37. Nakamoto, S.: Bitcoin: A peer-to-peer electronic cash system. Decentralized business review (2008)
38. Nethermind: Clear–prove anything about your Solidity smart contracts (2024). https://www.nethermind.io/blog/clear-prove-anything-about-your-solidity-smart-contracts
39. Nipkow, T., Wenzel, M., Paulson, L.C.: Isabelle/HOL: a proof assistant for higher-order logic. Springer (2002)
40. Paulson, L.C.: Theory ramsey (2004). https://isabelle.in.tum.de/website-Isabelle2021-1/dist/library/HOL/HOL-Library/Ramsey.html
41. Paulson, L.C.: A mechanised proof of gödel's incompleteness theorems using Nominal Isabelle. J. Autom. Reason. **55**, 1–37 (2015)
42. Pusceddu, D., Bartoletti, M.: Formalizing automated market makers in the Lean 4 theorem prover. arXiv preprint arXiv:2402.06064 (2024)
43. Reuters: How hackers stole $613 million in crypto tokens from poly network (2021). https://www.reuters.com/technology/how-hackers-stole-613-million-crypto-tokens-poly-network-2021-08-12/. Accessed Apr 2025
44. Setzer, A.: Modelling bitcoin in Agda. arXiv preprint arXiv:1804.06398 (2018)
45. Sun, T., Yu, W.: A formal verification framework for security issues of blockchain smart contracts. Electronics **9**(2), 255 (2020)
46. Thiemann, R., Yamada, A.: Formalizing Jordan normal forms in Isabelle/HOL. In: Proceedings of the 5th ACM SIGPLAN Conference on Certified Programs and Proofs, pp. 88–99 (2016)
47. Unruh, D.: scala-isabelle – a scala library for controlling isabelle/hol (2022). https://dominique-unruh.github.io/scala-isabelle/. Accessed Apr 2025
48. Wang, H., et al.: Lego-prover: Neural theorem proving with growing libraries. arXiv preprint arXiv:2310.00656 (2023)
49. Xin, H., et al.: Deepseek-prover: Advancing theorem proving in LLMs through large-scale synthetic data. arXiv preprint arXiv:2405.14333 (2024)
50. Yang, K., Deng, J.: Learning to prove theorems via interacting with proof assistants. In: International Conference on Machine Learning, pp. 6984–6994. PMLR (2019)

51. Yang, K., et al.: Leandojo: theorem proving with retrieval-augmented language models. Adv. Neural. Inf. Process. Syst. **36**, 21573–21612 (2023)
52. Yang, Z., Lei, H., Qian, W.: A hybrid formal verification system in coq for ensuring the reliability and security of Ethereum-based service smart contracts. IEEE Access **8**, 21411–21436 (2020)

Optimizing Smart Contract Testing via Neural-MCTS Test Prioritization

Morena Barboni, Filippo Lampa[(✉)], Andrea Morichetta, and Andrea Polini

University of Camerino, Via Madonna delle Carceri 7, Camerino 62032, Italy
{morena.barboni,filippo.lampa,andrea.morichetta,
andrea.polini}@unicam.it

Abstract. Smart contracts, as self-executing programs deployed on blockchain platforms, demand a high degree of reliability due to their immutable nature. Ensuring their correctness before deployment is crucial, as subsequent modifications are costly or impossible. By introducing artificial faults into contracts' code and measuring the ability of tests to detect them, mutation testing offers a rigorous approach to assessing the quality of test suites. However, the large number of mutants and exhaustive test executions required make mutation testing a resource-intensive operation. In this paper, we introduce ASCENT, a novel test prioritization technique designed to reduce the computational cost of mutation testing in Solidity-based decentralized applications. Unlike traditional methods that rely on prior domain knowledge or static heuristics, often yielding inconsistent performance across different Systems Under Test (SUTs), ASCENT utilizes a Neural Monte Carlo Tree Search (Neural-MCTS) algorithm to dynamically learn and adapt test execution strategies in real-time. By mapping test methods to MCTS states and using the number of tests required to kill a mutant as a reward signal, ASCENT incrementally refines a policy that prioritizes the most impactful tests early in the process. Our evaluation on five open-source Solidity projects, tested through the HardHat framework, shows that ASCENT consistently reduces the number of executed tests needed for effective mutation detection. Additionally, it achieves this without requiring prior knowledge of the SUT and maintains stable performance across projects of varying sizes and complexity.

Keywords: Mutation Testing · Test Prioritization · Reinforcement Learning · Monte Carlo Tree Search · Blockchain · Smart Contracts

1 Introduction

Due to its inherent reliability and transparency, blockchain architecture has paved the way for developing decentralized applications (DApps) in sensitive

This work was partially supported by project SERICS (PE00000014) under the MUR National Recovery and Resilience Plan funded by the European Union - NextGenerationEU, and by Fermo-Tech Extended.

W. Knottenbelt et al. (Eds.): Blocktea 2025, LNICST 669, pp. 19–36, 2026.
https://doi.org/10.1007/978-3-032-12335-0_2

domains where trust is essential. Smart contracts, by automating the actions required in a blockchain transaction, enable operations between parties without intermediaries while ensuring predefined guarantees. Being deployed on the blockchain, the trustworthiness of these contracts lies in their immutability, which, on the other hand, introduces the necessity of thorough testing before deployment to ensure their long-term reliability [8]. To address this need, *mutation testing* offers an effective way to evaluate the quality of test suites by introducing small changes into smart contract code and measuring whether the existing tests can detect them [12]. While this approach provides an in-depth assessment of a test suite's bug-detection capabilities [2], it also comes at a high cost. Generating a large number of mutants and executing extensive test runs can be time-consuming and resource-intensive [19,24]. This work presents ASCENT, a novel technique and tool for *test prioritization* intended to execute, on each mutant, sequences of tests that maximize the probability of detecting them. Unlike existing test prioritization techniques that rely on ad-hoc heuristics, precomputed structures, or pre-processing, often making them specific to the *System Under Test (SUT)*, ASCENT leverages the *Neural-MCTS algorithm* to learn program nuances continuously and adapt in real-time across the entire set of mutants. ASCENT frames the search for an optimal test execution sequence as an instance of Monte Carlo Tree Search, mapping test methods to MCTS states and using the number of tests required to kill each mutant as a reward signal. The approach balances exploitation of knowledge gained from past *episodes* (where an episode consists of a test prioritization instance targeting a single mutant) with exploration of potentially more effective test sequences. This evolving knowledge is retained within the policy and value networks, which gradually generalize and guide the search more accurately as the algorithm progresses. By framing the problem this way, ASCENT reduces the total number of test executions required in a real-time, system-agnostic manner, while maintaining high mutation detection effectiveness. This reduction makes mutation testing significantly more affordable and scalable, allowing developers to validate smart contracts more thoroughly using fewer resources. By lowering the resource barrier to rigorous testing, ASCENT contributes to the development of more reliable, secure, and trustworthy decentralized applications. The rest of this paper is organized as follows: Sect. 2 introduces the background knowledge on the key concepts underlying our study, namely mutation testing, test prioritization, and Neural-MCTS. Following, Sect. 3 goes through the core of ASCENT, detailing our approach, while Sect. 4 reports and discusses experimental setup, methodology, and results. Next, Sect. 5 outlines the existing studies in literature close to our problem. Finally, Sect. 6 lists the threats to validity, and Sect. 7 draws the conclusion of our work and suggests some future research directions.

2   Background

This section introduces key background concepts, covering mutation testing as discussed in Sect. 2.1, strategies for test prioritization presented in Sect. 2.2, the fundamentals of Monte Carlo Tree Search described in Sect. 2.3, and its evolution into the neural-augmented paradigm of Neural-MCTS, which is detailed in Sect. 2.4.

2.1   Mutation Testing

Mutation testing is a powerful technique whose objective is to evaluate the effectiveness of a test suite by introducing intentional faults (*i.e., mutants*) into the original code and assessing whether the tests can detect (*i.e., kill*) them. This technique provides a rigorous measure for test suite quality, making it especially valuable in high-stakes domains such as smart contract development [8,12]. Mutation testing relies on fault-injection rules called *mutation operators*, which systematically change the source code of a program to simulate realistic bugs. While some mutation operators are language-agnostic, contract-oriented languages like Solidity require specialized operators that account for their unique syntax and semantics. To meet this need, a number of tools, including Vertigo [18], SuMo [6,7,9], ReSuMo [5,10], and ContractMut [17], have been developed to generate Solidity-specific mutants. Despite its strengths, mutation testing faces a significant scalability issue. As more mutation operators are introduced to improve fault simulation, the number of possible mutants grows exponentially, especially when single statements can be mutated in multiple ways. This *combinatorial explosion* of mutants leads to high computational costs and makes it increasingly difficult to perform comprehensive test adequacy assessment when time and resources are limited.

2.2   Test Prioritization

Test prioritization improves efficiency by scheduling tests to maximize early fault detection, enabling partial execution of the test suite. In mutation testing, where each mutant requires a separate test run, this yields significant cumulative savings. Depending on the desired level of granularity, test prioritization can occur at the level of test files or individual methods. In this study, we focus on method-level prioritization to achieve finer granularity and maximize the impact of our approach. The criteria for determining the effectiveness of a test depend on the application domain and testing strategy. In the context of mutation testing, the problem of test prioritization can be formulated in two ways:

1. **Per-mutant prioritization:** Finding the optimal test order for a specific mutant.
2. **Global prioritization:** Finding a test order that optimizes detection across all mutants (or the remaining mutants not yet evaluated).

Both aim to find an optimal sequence $S \in \mathcal{P}$, where $\mathcal{P}$ is the set of test permutations and f is an evaluation function such that:

$$\forall S' \in \mathcal{P}, \quad f(S) \geq f(S') \quad \text{where} \quad f : \mathcal{P} \to \mathbb{R} \tag{1}$$

Here, f is an evaluation function that quantifies the effectiveness of a test sequence in achieving our testing goals. In test prioritization for mutation testing, this function can be adapted to account for either a single mutant (as in formulation 1) or a set of mutants, which may include all of them or only those yet to be analyzed (as in formulation 2). A common metric for assessing the effectiveness of test prioritization is the *Average Percentage of Faults Detected (APFD)*, introduced by Elbaum et al. [27], which tracks the cumulative percentage of faults detected as tests execute [14,23,33]. APFD is especially valuable in *global prioritization*, where a single test sequence is applied to all mutants. In this context, the metric reflects the cumulative bug detection rate after each test execution, effectively measuring how well a test ordering detects faults early. However, in *per-mutant prioritization*, APFD fails to capture incremental progress effectively. Instead, in this context, studies such as that of Zhang et al. [34] favor measuring effectiveness by tracking the number of tests required to kill each mutant, which provides a more precise assessment of prioritization progress.

2.3   Monte Carlo Tree Search

Monte Carlo Tree Search (MCTS) is a decision-making algorithm widely used for solving complex planning and search problems, particularly in large combinatorial spaces such as board games, robotics, and artificial intelligence applications [22]. These problems can be modeled as sequences of actions made within an *environment* (the system or context in which an agent operates) where each action leads to a new *state*, representing the current situation or configuration of that environment. MCTS explores the search space selectively, balancing *exploitation* (favoring actions that have previously led to good outcomes) and *exploration* (investigating less-visited actions that might yield better results) to focus on promising areas. The algorithm iteratively builds a search tree through four main steps:

Selection Starting from the root node, the algorithm traverses the tree by selecting child nodes that balance exploitation and exploration, typically using the *Upper Confidence Bound for Trees (UCT)* formula.

Expansion When a leaf node (unexplored state) is reached, new child nodes are added to the tree.

Simulation A *playout* from the new node simulates random moves until reaching a terminal state, yielding an estimated value for the state.

Backpropagation The result from the playout is propagated up the tree, updating statistics to refine future choices.

With repeated iterations, MCTS improves its estimates of action values, making it effective in large, intractable search spaces. However, traditional MCTS relies on random or heuristic rollouts, which can be inefficient in complex domains. To improve this, Neural Monte Carlo Tree Search (Neural-MCTS) integrates deep learning by replacing rollouts with learned policy and value predictions. This shift reduces simulation time to prediction time, allowing deeper or broader search within the same computational budget.

2.4 Neural-MCTS

In 2017, DeepMind introduced AlphaZero [31], a general-purpose reinforcement learning system that mastered complex board games such as Chess, Shogi, and Go without prior human knowledge. This breakthrough popularized Neural-MCTS, a paradigm combining deep learning with search-based planning for complex decision-making in large search spaces. Neural-MCTS employs two neural networks (often unified into a single model) for guiding Monte Carlo Tree Search: a *policy network* and a *value network*. These networks evaluate states and suggest promising actions to efficiently explore and prune the decision space. Trained via reinforcement learning, the networks predict both the policy (a probability distribution over legal moves) and the value function (the expected game outcome from a state), drawing training samples from a *replay buffer* that stores previous game experiences. Each experience includes game states, policy targets (from MCTS visit counts), and final game outcomes. A key innovation of Neural-MCTS is its independence from prior knowledge or hand-crafted heuristics. The system learns purely from self-play, storing statistics within the nodes of the MCTS tree, updating the neural network based on the outcomes, and refining its move selection strategy over time. As an anytime algorithm, Neural-MCTS improves progressively during search. At any moment, it can return the best move found so far, supporting time-flexible decisions while asymptotically approaching optimal play.

3 Neural-MCTS Test Prioritization

This section outlines our methodology for dynamic test prioritization using Neural-MCTS. Section 3.1 introduces the core concept of modeling test prioritization as a Monte Carlo Tree Search problem, guiding test selection in real-time. We define the state representation and the reward function used to assess prioritization effectiveness. Following, Sect. 3.2 describes the implementation framework, its modular architecture, and key configurable parameters.

3.1 Using Neural-MCTS for Test Prioritization

We model test prioritization as a discrete control problem, where each action corresponds to selecting a test. This framing enables the use of Monte Carlo Tree Search to guide test selection based on statistics from past executions. Neural-MCTS enhances this process by using policy and value networks to prune unpromising branches, focusing exploration on test sequences likely to detect faults. The system accumulates execution data as node-level statistics, informing future decisions and continuously refining its understanding of the System Under Test. Thus, rather than precomputing and returning a prioritized test suite, ASCENT prioritizes tests dynamically as they are executed, adapting to real-time outcomes. Figure 1 shows a fully expanded tree for a toy example with a set of four test methods $T = \{t_0, \ldots, t_3\}$. Each node represents a unique test

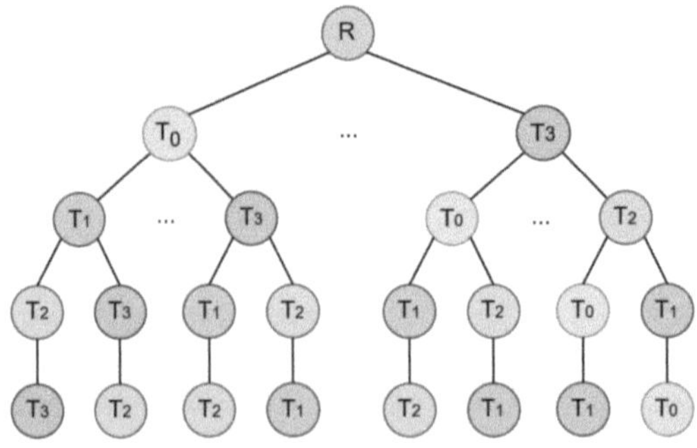

T_0	T_1	T_2	T_3
Test File:'Titn.test.ts'	Test File:'Titn.test.ts'	Test File:'MergeTgt.ts'	Test File:'Titn.test.ts'
Test method: 'should bridge tokens back...'	Test method: 'should send a token from...'	Test method:'should let a user to deposit TGT...'	Test method:'should allow withdrawal of...'

Fig. 1. Example of test method-to-node mapping in a fully expanded MCTS tree with four test methods.

method, with no test method repeated along any branch. A node's children correspond to remaining unselected tests, ensuring each sequence includes each test once. A node stores key MCTS statistics, including the sum of rewards, visit count, node value, and prior probabilities, along with the corresponding state of the environment. As illustrated in Fig. 2, the process iterates over the whole set of mutants $M = \{m_0, \ldots, m_{n-1}\}$, running one testing episode per mutant. For the first mutant, a test is selected uniformly at random from T to initialize the root node, and is immediately executed. For subsequent mutants, the root is selected using UCT based on accumulated statistics. The test execution sequence is then built incrementally using MCTS, which selects the next test by traversing the tree according to policy and value predictions. The search expands toward an unexecuted test, and among the expanded nodes, the most promising one is selected using visit statistics. The corresponding test is executed, and the result is stored in a replay buffer along with the observed reward. Periodically, the policy and value networks are updated using samples from this buffer. Node statistics are continuously updated during the process, which ends when the mutant is killed or all tests are executed. As shown in Fig. 1, tree size grows combinatorially, making it essential to fine-tune the search to focus only on the most promising test sequences.

State Representation of the Environment. We define $\Pi(T)$ as the set of all permutations over the complete test suite T, where each element represents a complete test execution sequence of length $|T|$, in which no test is repeated, for a given mutant. Let $\texttt{SeqID} : \mathbb{N} \rightarrow \Pi(T)$ be an enumeration function over all elements of $\Pi(T)$, such that $\texttt{SeqID}(z) = \sigma_z$ returns the z-th test execution

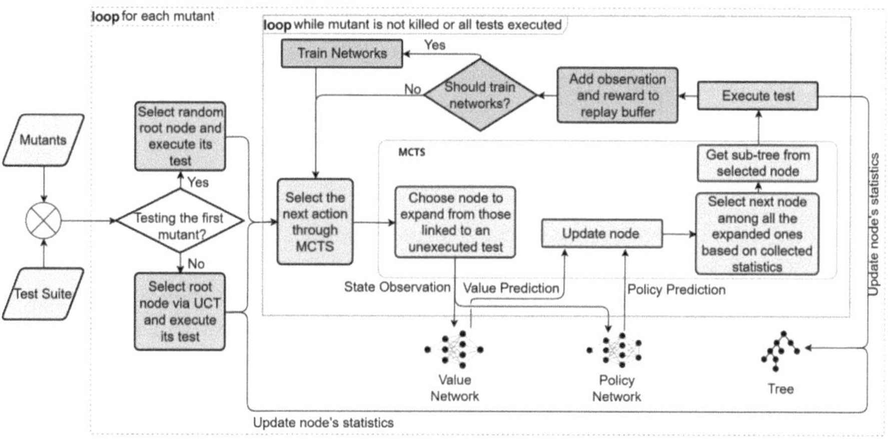

Fig. 2. Overview of the Neural-MCTS approach for real-time test prioritization.

sequence in the enumeration. Since we adopt a per-mutant prioritization strategy, we represent each state of the environment as a triplet $\mathcal{S} = \{k, g, \sigma\}$, where:

- k is the index of the test currently under evaluation,
- g is the index of the mutant under consideration,
- σ is a partial test sequence corresponding to the path from the root to the current node. It represents a prefix of $\sigma_z \in \Pi(T)$, where $\sigma_z = \texttt{SeqID}(z)$ denotes a full permutation that MCTS will eventually complete during the current episode.

Because the state $\mathcal{S}$ serves as input to the policy and value networks, the sequence σ must be transformed into a fixed-size representation. To this end, before passing $\mathcal{S}$ to the networks, we encode σ as a vector $V \in \mathbb{Z}^{|T|}$. Each position i, with $0 \leq i < |T|$, is assigned a value according to the following rule:

$$V[i] = \begin{cases} \sigma[i], & \text{if } i <= k \\ -1, & \text{otherwise} \end{cases} \tag{2}$$

In other words, the first $|\sigma|$ entries of V represent the test indices in the execution sequence σ, and the remaining positions are padded with -1 to enforce a uniform input size. This encoding ensures that each state is represented uniquely within the search tree, even when the same test appears at different positions across different sequences. While we adopt this representation in our study, adding features related to the System Under Test, mutation operator, or individual mutants could make the representation more expressive and potentially improve effectiveness.

Reward Function. Since our goal is to kill a mutant with as few tests as possible, we define the reward as the number of tests saved. Let α be a prefix of σ_z, denoting a partial test execution sequence applied to a mutant $m \in M$, and $kill(t, m)$ be a function that returns `true` if test t kills mutant m. Then, the reward $\mathcal{R}$ is defined as:

$$\mathcal{R} = \begin{cases} |T| - |\alpha|, & \text{if } kill(\alpha_{|\alpha|-1}, m) \\ 0, & \text{otherwise} \end{cases}$$

Here, $\alpha_{|\alpha|-1}$ refers to the last test executed in the sequence α. In the worst case, where all tests are executed without killing the mutant, the reward is zero. As execution progresses, Neural-MCTS converges toward optimal test prioritization, reducing the number of tests needed to detect faults while maintaining effectiveness.

3.2   The Framework

ASCENT[1] is implemented as a Python-based tool developed to validate the proposed approach. The framework is composed of the following main components:

1. **Prioritizer:** Prepares mutants, extracts relevant test methods with metadata, coordinates the mutant loop, and invokes the Neural-MCTS agent for prioritized test execution.
2. **Neural-MCTS Agent:** As the core decision-making component of the system, given a mutant and the set of tests, this module applies the MCTS algorithm to traverse the search tree and determine the optimal test execution sequence. Additionally, it provides observation-target training tuples to the neural network interface and maintains the shared search tree, used across all mutants. Tunable parameters include:

    Buffer Size Maximum training samples in replay buffer. Larger buffers improve generalization but may dilute recent data relevance. Samples are drawn randomly.

    Networks Update Delta Number of episodes (mutant evaluations) occurring between updates of the neural networks. This controls the learning frequency, balancing computational efficiency with responsiveness to new information.

    Batch Size Number of training samples drawn from the replay buffer at each network update. Larger batches can stabilize training through better gradient estimates but come at the cost of slower computation.

    Rollout Delay Episodes before the system starts to rely on neural network predictions instead of heuristic-guided rollouts, allowing initial experience accumulation.

    C Parameter Scalar constant used in the UCT formula to control the trade-off between exploration and exploitation. A higher value encourages exploration, which can be beneficial early in training or in sparse reward settings.

---

[1] https://github.com/filippo-lampa/ASCENT.

3. **Neural Networks Interface:** Prepares input observations and corresponding labels in a format suitable for the two neural networks. It encapsulates both the training loop and the logic for inference.

4 Validation

This section covers the methodology and findings related to the evaluation of our approach. In Sect. 4.1, we present our validation strategy, covering experimental design, network and agent configurations, and subject programs selection. Thereafter, Sect. 4.2 presents the results of the experiments conducted to validate ASCENT.

4.1 Experimental Setup

As previously mentioned, ASCENT aims to minimize the tests required to kill all mutants in a given SUT. We evaluated its effectiveness against a random test selection baseline across five publicly available Solidity projects. This section details our experimental setup and methodology.

Neural-MCTS Agent Parameters. The tunable parameters of the Neural-MCTS agent (introduced in Sect. 3.2) are designed to support effective learning across SUTs of varying size or complexity. Given the limited training data collectible during real-time execution, we selected these parameters to prioritize generalizability and stability during training. While this configuration performed consistently well across our diverse projects, further parameter tuning specific to individual SUTs may yield improved results.

Buffer Size: We set the replay buffer size equal to the total number of mutants to support our goal of prioritizing mutants globally. This design favors long-term memory over short-term data, enabling the agent to retain all experiences and generalize its learning across the entire mutant set.

Batch Size: We selected a batch size of 40. This batch size maintains low prioritization time while steadily reducing loss and improving model performance, demonstrating robustness against data shifts and outliers.

Network Update Delta: The network is updated after every episode (*i.e.*, update delta $= 1$). This frequent update schedule helps maximize the utility of the limited training data. Although frequent updates can risk overfitting, the relatively large batch size mitigates this by exposing the network to a broader sample distribution. This parameter can be increased for lower training times.

Rollout Delay: We set the rollout delay to 45 episodes. This ensures that the neural networks are not used to guide search until they have undergone at least one training iteration. A delay of 45 strikes a balance: setting it too high delays the benefit of informed search and risks polluting MCTS statistics with random data; setting it too low introduces unreliable early predictions. While this setting means that in very small projects (fewer than 45 mutants) the network is never used, these cases typically do not require prioritization due to their limited scale.

C Parameter: We use a C value of 1 in the UCT formula. Traditional MCTS applications often use a higher value (e.g., 2), but since our approach involves single-pass MCTS combined with online learning, excessive exploration can degrade performance by steering the search away from useful patterns. A lower C value encourages learned policy reliance while maintaining some exploration. However, values below 1 would cause the search to get stuck on known sequences, reducing diversity in test exploration.

Networks. We implemented the two networks (value and policy networks) as simple *feed-forward neural networks* using PyTorch [26]. Hidden layers are activated through *ReLU function* while *Adam optimizer*, with a learning rate of $10e-5$ for the policy network and $10e-4$ for the value network, is employed in training. Since the Value network outputs simpler values (the expected outcome of a state), a higher learning rate can still yield effective learning. In contrast, the Policy network outputs a probability distribution, making it more complex and sensitive, demanding a lower learning rate for stable training. Concerning the loss functions, the value network employs a custom mean-squared error loss. Since the training data is often highly imbalanced (the mutant is frequently not killed, and the reward is often zero, leading to underestimation of the value), we apply weighting to penalize underestimation errors more heavily. The custom loss is defined as:

$$L(\hat{y}, y) = \frac{1}{N} \sum_{i=1}^{N} \begin{cases} \alpha(y_i - \hat{y}_i)^2 & \text{if } y_i < \hat{y}_i \\ (y_i - \hat{y}_i)^2 & \text{if } y_i \geq \hat{y}_i \end{cases} \tag{3}$$

where α is a tunable parameter that controls the penalty for underestimation. The policy network uses cross-entropy loss to handle probability distributions.

Experimental Subjects. We evaluated ASCENT on five open-source Solidity projects from Code4rena [1] that rely on the Hardhat[2] testing framework. We chose subjects of varying sizes to assess the effectiveness of the approach in different contexts. To ensure diversity among evaluation subjects, we deliberately selected projects with distinct functional goals and avoided restricting our focus to DeFi DApps, despite their significant representation. Table 1 provides details

---

[2] Hardhat: https://hardhat.org.

about each selected project[3]. For each project, we report the mutation score obtained by running SuMo (i.e., the number of killed mutants over the total number of mutants), the total number of mutants generated, the number of test files in the project's test suite, and the total number of test methods across those files. Recall that a test file is a source file that includes one or more test methods, which are individual test cases typically targeting specific behaviors or conditions in the code. Despite the same test method may appear in multiple files, our prioritization approach treats identical methods as a single test, as rerunning the same logic on a mutant provides no additional benefit.

Table 1. Overview of the experimental subjects used for evaluation. The *MS* column reports the mutation score for each project, as obtained using the SuMo tool.

Project	MS (%)	Mutants	Test Files	Test Methods	Domain
SecondSwap	0.51	925	4	69	DeFi
NextGen	0.64	481	7	57	NFT
THORWallet	0.54	276	2	7	Wallet
BakerFi	0.55	3402	35	340	DeFi
Quadrata	0.83	504	12	107	Passport

Experimental Methodology. To evaluate the improvement offered by ASCENT over the baseline, we structured the experiments into three distinct steps:

1. **Mutant Generation** We used SuMo [9] to generate mutants for five real-world Solidity projects. SuMo first systematically generates mutants by applying a set of mutation operators to the source code. It then executes the original test suite against these mutants within the actual SUT, producing mutation analysis results. Each mutant is associated with metadata including the applied operator, the mutated code fragment, the affected function, and the set of tests that successfully killed it. Although ASCENT does not execute tests directly, we consider test outcomes based on real executions from SuMo to validate the tool, as ASCENT is agnostic to the testing framework used.

2. **Prioritized Testing** For each project, we performed prioritization on the test methods within the respective test suite files, using the mutants generated in the SuMo output file. Since live mutants are unknown a priori in real scenarios, our experiments were conducted using the entire set of mutants

---

[3] BakerFi - https://github.com/code-423n4/2024-12-bakerfi,
SecondSwap - https://github.com/code-423n4/2024-12-secondswap,
NextGen - https://github.com/code-423n4/2025-01-next-generation,
THORWallet - https://github.com/code-423n4/2025-02-thorwallet,
Quadrata - https://github.com/QuadrataNetwork/passport-contracts.

(i.e., without skipping live ones) to prevent additional information leakage and to check the capacity of the tool to address the imbalance in the training data. In this phase, we also evaluated the impact of different system and network parameters on the performance of the approach. Each experiment was repeated 10 times, with mutants shuffled before each run to ensure robustness and statistical significance. The results reported in this work are averaged over the ten experimental runs.

3. **Baseline Testing** We performed testing on the same five projects using a random baseline approach. The baseline randomly selects and executes tests on mutants. If a mutant is live after a test, the next test is executed; once a mutant is killed, the baseline proceeds to the next mutant. As for the previous phase, each baseline experiment was run 10 times, with mutants shuffled at the beginning of each execution. The final result is again the average of these 10 runs to ensure the validity and reliability of the baseline performance.

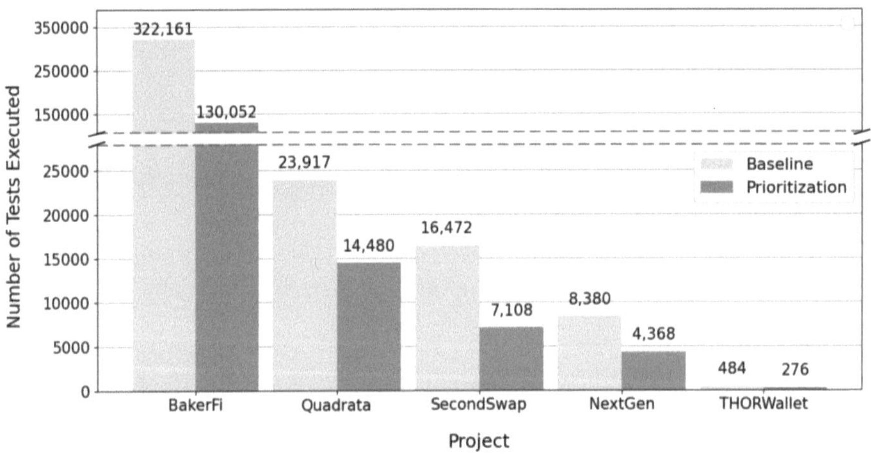

Fig. 3. Total Number of Tests Executed per Project Using the Randomized Baseline and ASCENT Approaches.

4.2   Results

Although the prioritization strategy was applied to the full set of mutants, we excluded live mutants (i.e., those that could not be killed by any test and were not detected by SuMo) from analysis, as their inability to be killed makes them irrelevant to evaluating prioritization effectiveness. Instead, we focus on the number of tests required to kill non-live mutants, where prioritization has real impact. Figure 3 compares the performance of our approach against the baseline across the five SUTs. In every case, ASCENT significantly reduces the number of tests needed to kill all mutants. As shown in Table 2, the percentage of improvement is consistently greater than or equal to 40%, regardless of the system's size, the number of mutants, or the test suite size. Unlike many existing approaches in the literature, ASCENT achieves this without any preprocessing, system-specific heuristics, or parameter tuning. Its performance remains robust across all subjects, without significantly underperforming on any project. Our results also reveal a trend: improvements scale with the number of *test methods* and *mutants*. This can be attributed to three factors: (1) larger test suites offer higher potential gains from prioritization, (2) more test methods increase opportunities for pattern discovery, and (3) more mutants help the approach identify broadly effective tests across different mutation operators.

Despite its large test suite, *Quadrata* shows smaller gains from prioritization compared to smaller projects, a seemingly counterintuitive result. Typically, larger suites offer greater potential for optimization. However, Quadrata also has a notably high mutation score (Table 1). This suggests that developers invested more effort into creating a thorough test suite, or that the mutants generated for this project were easier to kill. Either way, the test order has minimal impact, as most mutants are killed early regardless. This reflects a ceiling effect rather than a limitation of our method. Ultimately, these results suggest that the effectiveness of test prioritization is mainly influenced by the size of the test suite, but also by the distribution of mutant difficulty and how selectively tests can target them. When only a subset of tests are capable of killing the more difficult mutants, our approach becomes significantly more impactful.

Table 2. Test count reduction achieved with prioritization.

Project	Default	Prioritization	Improvement
BakerFi	322,161	130,052	60%
SecondSwap	16,472	7,108	57%
NextGen	8,380	4,368	48%
THORWallet	484	276	43%
Quadrata	23,917	14,480	40%

Reward Graph Analysis. Although experimental results show some degree of improvement over the baseline, the minimal state representation currently adopted, a simplistic reward signal, and the intentional exclusion of system- and network-level hyperparameter tuning to test generalization, cap the performance of the prioritization strategy. Figure 4 shows the evolution of the average reward over time, as well as the individual rewards assigned to each mutant during prioritization, focusing on the largest and best-performing SUT among those evaluated. In the initial iterations, the average reward distribution remains centered, resembling a normal distribution. After the first few iterations, it rapidly starts increasing until step 250, when it almost reaches a plateau and enters a slow learning phase. This behavior suggests that while the system is effectively learning in the early stages, it then prematurely starts converging towards a suboptimal solution, likely a local minimum. Tweaking the C parameter to gradually increase exploration over time could help the model continue investigating potentially valuable test sequences, rather than prematurely converging on suboptimal ones. This adjustment would allow the prioritization strategy to remain more adaptive through training, especially in later stages where the learning trend begins to plateau. Moreover, tuning the batch size considering the size of the SUT could also influence the model's capacity to avoid local minima. While the relatively small batch size employed in our experiments proved sufficient to outperform the baseline across all projects, it may still result in the model overfitting early patterns.

5   Related Work

Test case prioritization aims to improve testing efficiency by ordering tests to detect faults earlier [14]. Major techniques include coverage-based [27], requirement-based, risk-based, search-based, fault-based [15], history-based, and Markov chain-based approaches [11]. Khatibsyarbini et al. provide a comprehensive survey of these methods and their varying effectiveness across contexts [20]. A common limitation is their inconsistent performance across projects. Recent advances have introduced machine learning-based methods [25], which offer better adaptability to different systems under test. However, these techniques often require precomputed features, domain-specific tuning, or large, high-quality datasets, which limit their applicability in real-world environments.

Test Prioritization through Reinforcement Learning. Recent research has explored reinforcement learning (RL) for test prioritization to improve adaptability without requiring prior data. Though not strictly RL, Genetic Algorithms also address dynamic optimization problems without pre-existing datasets. Bajaj et al. systematically reviewed their application in regression testing [4]. Spieker et al. [32] applied deep RL to continuous integration (CI) environments, using test metadata and historical data to guide prioritization. Similarly, Bagherzadeh et al. ranked tests based on execution history and static code features [3]. Shi et al. extended Spieker's approach by incorporating a multi-objective reward function based on execution time and recent fault detection history [29]. While promising, these methods do not address mutation testing specifically, which presents unique challenges. Moreover, most rely on model-free RL techniques. Model-based RL is better suited to real-time mutation testing, as it enables more informed decision-making with fewer interactions, retaining the benefits of model-based reasoning without incurring its typical performance costs.

Test Prioritization and Mutation Testing. Many prior works on test prioritization and mutation testing focus on improving Regression Test Selection (RTS) by

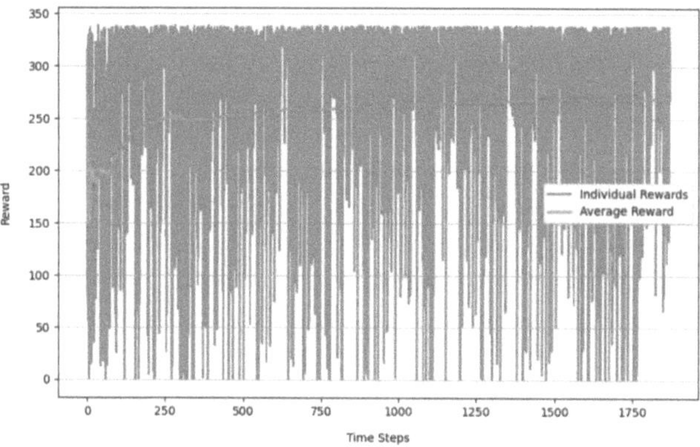

Fig. 4. Plot of individual rewards (green) and average reward (orange) across all mutants for the BakerFi project. (Color figure online)

identifying and re-executing only tests likely affected by code changes [10,13,35]. While effective in reducing costs, these methods address a different problem from intra-cycle test prioritization, which aims to optimize fault detection order within a single test run. In this context, Shin et al. [30] introduced a diversity-aware mutation adequacy metric that ranks tests based on how effectively they distinguish mutants, using mutation analysis as a prioritization surrogate. Lou et al. [21] applied RL to prioritize tests in CI environments, optimizing a reward function that favors early failure detection within time constraints. More directly aligned with our approach, Zhang et al. [34] proposed FaMT, which prioritizes tests for mutation analysis using multi-level coverage and power scores reflecting a test's historical mutant-killing effectiveness. While promising, these methods struggle with generalizability, showing inconsistent performance across projects.

6 Threats to Validity

In this section, we identify both internal and external threats that may affect the correctness and generalizability of our findings [28].

Internal Validity. Our framework relies on prior probabilities, predicted by the policy network, for action selection in the UCT exploration term. These priors are then used as targets for training the policy network, creating a feedback loop where action selection directly influences training targets. To mitigate this, we apply a rollout delay, postponing reliance on learned policies until sufficient experience is gathered. Another threat is the computational overhead of neural components, where training and inference times depend heavily on tuned hyperparameters like batch size and update frequency. We addressed this through careful parameter tuning to balance efficiency and performance.

External Validity. Our evaluation, limited to a fixed set of Solidity projects and SuMo mutation operators, may restrict the generalizability of results. While ASCENT is framework-agnostic in design, we only tested it using HardHat, leaving its effectiveness with other tools unverified. We ensured project diversity by selecting varying sizes and domains, but performance may vary with different testing frameworks or lower-quality test suites. Additionally, our state representation assumes a correlation between mutation operators and test behavior. If this assumption fails (e.g., in environments with redundant tests or many equivalent mutants [16]) the prioritization policy's effectiveness may diminish.

7   Conclusions and Future Work

Mutation testing is a powerful but computationally intensive technique due to the need to run full test suites against all mutants. Test prioritization mitigates this cost by executing the most impactful tests first. Existing methods often rely on fixed heuristics, limiting their adaptability. In this work, we introduced ASCENT, a test prioritization tool using a Neural Monte Carlo Tree Search (Neural-MCTS) algorithm. ASCENT operates in an online and real-time manner while effectively handling limited data availability, a common constraint in practical scenarios. We evaluated ASCENT on five open-source Solidity projects using HardHat. Results show a consistent reduction in the number of tests required for effective mutation analysis without compromising mutation scores. To test the generalization capability of our method, we maintained a fixed state representation and hyperparameters for both the system and the neural network. While this configuration was sufficient to outperform baseline techniques, our findings highlight the importance of tuning these components for optimal performance in production environments. Future work could explore richer state representations to capture deeper test and SUT characteristics, as well as assess the effect of different neural architectures and hyperparameters on performance. Efficiency may be improved through *alpha-beta pruning* to reduce the number of explored nodes during the search, or *cutoff thresholds* to better exploit MCTS's anytime nature. Additionally, replacing feedforward networks with *Recurrent Neural Networks (RNNs)* or *Transformer-based models* could better capture the sequential nature of test execution. Finally, future evaluations could incorporate comparisons with established test prioritization techniques, such as those discussed in Sect. 5 (e.g., coverage-based or fault-based heuristics), to enable a more comprehensive assessment of the approach's effectiveness.

References

1. Code4rena — code4rena.com. https://code4rena.com/ (2025)
2. Andrews, J.H., Briand, L.C., Labiche, Y., Namin, A.S.: Using mutation analysis for assessing and comparing testing coverage criteria. IEEE Trans. Software Eng. **32**(8), 608–624 (2006)

3. Bagherzadeh, M., Kahani, N., Briand, L.: Reinforcement learning for test case prioritization. IEEE Trans. Software Eng. **48**(8), 2836–2856 (2021)
4. Bajaj, A., Sangwan, O.P.: A systematic literature review of test case prioritization using genetic algorithms. IEEE Access **7**, 126355–126375 (2019)
5. Banescu, S., Barboni, M., Morichetta, A., Polini, A., Zulkoski, E.: Enhanced mutation testing of smart contracts in support of code inspection. In: 2024 IEEE International Conference on Blockchain and Cryptocurrency (ICBC), pp. 558–566 (2024). https://doi.org/10.1109/ICBC59979.2024.10634403
6. Barboni, M., Lampa, F., Morichetta, A., Polini, A., Zulkoski, E.: Alchemist: LLM-driven test generation using solidity mutants and the scientific method. In: IEEE International Conference on Blockchain and Cryptocurrency (ICBC) (2025)
7. Barboni, M., Lampa, F., Morichetta, A., Polini, A., Zulkoski, E.: Mutant-driven test generation for ethereum smart contracts via llms. In: IEEE International Conference on Artificial Intelligence Testing (AITest) (2025)
8. Barboni, M., Morichetta, A., Polini, A.: Smart contract testing: challenges and opportunities. In: Proceedings of the 5th International Workshop on Emerging Trends in Software Engineering for Blockchain, WETSEB@ICSE 2022, pp. 21–24. ACM (2022)
9. Barboni, M., Morichetta, A., Polini, A.: Sumo: a mutation testing approach and tool for the Ethereum blockchain. J. Syst. Softw. **193**, 111445 (2022)
10. Barboni, M., Morichetta, A., Polini, A., Casoni, F.: Resumo: a regression strategy and tool for mutation testing of solidity smart contracts. Software Qual. J. **32**(1), 225–253 (2024)
11. Barbosa, G., de Souza, É.F., dos Santos, L.B.R., da Silva, M., Balera, J.M., Vijaykumar, N.L.: A systematic literature review on prioritizing software test cases using markov chains. Inf. Softw. Technol. **147**, 106902 (2022)
12. Chen, H., Zhu, C., Zhang, L., Zhao, Y., Wang, L.: A survey of mutation based testing adequacy study on smart contract. In: 11th International Conference on Dependable Systems and Their Applications, DSA 2024, pp. 217–220. IEEE (2024)
13. Chen, L., Zhang, L.: Speeding up mutation testing via regression test selection: an extensive study. In: 11th IEEE International Conference on Software Testing, Verification and Validation, ICST 2018, pp. 58–69. IEEE Computer Society (2018)
14. Elbaum, S., Malishevsky, A.G., Rothermel, G.: Test case prioritization: a family of empirical studies. IEEE Trans. Softw. Eng. **28**(2), 159–182 (2002)
15. Farooq, F., Nadeem, A.: A fault based approach to test case prioritization. In: 2017 International Conference on Frontiers of Information Technology (FIT), pp. 52–57. IEEE (2017)
16. Grün, B.J.M., Schuler, D., Zeller, A.: The impact of equivalent mutants. In: 2009 International Conference on Software Testing, Verification, and Validation Workshops, pp. 192–199 (2009)
17. Hartel, P., Schumi, R.: Mutation testing of smart contracts at scale. In: International conference on tests and proofs, pp. 23–42. Springer (2020)
18. Honig, J.J., Everts, M.H., Huisman, M.: Practical mutation testing for smart contracts. In: Data Privacy Management, Cryptocurrencies and Blockchain Technology, pp. 289–303. Springer (2019)
19. Jia, Y., Harman, M.: An analysis and survey of the development of mutation testing. IEEE Trans. Software Eng. **37**(5), 649–678 (2010)
20. Khatibsyarbini, M., Isa, M.A., Jawawi, D.N., Tumeng, R.: Test case prioritization approaches in regression testing: A systematic literature review. Inf. Softw. Technol. **93**, 74–93 (2018)

21. Lou, Y., Hao, D., Zhang, L.: Mutation-based test-case prioritization in software evolution. In: 2015 IEEE 26th International Symposium on Software Reliability Engineering (ISSRE), pp. 46–57 (2015)
22. Metropolis, N., Ulam, S.: The monte carlo method. J. Am. Stat. Assoc. **44**(247), 335–341 (1949)
23. Mor, A.: Evaluate the effectiveness of test suite prioritization techniques using APFD metric. IOSR J. Comput. **16**(4), 47–51 (2014)
24. Offutt, A.J., Untch, R.H.: Mutation 2000: Uniting the orthogonal. Mutation testing for the new century **4** (2001)
25. Pan, R., Bagherzadeh, M., Ghaleb, T.A., Briand, L.: Test case selection and prioritization using machine learning: a systematic literature review. Empir. Softw. Eng. **27**(2), 29 (2022)
26. Paszke, A., et al.: Pytorch: An imperative style, high-performance deep learning library (2019). https://arxiv.org/abs/1912.01703
27. Rothermel, G., Untch, R.H., Chu, C., Harrold, M.J.: Prioritizing test cases for regression testing. IEEE Trans. Software Eng. **27**(10), 929–948 (2001)
28. Runeson, P., Höst, M.: Guidelines for conducting and reporting case study research in software engineering. Empir. Softw. Eng. **14**(2), 131–164 (2009)
29. Shi, T., Xiao, L., Wu, K.: Reinforcement learning based test case prioritization for enhancing the security of software. In: 2020 IEEE 7th International Conference on Data Science and Advanced Analytics (DSAA), pp. 663–672. IEEE (2020)
30. Shin, D., Yoo, S., Papadakis, M., Bae, D.H.: Empirical evaluation of mutation-based test case prioritization techniques. Softw. Test., Verif. Reliab. **29**(1–2), e1695 (2019)
31. Silver, D., et al.: Mastering chess and shogi by self-play with a general reinforcement learning algorithm. CoRR **abs/1712.01815** (2017). http://arxiv.org/abs/1712.01815
32. Spieker, H., Gotlieb, A., Marijan, D., Mossige, M.: Reinforcement learning for automatic test case prioritization and selection in continuous integration. In: Proceedings of the 26th ACM SIGSOFT International Symposium on Software Testing and Analysis, pp. 12–22 (2017)
33. Srivastava, P.R.: Test case prioritization. J. Theor. Appl. Inform. Technol. **4**(3) (2008)
34. Zhang, L., Marinov, D., Khurshid, S.: Faster mutation testing inspired by test prioritization and reduction. In: Proceedings of the 2013 International Symposium on Software Testing and Analysis, pp. 235–245. ISSTA 2013, Association for Computing Machinery, New York, NY, USA (2013)
35. Zhang, L., Marinov, D., Zhang, L., Khurshid, S.: Regression mutation testing. In: Heimdahl, M.P.E., Su, Z. (eds.) International Symposium on Software Testing and Analysis, ISSTA 2012, pp. 331–341. ACM (2012)

Advanced Large Language Models Prompting Strategies for Reentrancy Classification and Explanation in Smart Contracts

Matteo Rizzo[1], Alvise Spanò[1], Lorenzo Benetollo[1,2], Dalila Ressi[1(✉)], Andrea Gasparetto[1], and Sabina Rossi[1]

[1] Ca' Foscari University of Venice, Venice, Italy
{matteo.rizzo,alvise.spano,dalila.ressi,
andrea.gasparetto,sabina.rossi}@unive.it, lorenzo.benetollo@unicam.it
[2] University of Camerino, Camerino, Italy

Abstract. Reentrancy vulnerabilities pose a pervasive threat to blockchain ecosystems, demanding detection methods that are both highly accurate and produce trustworthy, human-verifiable explanations. While Large Language Models (LLMs) show promise, their opaque decision-making processes limit their reliability in this security-critical domain. We address this challenge by systematically evaluating two competing guidance strategies: grounding LLM analysis in external, structural evidence (via Retrieval-Augmented Generation) versus prescribing a human-expert-crafted, internal thought process (via Chain of Thought). A reasoning-optimized model enhanced by a Structurally-Aware RAG pipeline establishes a new state-of-the-art, surpassing traditional static analysis, deep learning, and other LLM baselines on a curated dataset of manually verified contracts. This evidence-grounded approach not only yields superior classification accuracy but, critically, produces transparent and actionable explanations that human experts judged as maximally correct and informative. By grounding automated analysis in verifiable evidence, our work delivers a validated blueprint for the next generation of AI-powered security tools.

Keywords: Smart contracts · Reentrancy · Large Language Models · Explainability

1 Introduction

Smart contracts are at the heart of the decentralized application ecosystem, yet their security remains a pressing concern. The infamous 2016 DAO hack, caused by a reentrancy vulnerability, stands as a sobering example of the financial and reputational damage that a single bug can inflict. Despite years of research and tool development, vulnerabilities such as reentrancy persist, exposing the limitations of conventional security analysis. Static analysis tools rely heavily on

© ICST Institute for Computer Sciences, Social Informatics and Telecommunications Engineering 2026
Published by Springer Nature Switzerland AG 2026. All Rights Reserved
W. Knottenbelt et al. (Eds.): Blocktea 2025, LNICST 669, pp. 37–56, 2026.
https://doi.org/10.1007/978-3-032-12335-0_3

rule-based logic, which often leads to a flood of false positives and limited adaptability. Dynamic tools, while more precise in execution, are constrained by path coverage and the generation of test inputs. Both approaches struggle to explain their findings in a way that is actionable and understandable to developers, often reducing their output to little more than warning flags without context.

Another major limitation of traditional tools is their reliance on fixed definitions of what constitutes a vulnerability. In the case of reentrancy, for instance, different tools employ varying interpretations. Slither, for example, distinguishes between four categories (Ether-stealing, non-Ether-stealing, benign, and event-reordering reentrancy) while other analyzers apply coarser or incompatible classifications. This lack of consensus on what is considered reentrant and what is not limits the adaptability of these tools when new attack patterns emerge or when nuanced interpretations of a vulnerability are required. Modifying a traditional analyzer to accommodate a novel reentrancy pattern would entail deep architectural changes as well as a major re-formalization of the underlying theoretical framework.

Large Language Models (LLMs) offer a radically different paradigm. Trained on massive corpora of code and text, these models are capable of recognizing patterns, reasoning about logic, and even generating natural-language explanations for their outputs—all without being explicitly programmed for the task.

This paper tackles that challenge head-on. Rather than relying on naïve prompting, we investigate how structured reasoning and code-aware retrieval can enhance the accuracy and reliability of LLMs in the context of smart contract security. We dissect how providing models with examples that reflect the actual structure of the code under analysis, rather than just its textual surface, can sharpen their diagnostic capabilities. We also study how guiding the model's reasoning through carefully designed prompting strategies can reduce logical errors and produce explanations that are both interpretable and verifiable [17]. Finally, we explore how combining these two approaches—reasoning guidance and structural context—can yield results that surpass the sum of their parts, moving closer to trustworthy, expert-level auditing powered by LLMs.

Our experiments on a curated benchmark of real-world, verified Solidity contracts demonstrate that these strategies not only improve classification accuracy but also foster explainability and reduce hallucination. The result is a system that not only detects reentrancy vulnerabilities but also explains them in transparent, correct, and verifiable ways.

The contributions of this paper follow:

- **Structural Equality for Retrieval Augmented Generation (RAG):** We propose a novel few-shot RAG strategy that retrieves examples based on the notion of structural similarity between programs, which is calculated by comparing either the Abstract Syntax Tree (AST) and the Control Flow Graph (CFG).
- **Expert-Crafted Chain-of-Thought (CoT):** We design a rigorous CoT prompting template, informed by domain expertise, to enforce a reasoning process that mirrors the logic followed by human security auditors.

– **Strategy Evaluation:** We combine structured CoT prompting with our RAG pipeline to create a hybrid approach that synergizes logical reasoning and relevant code context, delivering both accuracy and explainability.
– **Hallucination Mitigation:** We demonstrate empirically that our hybrid strategy significantly reduces LLM hallucination, marking a step toward safe and reliable LLM-based tools for smart contract auditing.

Our code repository is available for reproducibility at: https://github.com/ matteo-rizzo/advanced-llm-prompting-for-reentrancy.

2   Background

This section provides an overview of the foundational concepts for understanding our work. We begin by providing an informal definition of reentrancy as a vulnerability in Ethereum smart contracts, followed by a brief description of analysis techniques based on formal methods traditionally used for tampering with it. We finally introduce LLMs and the advanced prompting strategies—CoT and RAG—that form the basis of our proposed solution.

A smart contract is an immutable, self-executing program stored on a blockchain (in our case, Ethereum). While smart contracts are generally immutable—meaning their code cannot be altered once deployed—this immutability can be circumvented through design patterns such as proxy contracts, which have gained increasing popularity in recent years. Proxy contracts separate logic from storage, allowing upgrades to the contract's logic while preserving state. Despite this flexibility, pre-deployment security auditing remains crucial. Among the most studied vulnerabilities is *reentrancy*, especially in Ethereum. It occurs when a contract makes an external call to another, potentially malicious, contract before it has finalized its state-changing logic. Suppose the callee contract makes a recursive call back into the original function before it completes, allowing it to repeatedly execute a portion of the code, such as a withdrawal function, thereby draining the contract of its funds. The canonical flawed pattern, known as the "call-before-update" pattern, is illustrated by the following Solidity snippet:

```solidity
function withdraw(uint amount) public {
    // 1. Check if the user has enough balance
    require(balances[msg.sender] >= amount);

    // 2. Make the external call BEFORE updating the balance (VULNERABLE)
    (bool success, ) = msg.sender.call{value: amount}("");
    require(success, "Transfer failed.");

    // 3. Update the user's balance (too late)
    balances[msg.sender] -= amount;
}
```

To secure implementations the *Checks-Effects-Interactions (CEI)* pattern has been canonized by the Solidity community, which suggests programmer to perform all state changes (*Effects*) before external calls (*Interactions*) are made. Such pattern is only a good practice though, and two problems may incur: first, programmers may simply ignore it and still produce exploitable code; secondly, subtle scenarios or complex contracts may produce behaviors - hence, exhibit potential exploits - that are difficult to predict and analyze.

2.1 Formal Methods for Code Analysis

The primary methods for automated smart contract auditing have traditionally been static and dynamic analysis [4]. Tools for *static* analysis inspect the smart contract's source code or bytecode without executing it. They employ techniques such as control-flow graph analysis, symbolic execution, and syntax-directed pattern matching to identify potential vulnerabilities according to a predefined set of rules [7,14]. While effective at identifying many common anti-patterns, static analysis often suffers from a high rate of false positives and can miss complex or novel vulnerabilities not covered by its rule set [14].

Their counterpart are tools that perform *dynamic* analysis by executing the smart contract in a simulated environment to observe its behavior [8]. By sending a series of transactions to the contract, these tools (often referred to as fuzzers) explore different execution paths to uncover vulnerabilities that only manifest at runtime. However, their primary limitation is achieving complete path coverage; complex contracts with many possible states make it computationally infeasible to explore every possible execution trace, leading to potential false negatives [8]. A common weakness across both paradigms is their limited explanatory power, often leaving developers to decipher cryptic warnings [4].

2.2 Large Language Models for Code Analysis

LLMs are Deep Learning (DL) models pre-trained on vast corpora of text and code. This pre-training endows them with a robust, generalized understanding of language, syntax, and logical patterns. When applied to source code, LLMs can perform a variety of "code intelligence" tasks, such as code completion, translation, and bug detection, often with impressive *zero-shot* (no examples) or *few-shot* (a few examples) capabilities [1]. Their generative nature allows them to not only classify code but also to articulate the reasoning behind their decisions in natural language, a key advantage over traditional tools.

To steer LLM behavior toward more accurate and reliable outputs, several advanced prompting techniques have been developed. Our work focuses on two of the most prominent: *CoT* and *RAG*. The former is a form of prompting technique designed to elicit more complex reasoning from LLMs. Instead of asking for a direct answer, a CoT prompt encourages the model to generate a series of intermediate, logical steps that lead to the conclusion [19]. By externalizing the reasoning process, the model is less likely to make intuitive leaps and more likely to follow a coherent path, which has been shown to significantly improve performance on arithmetic, commonsense, and symbolic reasoning tasks. The generated chain of thought also provides a transparent window into the model's "thinking," making its output more interpretable and easier to debug. The latter, RAG, is a framework that grounds an LLM's output in external, verifiable knowledge, thereby reducing hallucinations and improving factual accuracy [11]. A standard RAG pipeline works in two stages. First, given a user query, a *retriever* module searches a knowledge base to find information relevant to the query. Second, the retrieved data is concatenated with the original query to form an expanded prompt, which is then fed to the LLM. This provides the model with relevant, in-session context, encouraging it to base its generated response on the provided evidence rather than relying solely on its internal, parametric knowledge.

3 Related Work

Reentrancy is one of the most critical and extensively studied vulnerabilities in Ethereum smart contracts. Detection techniques have evolved from traditional static and symbolic analyzers to Machine Learning (ML) models and, more recently, LLMs. We review these approaches across three categories: static and symbolic analysis, ML methods, and LLM-based systems, concluding with a discussion on structured prompting for explainable and verifiable reasoning.

3.1 Static Analysis and Symbolic Techniques

A wide range of static and symbolic tools has been proposed for auditing smart contracts. Early systems such as Oyente [14] pioneered the use of symbolic execution, control-flow analysis, and pattern-based vulnerability detection. While influential, many of these tools are no longer maintained or compatible with recent Solidity versions, particularly post-0.8.x. In this work, we focus on three widely adopted tools that are still actively maintained and support modern Solidity: Slither [7], Mythril [2], and Confuzzius [18]. Although not recent in origin, these analyzers remain relevant due to continued development and their distinct analysis strategies. Slither is a static analyzer that utilizes an SSA-based intermediate representation (SlithIR) and incorporates several detectors targeting various forms of reentrancy. Mythril employs symbolic execution and SMT solving to identify unsafe low-level calls lacking proper state updates. Confuzzius combines symbolic execution with evolutionary fuzzing, flagging suspicious traces involving storage access before and after external calls.

3.2 Learning-Based Detectors

ML approaches aim to address static analysis limitations such as high false positives and rigid pattern encoding. Traditional ML and DL techniques—including LSTMs, GNNs, and Transformer-based models like CodeBERT—have been applied to vulnerability classification with promising results [16]. These models are often trained on SmartBugs Wild [6], a large but weakly-labeled dataset, commonly annotated using the very static analyzers they aim to replace This feedback loop has led to inconsistent definitions of reentrancy and poor support for modern contracts.

Due to dataset imbalance and outdated syntax, it remains difficult to evaluate or generalize such models [15]. The lack of a standardized benchmark severely hinders meaningful comparisons across different architectures, particularly among DL and custom-designed models. Furthermore, most approaches are designed to detect a wide range of vulnerabilities, often without a specific focus on reentrancy, and frequently omit class-specific performance metrics, such as the per-class F1 score.

3.3 Large Language Models

Recent interest has turned to LLMs for contract vulnerability detection, particularly due to their dual capabilities in code understanding and natural language generation [13]. Single-stage prompts enable zero-shot classification, but models like GPT-4 still produce high false positive rates and hallucinated reasoning [10]. Moreover, LLMs' performance is highly task-dependent and often brittle when asked to reason over code transformations.

Multi-stage LLM architectures attempt to improve precision. GPTLens [10], for instance, separates vulnerability generation and critique using an adversarial "Auditor-Critic" loop. However, even these advanced techniques struggle with reentrancy, often due to the use of poor-quality labels and subtle semantic overlaps between patterns.

Our contribution lies in designing principled prompting strategies that integrate domain knowledge into LLM workflows. While generic CoT prompting elicits step-by-step reasoning [19], it does not ensure correctness or completeness in high-stakes domains, such as smart contract auditing. We introduce a procedural CoT framework derived from the CEI threat model for reentrancy, breaking down the reasoning process into verifiable steps such as identifying external calls and validating state update order. This approach aligns with recent structured prompting work [12], but applies it in a security-specific setting where correctness is critical.

To improve factual grounding, we incorporate a structurally-aware Retrieval-Augmented Generation (RAG) mechanism [20]. While prior RAG methods rely on semantic similarity, this can mislead LLMs in logic-sensitive tasks. Instead, we compute structural similarity using classic program analysis tools; specifically, CFGs and ASTs extracted with Slither and compared using the Weisfeiler-Lehman kernel. While graph-based similarity has been used for clone detection, its use as a retrieval filter for RAG in smart contract analysis is novel and effective. This hybrid approach—symbolically structured CoT reasoning combined with retrieval guided by code structure—represents a neuro-symbolic direction for vulnerability detection. By grounding explanations in verifiable logic and controlling evidence via structural similarity, we aim to mitigate the opacity and unreliability that have plagued prior ML and LLM-based methods.

4   Methodology

Our methodological approach first establishes performance baselines across several paradigms. Then it assesses a series of prompting strategies engineered to enhance the LLM's logical fidelity and factual grounding. All experiments are anchored by a manually validated benchmark dataset and are evaluated via a protocol measuring both predictive accuracy and the qualitative utility of the generated explanations. A consistent set of formal principles for identifying reentrancy (e.g., CEI pattern adherence, valid reentrancy guard patterns) was provided to the LLMs in all relevant experiments to ensure consistency. Figure 1 illustrates the complete methodological workflow.

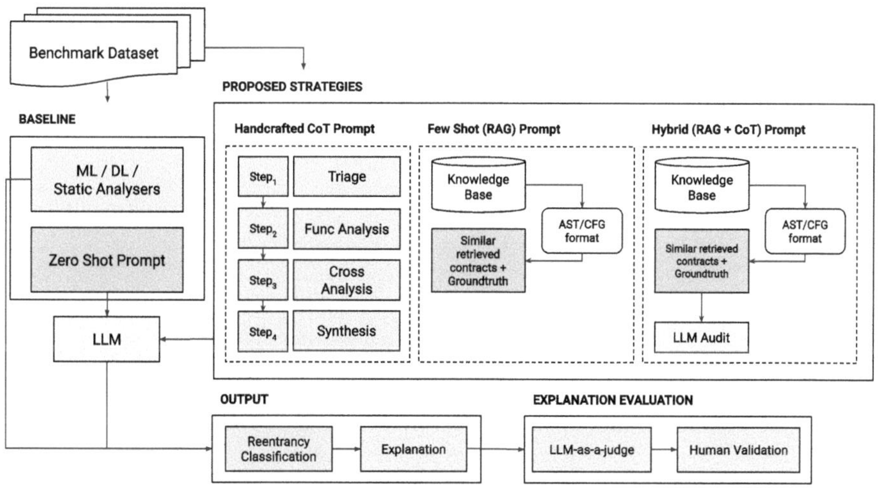

Fig. 1. Methodology workflow.

4.1   Reentrancy Detection Principles

To ensure a consistent and rigorous analytical standard across all experimental arms—from human expert validation to our LLM-based strategies—we established a formal set of reentrancy detection principles. This framework moves beyond naive pattern matching to incorporate a nuanced understanding of smart contract execution logic, mitigation techniques, and plausible exploitability.

At its core, our framework is built upon a strict definition of the CEI pattern. A contract is considered to adhere to this pattern if all state modifications are unconditionally completed *before* any external call within a given logical operation. For this purpose, an *Effect* is strictly defined as a contract state modification via the assignment operator. Operations such as event emissions or `require`/`assert` statements are not considered Effects.

Conversely, an *Interaction* is narrowly defined as an external call that can shift control flow to a potentially malicious contract. This includes low-level primitives like `.call` and `.delegatecall`, as well as any method invocation on an external contract or interface type. Primitives that do not transfer execution control in a reentrant manner, such as `.staticcall`, or that have built-in gas limitations that prevent reentrancy, like native `.send` and `.transfer`, are explicitly excluded from this definition.

The presence of a potential CEI violation is a necessary, but not sufficient, condition for vulnerability classification. Our framework requires the identification of a *plausible exploit path* where reentrancy leads to a tangible, harmful outcome, which may include not only theft of assets but also critical state inconsistencies that break contract logic.

Finally, the framework accounts for common mitigation strategies. A function protected by a correctly implemented and applied reentrancy guard (e.g., a standard `nonReentrant` modifier or a custom mutex) is generally considered safe from re-entering itself. However, in cases of *cross-function reentrancy*—where an external call in function `A` allows re-entry into a different function `B` that shares state with `A`—the protective mechanism must correctly guard all relevant functions in the potential execution path to be considered effective.

4.2   Benchmark Construction and Validation

The cornerstone of this investigation is a benchmark dataset constructed to address critical deficiencies in extant resources. An initial corpus was aggregated from three established sources [3,5,9] and subsequently underwent deduplication and compilation filtering. The principal contribution resides in a manual verification phase conducted by three domain experts, following a predefined rubric based on a formal definition of reentrancy. This audit revealed profound inaccuracies in prior labels; notably, 28 contracts previously designated as reentrant were confirmed to be safe, while 5 labeled safe were found to contain vulnerabilities. To quantify the reliability of this process, we measured the inter-rater reliability before a final consensus discussion, achieving a Fleiss' Kappa of 0.89, indicating substantial agreement. This exacting process yielded our final benchmark of 436 contracts (122 reentrant, 314 safe), providing a high-fidelity ground truth.

To contextualize the performance of our proposed approach, we compare it against a diverse set of strong baselines spanning traditional program analysis, classical and neural ML, and recent zero-shot language models. For benchmarking against established, non-learning techniques, we evaluated a portfolio of three prominent analyzers: *Slither*, *Mythril*, and *Confuzzious*. These were deliberately selected to represent the field's dominant paradigms: static analysis, symbolic execution, and fuzzing, respectively. The tools were run using their default configurations via the SmartBugs framework to establish a fair and reproducible benchmark of their standard, out-of-the-box performance.

We also investigated seven traditional ML models (Gradient Boosting, Gaussian Naive Bayes, K-Nearest Neighbors, Logistic Regression, Random Forest, Support Vector Machine, Extreme Gradient Boosting) and three DL architectures (Feed Forward Neural Network, Bidirectional Long Short Term Memory, and CodeBERT). To ensure competitive performance, all traditional models underwent hyperparameter optimization using a grid search.

For LLMs, we evaluated the untuned capabilities of six models: GPT-4o, GPT-4.1, GPT-4.1-mini, GPT-4.1-nano, o3-mini, and o4-mini. We deliberately exclude fine-tuning to isolate the effects of in-context learning, reserving a direct comparison against it for future work. To enhance LLM performance beyond zero-shot capabilities, we explore three advanced prompting strategies designed to inject structural priors, expert reasoning patterns, or both. These approaches aim to systematically guide the model toward accurate and interpretable assessments of vulnerability.

Structurally-Aware RAG. This strategy grounds the LLM with in-context examples. For a target contract, our pipeline retrieves the top-k structurally analogous contracts ($k = 3$, determined empirically in Sect. 5.1) based on the graph similarity of their ASTs and CFGs. The source code of these examples is then provided to the LLM as context for its analysis.

Expert-Crafted CoT. This strategy implements the four-step audit process not as a single monolithic prompt, but as a programmatic chain of four sequential LLM calls, where the output of one step is consumed as the input for the next. The sequence enforces a formal decomposition of the problem: (1) a *Triage* step identifies all functions with external calls; (2) a localized *Function Analysis* step assesses each function individually; (3) a *Cross Function Analysis* step analyzes the interaction between these functions; and (4) a final *Synthesis* step aggregates all intermediate findings into a conclusive verdict.

Hybrid (CoT + RAG) Strategy. This strategy integrates evidence with reasoning through a two-stage context enrichment process. First, in a preliminary step, a separate LLM instance generates a detailed security audit for each of the $k = 3$ retrieved examples and their corresponding labels, explaining *why* they are safe or vulnerable according to a standardized template. Second, the primary LLM is tasked with analyzing the target contract, but it is provided with these pre-computed, structured analyses as its context, rather than raw source code. This approach provides a set of worked examples, demonstrating how to apply the reasoning principles to concrete cases before the model begins its analysis.

To rigorously evaluate model performance, we designed a two-part protocol that considers both *predictive accuracy* and the *quality of generated explanations*. This ensures a comprehensive assessment—capturing not only what the models predict, but also how and why they arrive at their conclusions. Predictive performance was measured using standard macro-averaged metrics—precision, recall, and F1-score—calculated over a 3-fold cross-validation setup to ensure robustness across samples. To assess the quality of explanations, we adopted a two-stage process. First, an automated evaluation employed an *LLM-as-a-Judge* (specifically, o4-mini) to rate the explanations according to a structured rubric.

This rubric was aligned with the same formal criteria used during task design. It evaluated each explanation across three dimensions: correctness (factual accuracy), informativeness (depth and helpfulness), and pertinence (conciseness and relevance). In the second stage, a human expert evaluation was conducted by three security professionals on a randomly selected sample of 88 explanations from one of the cross-validation test splits. The human experts were required to ground their evaluation on the same rubric employed by the LLM-as-a-Judge. We used the two-sided Wilcoxon signed-rank test ($p < 0.05$) to assess statistical significance in the ordinal ratings.

4.3   Implementation and Reproducibility

Implementations relied on standard libraries: traditional models used `scikit-learn` (v1.6.0); DL models used `PyTorch` (v2.4.1). The BiLSTM/FFNN models were trained for 50 epochs (batch size 32, AdamW, LR 1×10^{-4}), while CodeBERT was fine-tuned for 5 epochs (batch size 16, LR 2×10^{-5}) from the `microsoft/codebert-base` checkpoint.

The RAG pipeline used `Slither` (v0.9.0) for AST/CFG generation and `GraKeL` (v0.1.8) with the Weisfeiler-Lehman kernel (3 iterations) for graph similarity measurement. All LLM interactions were conducted at a temperature of 0. To ensure full transparency and facilitate replication, all source code, data, and the precise, structured prompt templates used to implement the described strategies are publicly available in our code repository.

5   Results

We present our evaluation results along two dimensions: classification accuracy and explanation quality. Accuracy compares the predictive performance of traditional, neural, static analysis, and generative models, while explanation quality—measured via automated metrics and a user study—assesses correctness, informativeness, and relevance.

5.1   Example Retrieval

The effectiveness of the RAG approach critically depends on retrieving an appropriate number of relevant examples, controlled by the parameter k. Selecting an optimal k requires balancing the benefits of contextual information against the risk of introducing noise or conflicting examples. To determine the best value, we conducted a sensitivity analysis by varying k from 1 to 7 and measuring its effect on classification accuracy and preliminary explanation quality, using GPT-4.1-nano on a single test split.

These experiments were conducted using the RAG setup across different input data representations derived from AST, CFG, and their combination (i.e., a weighted average of the individual similarity scores). Our findings, summarized graphically in Fig. 2, indicate a consistent trend: model performance generally improves as k increases from 1 to 3. However, for values of k greater than 3, we observed a tendency for F1 performance to degrade. This suggests that while retrieving a small number of highly relevant examples ($k \leq 3$) enhances the model's context, incorporating more examples ($k > 3$) increasingly introduces less pertinent information, potentially confusing the model or diluting the signal from the most relevant retrieved documents. Based on this empirical analysis, we selected $k = 3$ as the optimal number of retrieved examples for all subsequent RAG experiments reported in this study. This value represents the best-observed trade-off between providing sufficient context and minimizing noise.

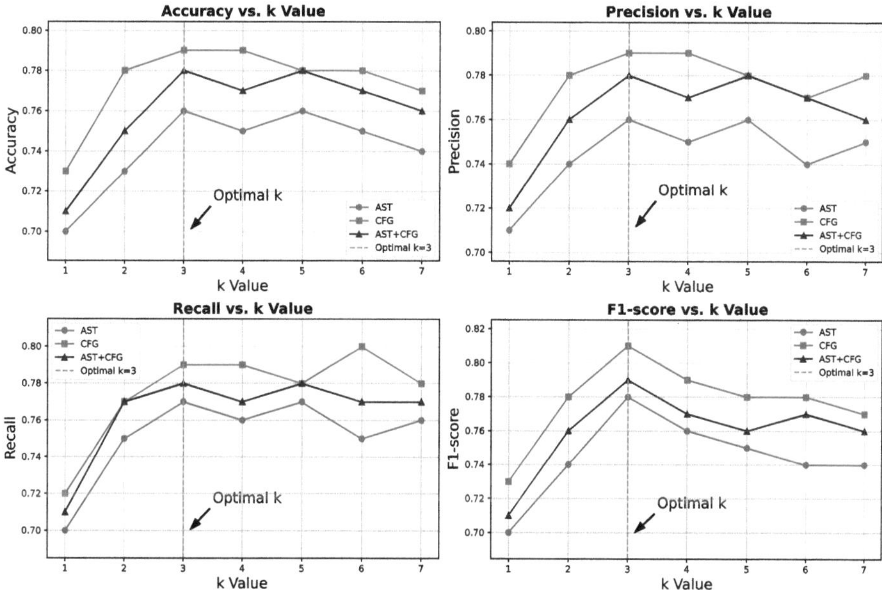

Fig. 2. Impact of the number of retrieved examples (k) on model performance across different data representations.

To enhance our Structurally-Aware RAG pipeline, we conducted preliminary experiments to determine which structural representation most effectively captures contract similarity. Our central hypothesis is that the choice of structural encoding directly influences the relevance of retrieved examples, which in turn affects the LLM's downstream analysis. We evaluated three representations: the AST, the CFG, and a combined AST+CFG approach (using averaged similarity scores). For clarity, we report results for GPT-4.1, GPT-4.1-mini, and GPT-4.1-nano in Table 1, representing large, medium, and small model sizes, respectively.

Across all model scales, we observed a consistent trend: retrieval based on CFG similarity outperforms both AST and combined representations. This advantage is particularly pronounced for GPT-4.1-nano and GPT-4.1-mini, and remains stable even for the larger GPT-4.1 model, where CFG-based retrieval yields the highest F1 score with the lowest standard deviation.

This result highlights an important insight: while vulnerability detection is ultimately carried out by the LLM analyzing full source code, the retrieval stage plays a crucial role in shaping the quality of that analysis. In the case of reentrancy, which depends on the execution order of operations—such as an external call preceding a state update—the CFG provides a better signal for identifying structurally similar contracts. Although our CFGs are not semantically annotated, the node labels generated by Slither (e.g., indicating low-level calls) are preserved in the graph and leveraged during similarity computation via the Weisfeiler-Lehman kernel. As a result, the CFG captures both execution flow and lightweight semantic cues that guide retrieval more effectively than syntax-based approaches.

Interestingly, we found that considering both AST and CFG similarities did not improve performance over CFG alone. We hypothesize this may be due to AST introducing redundant or less relevant information, which can dilute the more task-relevant control flow signals captured by the CFG. Additionally, without a more sophisticated fusion method, the averaged representation may blur the distinct structural signals, ultimately reducing retrieval precision.

Given these findings, we selected the CFG as the default structural representation for all subsequent experiments involving RAG and Hybrid retrieval strategies.

Table 1. RAG strategies using different structural representations. Values are reported as Mean (Standard Deviation). The best result for each model is in bold.

Model	Representation	Accuracy	Precision	Recall	F1 Score
GPT-4.1	AST + CFG	0.91 (0.03)	0.92 (0.03)	0.91 (0.03)	0.91 (0.03)
	AST	0.92 (0.03)	0.92 (0.03)	0.92 (0.03)	0.92 (0.03)
	CFG	**0.92(0.02)**	**0.92(0.01)**	**0.92(0.02)**	**0.92(0.01)**
GPT-4.1-mini	AST + CFG	0.85 (0.00)	0.86 (0.02)	0.85 (0.00)	0.84 (0.00)
	AST	0.85 (0.01)	0.86 (0.01)	0.85 (0.01)	0.84 (0.02)
	CFG	**0.88(0.01)**	**0.88(0.01)**	**0.88(0.01)**	**0.88(0.01)**
GPT-4.1-nano	AST + CFG	0.74 (0.01)	0.75 (0.04)	0.74 (0.01)	0.66 (0.01)
	AST	0.73 (0.02)	0.73 (0.07)	0.73 (0.02)	0.66 (0.02)
	CFG	**0.81(0.01)**	**0.82(0.02)**	**0.81(0.01)**	**0.79(0.01)**

5.2 Accuracy Evaluation

Our empirical evaluation reveals a clear hierarchy of efficacy among competing methodologies for reentrancy detection. The findings, summarized in Table 2, not only quantify the performance of different approaches but also yield critical

Table 2. Overall performance comparison across all model families and strategies. Learning-based model results are reported as Mean (Standard Deviation), best per strategy in *italic* and overall best in **bold**.

Approach	Strategy	Accuracy	Precision	Recall	F1 Score
Large Language Models					
o3-mini	Baseline	0.96 (0.01)	0.96 (0.01)	0.96 (0.01)	0.96 (0.01)
	Baseline + CoT	0.94 (0.01)	0.95 (0.01)	0.94 (0.01)	0.95 (0.01)
	RAG	**0.97(0.01)**	**0.97(0.01)**	**0.97(0.01)**	**0.97(0.01)**
	RAG + CoT	0.94 (0.01)	0.95 (0.01)	0.94 (0.01)	0.94 (0.01)
o4-mini	Baseline	0.93 (0.02)	0.94 (0.01)	0.93 (0.02)	0.93 (0.02)
	Baseline + CoT	*0.95 (0.01)*	*0.95 (0.01)*	*0.95 (0.01)*	*0.95 (0.01)*
	RAG	0.94 (0.02)	0.94 (0.02)	0.94 (0.02)	0.94 (0.02)
	RAG + CoT	0.94 (0.02)	0.95 (0.02)	0.94 (0.02)	0.94 (0.02)
GPT-4.1	Baseline	0.87 (0.02)	0.90 (0.01)	0.87 (0.02)	0.88 (0.02)
	Baseline + CoT	0.87 (0.03)	0.90 (0.02)	0.87 (0.03)	0.87 (0.02)
	RAG	*0.92 (0.02)*	*0.92 (0.01)*	*0.92 (0.02)*	*0.92 (0.01)*
	RAG + CoT	*0.92 (0.01)*	*0.92 (0.00)*	*0.92 (0.01)*	*0.92 (0.01)*
GPT-4.1-mini	Baseline	0.86 (0.01)	0.88 (0.01)	0.86 (0.01)	0.85 (0.02)
	Baseline + CoT	*0.90 (0.01)*	*0.91 (0.02)*	*0.90 (0.01)*	*0.90 (0.01)*
	RAG	0.88 (0.01)	0.88 (0.01)	0.88 (0.01)	0.88 (0.01)
	RAG + CoT	0.88 (0.01)	0.88 (0.01)	0.88 (0.01)	0.88 (0.01)
GPT-4.1-nano	Baseline	0.72 (0.00)	0.61 (0.13)	0.72 (0.00)	0.61 (0.01)
	Baseline + CoT	0.71 (0.02)	0.74 (0.01)	0.71 (0.02)	0.72 (0.02)
	RAG	*0.81 (0.01)*	*0.82 (0.02)*	*0.81 (0.01)*	*0.79 (0.01)*
	RAG + CoT	0.80 (0.01)	0.80 (0.01)	0.80 (0.01)	0.77 (0.02)
GPT-4o	Baseline	0.85 (0.02)	0.89 (0.02)	0.85 (0.02)	0.86 (0.02)
	Baseline + CoT	0.86 (0.03)	0.90 (0.02)	0.86 (0.03)	0.86 (0.03)
	RAG	*0.92 (0.01)*	0.92 (0.01)	*0.92 (0.01)*	0.92 (0.01)
	RAG + CoT	*0.92 (0.01)*	*0.93 (0.01)*	*0.92 (0.01)*	*0.93 (0.01)*
Traditional and DL Baselines					
Traditional ML	Gradient Boosting	0.90 (0.04)	0.87 (0.04)	0.76 (0.11)	0.81 (0.05)
	Gaussian NB	0.82 (0.05)	0.70 (0.06)	0.65 (0.12)	0.67 (0.07)
	KNN	0.88 (0.01)	0.85 (0.13)	0.74 (0.13)	0.78 (0.01)
	Logistic Regression	0.80 (0.06)	0.93 (0.12)	0.33 (0.12)	0.47 (0.12)
	Random Forest	0.90 (0.04)	0.90 (0.07)	0.73 (0.13)	0.80 (0.07)
	SVM	0.84 (0.04)	**0.93(0.12)**	0.51 (0.16)	0.64 (0.09)
	XGBoost	*0.91 (0.02)*	0.88 (0.08)	*0.79 (0.10)*	*0.83 (0.02)*
Deep Learning	CodeBERT	0.90 (0.13)	0.82 (0.24)	**0.96(0.03)**	**0.87(0.14)**
	LSTM	0.86 (0.12)	0.76 (0.17)	**0.96(0.03)**	0.83 (0.11)
	FFNN	**0.96(0.01)**	*0.85 (0.03)*	0.89 (0.03)	0.86 (0.02)
Static Analysis Tool Baselines					
Static Analysis Tools	Confuzzius	**0.88**	**0.94**	0.63	**0.75**
	Mythril	0.75	0.61	0.31	0.41
	Slither	0.86	0.82	**0.64**	0.72

insights into the trade-offs between model architecture, prompting strategy, and computational cost.

The central finding of our study is that LLMs, when properly guided, establish a new state-of-the-art. A crucial distinction emerges between the general-purpose GPT series and the reasoning-optimized o series. While the larger GPT-4o is a powerful generalist, the o3-mini model, particularly when augmented with our Structurally-Aware RAG strategy, achieved the highest overall F1 Score.

This performance divergence stems from their different design philosophies. GPT models are optimized for broad applicability, whereas o models are explicitly trained to excel at multi-step logical problems. This inherent specialization gives o3-mini a significant advantage, allowing it to achieve an exceptional baseline score even without complex prompting.

This distinction also explains the nuanced impact of our prompting strategies. The CoT framework, designed to impose a logical structure, provides a clear benefit to some generalist GPT models but shows diminishing returns for the o series. This suggests that the o series, having been trained to generate its own optimized reasoning paths, can experience "procedural interference" from an externally enforced workflow.

Conversely, while RAG provided the highest performance ceiling, its universal effectiveness is not absolute. The primary performance bottleneck for top-tier models was a lack of specific domain knowledge, which RAG directly addresses. However, for smaller models, the core limitation may be reasoning capacity itself, a factor that RAG cannot fully remediate. The frequent failure of the hybrid RAG+CoT strategy to outperform RAG alone further suggests a phenomenon of *constraint-induced sub-optimality*, where a rigid procedure limits a powerful model's ability to synthesize the rich information flexibly embedded by RAG-provided exemplars.

Discussion. The inclusion of the smaller GPT-4.1-mini and GPT-4.1-nano models illuminates a critical dimension for practical application: the trade-off between performance and resource efficiency. These faster, cheaper models provide valuable insights into the minimum viable capabilities for this task.

The **GPT-4.1-mini** model emerges as a highly compelling option. With a simple CoT strategy, it achieved an F1-score outperforming the baseline results of the much larger GPT-4.1 and GPT-4o models. This finding is significant, as it suggests that for moderately sized models, a structured reasoning framework (CoT) can be more effective than providing raw knowledge (RAG), likely because it scaffolds the model's more limited intrinsic reasoning capabilities. For organizations where the cost and latency of flagship models are prohibitive, GPT-4.1-mini with CoT represents a "sweet spot", offering robust performance that far exceeds traditional baselines at a fraction of the computational budget.

The **GPT-4.1-nano** model defines the lower bound of effectiveness. With a top F1-score using RAG, its performance is substantially weaker than all other LLMs. This demonstrates that there is a "performance floor"—a minimum threshold of model scale and complexity required to move beyond surface-level pattern matching to the deeper semantic analysis necessary for this task. Even the best prompting strategy cannot fully compensate for a fundamental lack of reasoning power. Tellingly, the nano model's performance is only marginally better than our best static analysis baseline (i.e., Confuzzius), highlighting that at this small scale, the LLM's advantage begins to erode.

As a final remark, we delve now into a comparative analysis against our baselines models, which elucidates the specific failure modes of previous-generation techniques and underscores the nature of the LLM's advantage.

The DL baselines, such as `CodeBERT`, exhibited a characteristic high-recall, low-precision profile, achieving a recall of 0.96 but a much lower F1-score. This pattern suggests that such models are adept at learning the *syntactic correlates* of vulnerabilities—for example, the presence of an external call within a function—but fail to grasp the deeper, temporal semantics required to distinguish a benign call from a reentrant one (i.e., whether the call occurs *before* a state update). In contrast, the high F1-scores of appropriately prompted LLMs imply they are successfully capturing this essential logic.

The static analysis tools, foundational to current security practices, were significantly outperformed by nearly all learning-based models. Their performance, characterized by low F1-scores and particularly poor recall, highlights the inherent brittleness of heuristic-based detection. These tools rely on predefined patterns that struggle to generalize. This "semantic gap" between rigid heuristics and complex reality is precisely what modern LLMs, even the cost-effective GPT-4.1-mini, are equipped to bridge.

5.3   Explainability Evaluation

Beyond predictive accuracy, a critical dimension of our evaluation was the quality and utility of the explanations generated by our LLM strategies. A correct classification is of limited value in a security context if the underlying reasoning is flawed or opaque. To this end, we employed a dual-protocol evaluation, combining definitive human expert ratings with scalable LLM-as-a-Judge assessments to create a comprehensive picture of explainability.

Our human expert evaluation (Table 3, based on the explanations by o3-mini) immediately revealed that how an explanation is generated has a profound impact on its utility. The explanations from the Structurally-Aware RAG strategy were judged as significantly more valuable than those from the baseline zero-shot approach, particularly in Informativeness. This numerical gap is not academic; it represents a fundamental difference in function. A baseline explanation provides a verdict that a developer must then independently verify. A RAG-generated explanation, by contrast, provides a verdict *along with* verifiable evidence in the form of an analogous contract. This transforms the AI's output from a mere claim to be scrutinized into a pedagogical tool that helps the developer understand the *why* behind the vulnerability, directly accelerating remediation and learning.

Such a grounding in evidence is also crucial for building user trust. The higher Correctness score for RAG indicates that grounding the LLM in real-world examples measurably reduces the risk of factual hallucination, giving developers confidence in the analysis. Interestingly, the baseline's marginally higher Pertinence score highlights a subtle but important user preference for conciseness, a factor we dissected more deeply in our automated evaluation.

Table 3. Comparison of Qualitative Explanation Metrics: BASELINE vs. RAG o3-mini. Values are reported as Mean (Standard Deviation) on a 1–5 scale. The best performing strategy for each metric is highlighted in **bold**.

Metric	Baseline	RAG
Correctness	4.38 (0.94)	**4.43 (0.84)**
Informativeness	4.14 (0.70)	**4.72 (0.57)**
Pertinence	**4.37 (0.87)**	4.31 (0.84)

Discussion. The LLM-as-a-Judge assessment, with its per-model breakdown (Table 4), allows for a fine-grained analysis of how prompting strategies interact with different model architectures and capabilities.

The results reveal that evidence-grounding is a universally dominant principle. Across all models, from the high-performing o3-mini to the compact GPT-4.1-nano, the Structurally-Aware RAG strategy consistently delivered the best balance of Correctness and Pertinence. For instance, RAG elevated the correctness of GPT-4.1-nano from a baseline of 3.53 to 4.42, demonstrating its power to set a higher quality floor even for smaller models. This confirms that providing verifiable, contextual evidence is the most robust path to generating trustworthy and efficient explanations.

Conversely, the impact of the CoT framework is highly dependent on the model's underlying architecture. For the reasoning-optimized o models, the benefits of CoT were marginal, often outweighed by a drop in Pertinence, confirming our "procedural interference" hypothesis for these specialized models. In stark contrast, the generalist GPT models showed significant gains in Informativeness when CoT was applied. This suggests that for less specialized models, the explicit scaffolding of CoT is crucial for generating a more logical output.

The analysis also solidifies a fundamental trade-off between Informativeness and Pertinence. For every model tested, the hybrid RAG + CoT strategy produced the most exhaustively detailed explanations, consistently achieving the highest Informativeness scores. However, this same verbosity consistently resulted in one of the lowest Pertinence scores. This finding demonstrates that the verbosity induced by CoT is a systemic characteristic of the methodology itself, creating a critical design tension for developers of explainable AI systems: maximizing detail can directly harm conciseness.

In synthesis, our dual evaluation converges on a clear and impactful conclusion. The most effective and trustworthy AI security tools are not those that attempt to rigidly replicate a human's entire thought process (CoT), but those that emulate a human expert's use of evidence (RAG). By grounding its analysis in concrete, verifiable examples, the Structurally-Aware RAG strategy produces explanations that are correct, insightful, and efficiently actionable, fostering a collaborative relationship between the developer and the AI tool.

5.4   Limitations

Several limitations define the scope of our findings. Our study focuses exclusively on reentrancy in Solidity; thus, the generalizability of our methods to other vulnerability classes or blockchain ecosystems remains an open question. The reliance on proprietary, black-box LLMs also presents challenges for long-term reproducibility and introduces practical constraints, including cost and latency, for real-time applications. Finally, our methodology is confined to static source

Table 4. Per-Model LLM-as-a-Judge Evaluation of Generated Explanations. Values are reported as Mean (Standard Deviation) on a 1–5 scale. The best-performing strategy for each model and metric is highlighted in *italic*, with the overall best strategy in **bold**.

Model	Strategy	Correctness	Informativeness	Pertinence
o3-mini	Baseline	4.61 (0.75)	4.03 (0.90)	4.71 (0.60)
	Baseline + CoT	4.72 (0.65)	4.55 (0.70)	4.45 (0.80)
	RAG	**4.91 (0.40)**	4.83 (0.50)	**4.85 (0.45)**
	RAG + CoT	4.84 (0.45)	**4.93 (0.40)**	4.22 (0.95)
o4-mini	Baseline	4.43 (0.80)	3.81 (1.05)	4.65 (0.65)
	Baseline + CoT	4.65 (0.70)	4.41 (0.80)	4.31 (0.85)
	RAG	*4.83 (0.50)*	4.71 (0.60)	*4.77 (0.55)*
	RAG + CoT	4.76 (0.55)	*4.81 (0.50)*	4.15 (1.00)
GPT-4.1	Baseline	3.82 (1.10)	3.05 (1.20)	4.21 (0.85)
	Baseline + CoT	4.25 (0.95)	4.08 (0.90)	4.03 (0.90)
	RAG	*4.71 (0.65)*	4.54 (0.75)	*4.63 (0.70)*
	RAG + CoT	4.64 (0.70)	*4.66 (0.65)*	3.88 (1.15)
GPT-4.1-mini	Baseline	3.91 (1.05)	3.25 (1.15)	4.25 (0.80)
	Baseline + CoT	4.33 (0.90)	4.15 (0.95)	4.08 (0.85)
	RAG	*4.68 (0.68)*	4.51 (0.78)	*4.66 (0.65)*
	RAG + CoT	4.55 (0.72)	*4.63 (0.68)*	3.95 (1.10)
GPT-4.1-nano	Baseline	3.53 (1.20)	2.51 (1.30)	4.05 (0.95)
	Baseline + CoT	3.88 (1.10)	3.55 (1.10)	3.81 (1.00)
	RAG	*4.42 (0.80)*	4.23 (0.90)	*4.45 (0.80)*
	RAG + CoT	4.31 (0.85)	*4.35 (0.80)*	3.64 (1.25)
GPT-4o	Baseline	3.75 (1.15)	2.89 (1.25)	4.13 (0.90)
	Baseline + CoT	4.11 (1.00)	3.84 (1.00)	3.91 (0.95)
	RAG	*4.65 (0.70)*	4.42 (0.80)	*4.55 (0.75)*
	RAG + CoT	4.58 (0.75)	*4.59 (0.70)*	3.71 (1.20)

code analysis. It does not account for dynamic, on-chain states or complex multi-contract interactions, which can be the source of emergent exploits.

6   Conclusions

This work demonstrates that LLMs, guided by our Structurally-Aware RAG strategy, establish a new state-of-the-art in smart contract reentrancy detection, surpassing traditional ML, DL, and static analysis baselines. We reveal that for complex code analysis, grounding specialized reasoning models in factual, structural precedents is more effective than prescribing a rigid thought process. Crucially, this evidence-grounded approach not only maximizes accuracy but also yields trustworthy, actionable explanations necessary for real-world adoption.

Our findings open several promising avenues for future research. A crucial next step is to assess the generalizability of our Structurally-Aware RAG approach, extending it beyond reentrancy to a wider spectrum of vulnerabilities and other programming languages to validate its broader utility. Methodologically, we see significant potential in exploring more advanced program representations, such as Program Dependence Graphs, for retrieval and in developing methods for the automated optimization of prompt frameworks. Furthermore, the current one-shot paradigm could be evolved into interactive, conversational auditing systems where security experts can dialogue with the AI, enabling a more dynamic human-in-the-loop analysis. Ultimately, addressing the practical constraints of latency and cost through model distillation and other optimization techniques will be crucial for developing smaller, more efficient models suitable for real-time deployment in continuous integration/deployment pipelines.

Acknowledgments. This paper was funded by Veneto Agricoltura within the scope of the project "Guaranteeing the continuity of the agri-foodchain: the digitization of wholesale markets". This study was also carried out within the PE0000014 - Security and Rights in the CyberSpace (SERICS) and received funding from the European Union Next-GenerationEU - National Recovery and Resilience Plan (NRRP) MISSION 4 COMPONENT 2, INVESTIMENT 1.3 CUP N. H73C22000890001. This work has been also partially supported by the Research Project INDAM GNCS 2025 - CUP E53C24001950001 - "Modelli e Analisi per sistemi Reversibili e Quantistici (MARQ)" and by the Project PRIN 2020 - CUP N. 20202FCJMH "NiRvAna - Noninterference and Reversibility Analysis in Private Blockchains". This manuscript reflects only the authors' views and opinions, neither the European Union nor the European Commission can be considered responsible for them.

References

1. Chen, J., Wang, L., Zhu, H., Sheng, V.S.: CLEP: A novel contrastive learning method for evolutionary reentrancy vulnerability detection. In: Walsh, T., Shah, J., Kolter, Z., eds., Proceedings of the AAAI Conference on Artificial Intelligence, vol. 39, pp. 67–74. Association for the Advancement of Artificial Intelligence (AAAI), (Apr 2025)

2. ConsenSys. Mythril: Symbolic-execution-based security analysis tool for EVM bytecode. https://github.com/ConsenSysDiligence/mythril. Accessed 30 June 2025
3. GitHub Contributors. GitHub - xf97/HuangGai at v1.0.0. https://github.com/ xf97/HuangGai/tree/v1.0.0. Accessed 29 May 2025
4. Di Angelo, M., Salzer, G.: A survey of tools for analyzing Ethereum smart contracts. In: 2020 IEEE International Conference on Decentralized Applications and Infrastructures (DAPPCON), pp. 115–120. IEEE (2020)
5. Di Angelo, M., Salzer, G.: Consolidation of ground truth sets for weakness detection in smart contracts, vol. 13953, pp. 439–455. Springer Science+Business Media (Dec 2023)
6. Durieux, T., Ferreira, J.F., Abreu, R., Cruz, P.: Empirical review of automated analysis tools on 47,587 Ethereum smart contracts. In: Rothermel, G., Bae, D.-H., eds., Proceedings of the ACM/IEEE 42nd International conference on software engineering, pp. 530–541. ACM (June 2020)
7. Feist, J., Grieco, G., Groce, A.: Slither: a static analysis framework for smart contracts. In: Proceedings of the 2nd International Workshop on Emerging Trends in Software Engineering for Blockchain, pp. 8–15. IEEE / ACM (May 2019)
8. Grieco, G., Maffei, M., Schneidewind, C.: Echidna: A fast smart contract fuzzer. In: 2020 IEEE European Symposium on Security and Privacy Workshops (EuroS&PW), pp. 435–444. IEEE (2020)
9. Guo, L., Huang, H., Zhao, L., Wang, P., Jiang, S., Chunhua, S.: Reentrancy vulnerability detection based on graph convolutional networks and expert patterns under subspace mapping. Comput. Secur. **142**, 103894 (2024)
10. Hu, S., Huang, T., İlhan, F., Tekin, S.F., Liu, L.: Large language model-powered smart contract vulnerability detection: new perspectives. In: 2023 5th IEEE International Conference on Trust, Privacy and Security in Intelligent Systems and Applications (TPS-ISA), pp. 297–306, Los Alamitos, CA, USA, November 2023. IEEE Computer Society
11. Lewis, P., et al.: Retrieval-augmented generation for knowledge-intensive NLP tasks. In: Larochelle, H., Ranzato, M., Hadsell, R., Balcan, M.-F., Lin, H.-T., eds., Advances in Neural Information Processing Systems **33**, 9459–9474 (2020)
12. Li, J., Li, G., Li, Y., Jin, Z.: Structured chain-of-thought prompting for code generation. ACM Trans. Softw. Eng. Methodol. **34**(2), 1–23 (2025)
13. Li, Z., Li, X., Li, W. and Wang, X.: SCALM: detecting bad practices in smart contracts through LLMs. In: Walsh, T., Shah, J., Kolter, Z., eds., Proceedings of the AAAI Conference on Artificial Intelligence, vol. 39, pp. 470–477. Association for the Advancement of Artificial Intelligence (AAAI) (Feb 2025)
14. Luu, L., Chu, D.H., Olickel, H., Saxena, P., Hobor, A.: Making smart contracts smarter. In: Weippl, E.R., Katzenbeisser, S., Kruegel, C., Myers, A.C., Halevi, S., eds., Proceedings of the 2016 ACM SIGSAC Conference on Computer and Communications Security, pp. 254–269. ACM (Oct 2016)
15. Ressi, D., Spanó A., Benetollo, L., Piazza, C., Bugliesi, M., Rossi, S.: Vulnerability detection in Ethereum smart contracts via machine learning: a qualitative analysis. arXiv preprint arXiv:2407.18639 (July 2024)
16. Rizzo, M., Ressi, D., Gasparetto, A., Rossi, S.: A comparison of machine learning techniques for Ethereum smart contract vulnerability detection. In: Porello, D., Vinci, C., Zavatteri, M., eds., Short Paper Proceedings of the 6th International Workshop on Artificial Intelligence and Formal Verification, Logic, Automata, and Synthesis, OVERLAY 2024, vol. 3904, pp. 119–126. CEUR-WS.org (2024)

17. Rizzo, M., Veneri, A., Albarelli, A., Lucchese, C., Nobile, M., Conati, C.: A theoretical framework for AI models explainability with application in biomedicine. In: 2023 IEEE Conference on Computational Intelligence in Bioinformatics and Computational Biology (CIBCB), pp. 1–9. IEEE (Aug 2023)
18. Torres, C.F., Iannillo, A.K., Gervais, A., State, R.: Confuzzius: a data dependency-aware hybrid fuzzer for smart contracts. In: 2021 IEEE European Symposium on Security and Privacy (EuroS&P), pp. 103–119. IEEE (Sept 2021)
19. Wei, J., et al.: Chain-of-thought prompting elicits reasoning in large language models. In: Sanmi Koyejo, S., Mohamed, A., Danielle Belgrave, A K., Cho, Oh, A., eds., Proceedings of the 36th International Conference on Neural Information Processing Systems, NIPS '22, Red Hook, NY, USA, January 2022. Curran Associates Inc (Jan 2022)
20. Yu, J.: Retrieval augmented generation integrated large language models in smart contract vulnerability detection. arXiv preprint (July 2024)

Protocol and Security

Fast Blocks and Furious Adjustments: Satoshi Drift

Demetris Kyriacou[1]([✉]), Matthieu Babak[2], Iain Stewart[1],
and William J Knottenbelt[1]

[1] Imperial College London, London, UK
`demetris.kyriacou22@imperial.ac.uk`
[2] ENSTA Paris, Palaiseau, France

Abstract. Difficulty adjustment algorithms (DAAs) are a vital component of every Proof-of-Work (PoW) blockchain. They regulate mining difficulty which in turn modulates interblock times. Maintaining a stable block-production rate and consistent transaction throughput is crucial for the smooth operation of a blockchain and can positively affect its reputation. The challenging part of a DAA is that the actual blockchain hash rate is unknown. Therefore, difficulty adjustments must be based on historical data, estimations and/or predictions. For Bitcoin (BTC), things are relatively simple. The vast hash power of Bitcoin's network makes it largely immune to fluctuations, allowing the difficulty to be adjusted infrequently (approx. every two weeks) without affecting throughput. On the other hand, the rest of the PoW blockchains, such as Bitcoin Cash (BCH), are more susceptible to hash power fluctuations and require a more adaptive DAA which adjusts the mining difficulty after every block. Such DAAs already exist, have been battle-tested and have proven effective at maintaining average interblock times close to the target. Nevertheless, to our knowledge, no DAA successfully addresses the problem of accumulated drift. In fact, both BTC and BCH halvings of April 2024 occurred almost 9 months ahead of schedule due to this drift. In this paper, we propose a novel yet very simple DAA based on a negative exponential filter that not only keeps the block-production rate stable in the long run but also eliminates any already-accumulated drift.

Keywords: Difficulty Adjustment Algorithm · Mining difficulty · Proof of Work · Bitcoin Cash

1 Introduction

Over recent years, various difficulty adjustment algorithms (DAAs) have been proposed and implemented in blockchains that support Proof-of-Work (PoW) consensus mechanisms. Some of them proved to be stable and robust while others deteriorated to relics amidst disaster.

© ICST Institute for Computer Sciences, Social Informatics and Telecommunications Engineering 2026
Published by Springer Nature Switzerland AG 2026. All Rights Reserved
W. Knottenbelt et al. (Eds.): Blocktea 2025, LNICST 669, pp. 59–79, 2026.
https://doi.org/10.1007/978-3-032-12335-0_4

The primary purpose of a DAA is to regulate interblock times of a PoW blockchain by adjusting the difficulty of mining a block. In an ideal world where the real total hash rate of a blockchain network is known, adjusting difficulty would be trivial. In practice, however, the hash rate of a network is unobservable and can only be estimated using data about previously mined blocks such as interblock times and past difficulties. Although some miners proudly and openly declare their hash power, some of them remain rather cryptic. Additionally, there are miners who are not always loyal to mining on a single blockchain but instead perform what is called coin-hopping strategies to maximise their profit [16]. Interestingly, the hash power behavior of the network resembles that of financial markets. Both are driven by underlying human, technological, and architectural components. Another common trait is that poorly designed algorithms or subtle interactions between algorithms can disrupt their orderly regulation [3].

However, even if the DAA does a good job in controlling interblock times in short-term, there is another problem than can be gradually developed in long-term. *Drift* or *skew* is created when blocks are, on average, being mined faster or slower than normal. For BTC it happens mainly because the DAA cannot keep up with the increase of hash rate due to increase in mining popularity and hardware capabilities. Consequently, it accumulates drift every time there is a major leap forward in mining technology.

In August 2017, disputes within the Bitcoin community over scalability and functionality led to the creation of Bitcoin Cash (BCH) [24,25] as a hard fork. After the hard fork, Bitcoin Cash continued its own, more turbulent path, as an independent blockchain and experienced another schism as a result of Bitcoin Cash's hash war [17]. The blockchain was split into what is still referred to as Bitcoin Cash (BCH) [6] and Bitcoin SV (BSV) [7]. This paper focuses on the former. To this day, BTC uses its original DAA with biweekly difficulty adjustments, while BCH has experimented with various DAAs that adjust the mining difficulty at every block [4,9]. Both of them though have piled on more drift to the inherited pre-fork drift and, as result, their halvings on April 2024 happened almost 9 months prior to their originally-scheduled dates.

In this paper, we choose to focus on BCH due to its unsettled past of DAAs along with the fact that it represents one of the most popular PoW blockchains whose mining difficulty is adjusted at every block. Additionally, BCH's vulnerability to hash rate fluctuations make it more challenging and interesting to investigate. Lastly, our research builds on previous work by Ilie et al. [13].

Concretely, we present an innovative DAA that alleviates the problem of drift by gradually eradicating any that has already been accrued. Although designed primarily for BCH, our DAA is compatible with most PoW blockchains that adjust their mining difficulty at every block. Furthermore, the responsiveness of the DAA can be adjusted using a smoothing factor. Initially, we perform an empirical analysis on the various DAAs used in BCH. We investigate methods of evaluating performance of DAAs and reveal flaws and weaknesses of each one. Moreover, we define our novel DAA based on a negative exponential filter and explain the rationale for its tunable parameters. Finally, we substantiate our findings with simulations that verify the robust performance of our DAA and compare it to the existing DAA of BCH.

2   Related Work

Bitcoin Cash has adopted multiple DAAs since the hard fork with Bitcoin; all of them are analysed in depth in Sect. 4. A noteworthy proposal for BCH that was never adopted was Amaury Sechet's Grasberg DAA [1]. Grasberg DAA was based on a negative exponential filter and included a drift correction mechanism. It aimed to ensure a stable and more predictable block-production rate and minimise the profit gap between loyal mining and coin-hopping mining. However, the proposal was rejected as it was deemed too complicated and inadequately substantiated. Furthermore, few members of the BCH community argued against the need for drift correction [11,15,20]. The main difference between our DAA and Grasberg is that ours is very simple, as we only make a minor adjustment to the current DAA to achieve drift correction. Additionally, our DAA converges to the current DAA as the drift converges to 0. In addition, we provide a detailed analysis of the mathematical background, as well as extensive simulations.

3   Background

3.1   Hash Rate

Hash rate is a measurement of a computational unit's ability to produce outputs of a hashing function. It is calculated as hashes per second and in blockchain terms it is the main method of evaluating computational power [14]. Therefore, throughout this paper, the terms hash rate, hash power and computational power will be used interchangeably.

3.2   Proof of Work (PoW) Mining

Each valid block consists of a collection of transactions along with a header that contains important information about the block such as its timestamp and the root hash of transactions. One of the block header fields is called *nonce*. The sole purpose of a nonce is to pseudorandomly alternate the output of a hash function that takes block header as input. By requiring the hash of a block header to be smaller than a predefined threshold or *target*, the trivial process of creating a block becomes a challenging cryptographic puzzle called PoW mining [10,21]. PoW is based on the idea that mining a block is computationally demanding, so that no malicious user has the ability to mine blocks faster than the rest of the network. The only way a malicious user can do that is by possessing at least 51% of network's computational power [8].

3.3 Target

Target is a numerical value that a hashed block header must be less than or equal to in order for a new block to be mined successfully [23]. The probability of a hash being smaller than or equal to the target is:

$$P(hash \leq target) = \frac{target + 1}{2^{256}}$$

where every hash has 2^{256} possible outputs $[0, 2^{256} - 1]$

Also, each attempt to mine a block is a Bernoulli trial with a probability of success equal to $\frac{target+1}{2^{256}}$. Thus, the expected work or the number of hashes to mine a single block is:

$$\mathbb{E}[W] = 2^{256}/(target + 1) \approx 2^{256}/target$$

3.4 Difficulty

The idea that a higher target means that it is more difficult to mine a block while a lower target means it is easier can be perceived as somewhat counter-intuitive. Thus, the notion of *difficulty* was introduced. Difficulty represents how difficult it is to mine a block using some current target relative to how difficult it would have been if the highest possible target was used [23]. The maximum target is equal to the target of the very first block of Bitcoin and is almost equal to 2^{224}.

$$D = \frac{max\_target}{target} = \frac{first\ block's\ target}{target} \approx \frac{2^{224}}{target}$$

Expected number of hashes to mine a single block can also be expressed as:

$$\mathbb{E}[W] = D \cdot 2^{32}$$

Notably, if the real hash rate H_n at any given time was observable and since the ideal interblock time T is constant, setting the difficulty for each block would be trivial:

$$D_n \cdot 2^{32} = \mathbb{E}[W] = H_n \cdot T$$

However, in reality it is unattainable to observe the actual hash rate of the network *a priori*. In fact, it is impossible to precisely calculate the real hash rate even *a posteriori*. For this reason, designing a robust DAA poses a challenge.

3.5 Difficulty Adjustment Algorithm (DAA)

A Difficulty Adjustment Algorithm (DAA) is a vital element of every PoW blockchain. Its main task is to control mining difficulty to modulate the time between the creation of every new block in the blockchain.

In the short term, a DAA should ensure a stable block-production rate and relatively steady transaction throughput which makes the blockchain dependable. The reliability of a blockchain improves user experience but is also reflected in its coin's value. In the long run, a DAA controls coin issuance, timing of the halvings, and miners' profit. By lowering miners' reward, scarcity is maintained and this is a measure to protect from inflationary effects. Moreover, lowering supply increases demand and affects the price of the coins [18].

Today, more than fifteen years later, Bitcoin is the most well-established cryptocurrency and its network hash power is vast and invariant to minor oscillations. As a result, its primitive original DAA [21] that adjusts mining difficulty on a biweekly basis is sufficient. But, alas, not every PoW blockchain enjoys the same broad and stable support by miners as BTC. Almost all PoW altcoins are plagued by highly volatile hash power, mainly due to coin-hopping strategies, and cannot afford to wait a fortnight to alter mining difficulty.

There are multiple factors that influence a miner's coin-hopping strategy, like mining difficulty or coin value, but the main motive is single and clear, maximising profit. Since various PoW blockchains use the same mining mechanism, it is only a matter of flipping a switch for a miner to "hop" to mining the most profitable coin at any given time [16].

Coin-hopping is when a miner switches the entirety or a part of his hash power from mining one coin to another. Hence, this switch alters the total hash power of both blockchain networks. When performed on a large scale, coin-hopping can cause serious fluctuations in an altcoin network's total hash rate and DAAs are required to be able to keep up with this. As a result, numerous DAAs were developed during the previous decade, many of which proved to be resistant to hash rate fluctuations and capable of maintaining relatively stable block-production rates. What was not accounted for though is the long-term effect of DAAs' inability to keep up with the general increase of hash power in blockchains, primarily due to technology advances.

3.6   Drift (Skew)

Satoshi Nakamoto foresaw the increasing hardware speed and mining interest back in 2008 when the Bitcoin whitepaper was issued [21]. Indeed, as you can see in Fig. 1, BTC's difficulty has a tendency to increase over the years. Furthermore, there are two obvious rapid jumps in difficulty. The first was around 2010 with the introduction of GPU mining, and the second was around 2013 with the introduction of ASIC mining.

Of course, BTC's DAA was able to cope with the difficulty increase and restore the order of block-production rate without significant impact on transaction throughput. However, as shown in Fig. 2, drift was gradually built up because – on average – blocks were mined faster than every 10 min. BTC's DAA remained the same and was never adjusted to mitigate the problem of drift. As a result, the 2nd, 3rd and 4th BTC halvings occurred 139, 234 and 252 days (respectively) ahead of schedule (see Fig. 2 or Table 1 in Appendix A). Meanwhile, when BCH forked out of BTC in August 2017, it inherited any already-accumulated drift. Its stormy quest to find a suitable DAA only made the drift problem worse. Thus, BCH's 3rd and 4th halvings happened 267 and 269 days (respectively) ahead of their ideal time (see Fig. 2 or Table 1 in Appendix A).

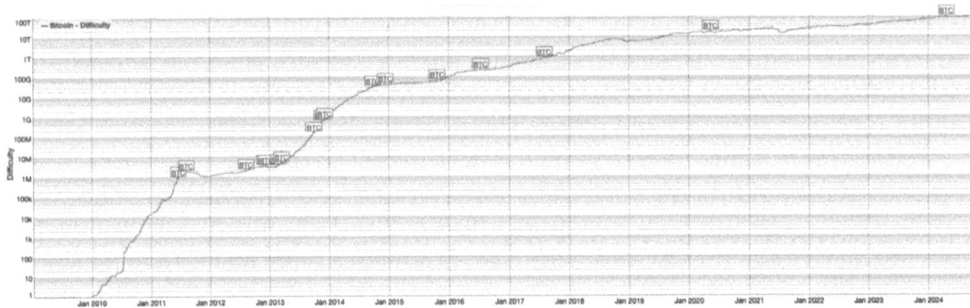

Fig. 1. BTC difficulty history, source: https://bitinfocharts.com/comparison/bitcoin-difficulty.html

4   Current and Legacy DAAs of BCH

4.1   BTC DAA

Prior to the August 2017 fork, Bitcoin Cash used Bitcoin's DAA according to which the mining difficulty is updated every 2016 blocks. The DAA formula prevents extreme changes in difficulty by capping adjustments, allowing the new difficulty to be no more than four times higher or lower than the previous value [22]. This DAA has allowed Bitcoin network to maintain a stable block-generation rate of approximately one block every ten minutes. The formula is:

$$D_{new} = D_{current} \cdot \max\left(\min\left(\frac{1,209,600}{t}, 4 \right), 0.25 \right) \tag{1}$$

where:

- D_{new} is the difficulty of the next 2016 blocks.
- $D_{current}$ is the difficulty of the previous 2016 blocks.
- t represents the time difference in seconds between the timestamps of the latest block (B_n) and the 2016th previous block (B_{n-2015}).

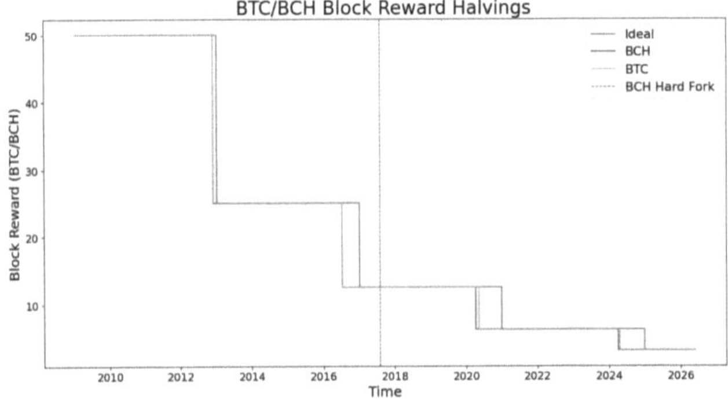

Fig. 2. BTC/BCH Block Reward Halvings.

- 1,209,600 s is the expected time to mine 2016 blocks at a rate of one block every ten minutes.
- The factor is constrained between 0.25 and 4 to prevent drastic changes.

As shown in Figs. 3 and 4, this DAA works very well for BTC. The block time distribution is converging to Poisson distribution and there is no autocorrelation between interblock times (i.e. correlation between the time series of interblock times and a delayed copy of itself). As explained in previous sections though, it is not viable for most altcoins and it does not solve the drift problem.

4.2 Emergency DAA (EDA)

In anticipation of the BTC–BCH fork, the BCH community decided that a new DAA was needed to ensure the survival of Bitcoin Cash. Although it was impossible to accurately predict the post-fork hash power of the new blockchain, it was certain that BTC would keep the lion's share. There was also a great uncertainty about the effect of the split on BCH's value [2]. Hence, emergency DAA was an adjustment to the original DAA that lowered difficulty immediately if there was a huge drop in hash power. More specifically, if the interval between the median time past (MTP) of the current block n and the MTP of block $n-6$ was greater than 12 h, the difficulty would drop directly by 20% [22].

4.3 CW-144

Bitcoin cash survived the split with the help of EDA DAA but it did not come away intact. As anticipated, the network's hash power experienced a free fall and left the blockchain vulnerable to fluctuations. Figures 3 and 4 reveal the extent of hash rate fluctuation and the desperate need for a more stable DAA. Amaury Sechet's CW-144 [5] was promising to provide just that. CW-144 was activated on November 2017, only three months after the activation of the EDA.

CW-144 adjusted difficulty after each block and used a 144-period simple moving average to estimate hash rate [22]. The formula used to calculate the new difficulty for each block is:

$$D_n = \widehat{H_n} \cdot T = \frac{\sum_{i=old}^{new} D_i}{T_{elapsed}} \cdot T \tag{2}$$

where:

- $\widehat{H_n}$ is the estimated hash rate after mining the n-th block.
- T is the ideal time between two blocks, i.e., 10 min.
- B_{new} is the block with the median timestamp between the latest block B_n and the previous two B_{n-1} and B_{n-2}.
- B_{old} is the block with median timestamp between blocks B_{n-144}, B_{n-145} and B_{n-146}.
- $T_{elapsed}$ is the elapsed time between B_{new} and B_{old}.

As shown in Fig. 4, CW-144 achieved an average interblock time close to optimal. However, it caused a serious autocorrelation issue. In simple words, CW-144 caused large and consistent oscillations in hash rate and difficulty throughout the day. This created brief periods of low difficulty and large numbers of new blocks, and large periods of high difficulty and low number of new blocks. As a result, not only did it not protect BCH from coin-hopping but it made it more vulnerable to it instead. On top of that, the BCH–BSV fork happened, causing even more stability issues to the remaining BCH network as can be seen in Fig. 3.

4.4   ASERT/NEFDA

By 2020 it was obvious that BCH's DAA was suffering and was in urgent need of an upgrade. A few different solutions were put forward, and after a heated debate within BCH community, it was decided to adopt a proposal that used a negative exponential filter. Two very similar proposals were submitted independently by two separate teams under different names, ASERT [12,19] and NEFDA [13].

NEFDA's formula is:

$$D_n = \widehat{H_n} \cdot T = \frac{1}{S} \sum_{i=0}^{n-1} D_i e^{\frac{t_i - t_n}{S}} \cdot T \tag{3}$$

where:

- $\widehat{H_n}$ is the estimated hash rate after mining the n-th block.

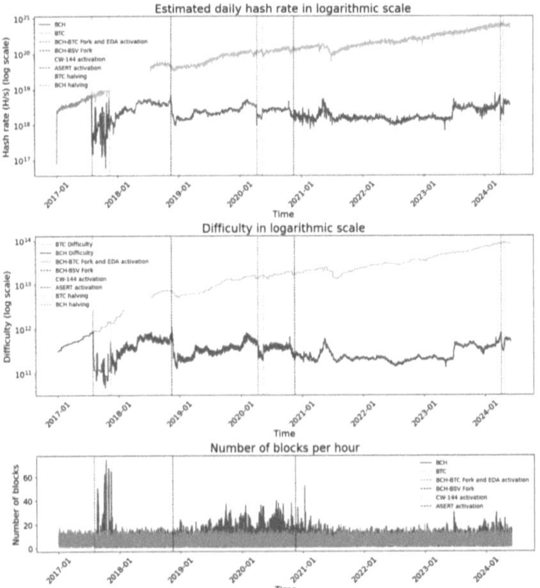

Fig. 3. BTC–BCH historical data comparison.

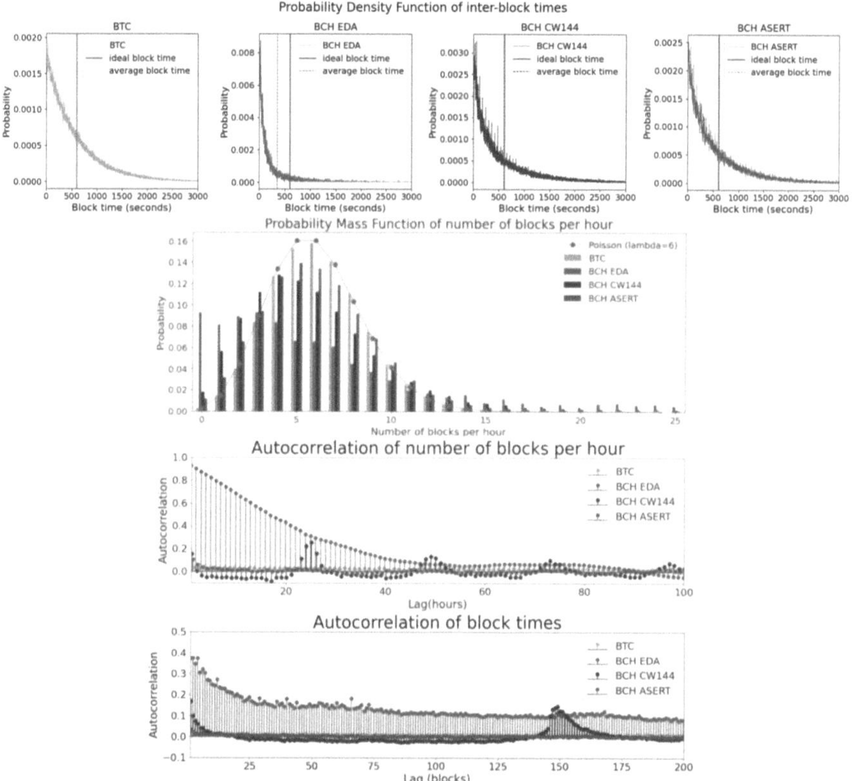

Fig. 4. DAA block time, and autocorrelation comparisons.

- T is the ideal time between two blocks, i.e., 10 min.
- S is the smoothing factor.
- D_i is the difficulty after mining block i.
- t_i is the timestamp of block i.

Figures 3–4 show that NEFDA (ASERT) helped stabilise the BCH hash rate, brought the block time distribution much closer to ideal, and solved the autocorrelation problem. Furthermore, due to hash rate stabilisation, it did not introduce any significant additional drift. However, it did not mitigate the problem either, and the blockchain is still exposed to further drift accumulation in the next leap in mining technology.

5   Modified NEFDA (NEF(DA)^2)

To combat the drift problem, we propose a modified version of NEFDA which we call *NEFDA with Drift Adjustment* (NEF(DA)^2). This novel algorithm has one critical adjustment over its predecessor: the ideal interval between blocks is no longer constant. Instead, the ideal interval is a variable that adapts to drift, i.e. long-term deviation from target interblock timing. NEF(DA)^2 formula is:

$$D_n = \widehat{H_n} \cdot T_n = \frac{1}{S} \left[\sum_{i=0}^{n-1} D_i e^{\frac{t_i - t_n}{S}} \right] \cdot T e^{\frac{t_0 - t_n + nT}{S}} \tag{4}$$

where:

- $\widehat{H_n}$ is the estimated hash rate after mining the n-th block.
- T_n is the goal time to mine the next block.
- T is the ideal time between two blocks, i.e., $10\,\text{min}$.
- S is the smoothing factor.
- D_i is the difficulty after mining block i.
- t_i is the timestamp of block i.

NEF(DA)^2 eliminates drift by continuously adjusting difficulty in response to the network's estimated hash rate as well as accumulated drift. Mathematically, the drift is given by:

$$drift = t_n - (t_0 + nT)$$

- t_0 being the Genesis time.

Starting from Eq. (4) we can derive (see Appendix B) the following recursive formula:

$$D_n = D_{n-1} \left[1 + \frac{T}{S} \cdot e^{\frac{t_0 - t_{n-1} + (n-1)T}{S}} \right] \cdot e^{\frac{2(t_{n-1} - t_n) + T}{S}} \tag{5}$$

To highlight differences, we recall the equivalent NEFDA [13] formula:

$$D_n = D_{n-1} \left(1 + \frac{T}{S} \right) \cdot e^{\frac{t_{n-1} - t_n}{S}} \tag{NEFDA}$$

To illustrate the effect of the drift correction term, let us assume that the most recent block was mined exactly on time and $t_n - t_{n-1} = T$. Therefore:

$$\frac{t_{n-1} - t_n}{S} = \frac{2(t_{n-1} - t_n) + T}{S}$$

indicating that when the latest interblock time is equal to the ideal, for both DAAs, the negative exponential filter term is:

$$e^{-\frac{T}{S}}$$

Using the assumption $1 + \frac{T}{S} \approx e^{\frac{T}{S}}$, the following holds for NEFDA:

$$D_n = D_{n-1} \cdot e^{\frac{T}{S}} \cdot e^{-\frac{T}{S}} = D_{n-1}$$

which means that in this case the difficulty will remain unchanged regardless of any accumulated drift. In contrast, NEF(DA)^2 yields:

$$D_n = D_{n-1} \left[1 + \frac{T}{S} \cdot e^{\frac{t_0 - t_{n-1} + (n-1)T}{S}} \right] \cdot e^{-\frac{T}{S}}$$

If $(n-1)T + t_0 - t_{n-1} = 0$, i.e. there is no drift, NEF(DA)^2 reduces to NEFDA. However, if $(n-1)T + t_0 - t_{n-1} \neq 0$, we encounter two possible scenarios:

1. **Ahead of Schedule**: In this case:

$$t_{n-1} - t_0 \leq (n-1)T \quad \leftrightarrow \quad t_0 - t_{n-1} + (n-1)T \geq 0$$

$$\implies \quad e^{\frac{t_0 - t_{n-1} + (n-1)T}{S}} \geq 1$$

Thus implying:

$$D_n \geq D_{n-1}\left(1 + \frac{T}{S}\right) \cdot e^{-\frac{T}{S}} = D_{n-1}$$

thereby increasing difficulty to counteract drift.

2. **Behind Schedule**: In this case, the reverse logic applies:

$$t_{n-1} - t_0 \geq (n-1)T \quad \leftrightarrow \quad t_0 - t_{n-1} + (n-1)T \leq 0$$

$$\implies \quad e^{\frac{t_0 - t_{n-1} + (n-1)T}{S}} \leq 1$$

which implies:

$$D_n \leq D_{n-1}\left(1 + \frac{T}{S}\right) \cdot e^{-\frac{T}{S}} = D_{n-1}$$

resulting in a decrease in difficulty to compensate for the lag.

Therefore, our proposed NEF(DA)^2 algorithm allows dynamic tuning of difficulty not only based on the estimated hash rate but also based on the accumulated historical drift. The main benefit of NEF(DA)^2 is its simplicity, as it achieves drift correction with a very subtle change in complexity compared to NEFDA (modifying only a couple of code lines). Consequently, it ensures very stable and predictable long-term block production. Meanwhile, it inherits all of NEFDA's desired properties and reduces to it as soon as drift is eliminated. Lastly, we acknowledge the necessity of temporarily overshooting difficulty to correct drift, which might not be popular with miners in the short term, but does put the block production schedule back on track.

6 Simulation

As a next step, we develop a simulation that replicates the block-production procedure and implements NEFDA and NEF(DA)^2 DAAs. Then we use the simulation data to extract information and create visualisations to compare the behaviour of the two algorithms. The code for simulation and visualisation can be found in an open source repository[1].

For each simulation, we run the block-production procedure for a nominal duration of 15 years using the same hash rate function twice, one for each DAA. This produces a list of all the blocks that were created along with data (timestamps, difficulties, total work) and metadata (interblock times, drift, hash rate).

For the visualisation, we start by creating block time distribution graphs to ensure that NEF(DA)^2 follows the desired Poisson distribution similarly to

---

[1] https://github.com/demKyr/BCH-DAA.

NEFDA. Consequently, we juxtapose the autocorrelation of the algorithms to illustrate the lack of periodic pattern between interblock times. Lastly, we plot drift, difficulty and average block time per day against hash rate to compare the two DAAs.

The main purpose of the simulations is to exemplify the great impact of $NEF(DA)^2$ and to experimentally prove that it solves the drift problem while at the same time inherits all the beneficial properties of NEFDA. Fig. 5 demonstrates the code elegance and simplicity of $NEF(DA)^2$. Appendix C contains additional simulations.

```
#ifdef NEFDA
    candidate.target = 1.0/(estimated_hash_rate*IDEAL_INTERBLOCK_TIME);
#endif

#ifdef MODIFIED_NEFDA
    double skew = t-(GENESIS_TIME+(n+1)*IDEAL_INTERBLOCK_TIME);
    candidate.target = 1.0/(estimated_hash_rate*IDEAL_INTERBLOCK_TIME)*exp(skew/SHADOW_OF_FUTURE_TIMESCALE);
#endif
```

Fig. 5. Code changes from NEFDA to $NEF(DA)^2$.

6.1   Non-adaptive Hash Rate

For this part, we use predetermined hash rate functions that do not adapt to changes in difficulty. Such simulations compare the response of the two DAAs to different hash rate behaviours like instant changes, linear growth, exponential growth or oscillations.

To avoid repetition, we only present the block time distribution and autocorrelation graphs for the first hash rate function. For this section, those graphs are used to ensure that both algorithms have similar behaviour in terms of block time distribution and autocorrelation.

Staircase Hash Rate Function. Hash rate is increased twice by one order of magnitude each time and replicates hash rate increases like the ones from the transition to GPU mining (2010) and then to ASIC mining (2013).

As shown in Figs. 6 and 7, both DAAs follow the same distribution and have similar autocorrelation. However, as shown in Fig. 8, $NEF(DA)^2$ can quickly absorb the shock from the sudden change in hash rate and eliminate any drift while NEFDA never recovers. Moreover, $NEF(DA)^2$ achieves this with only a slight ephemeral adjustment of difficulty.

Rectangular Hash Rate Function. This hash rate function creates a sudden increase of hash power by a factor of 30 and a subsequent drop to initial hash rate. As shown in Fig. 9, $NEF(DA)^2$ can effectively respond to both rises and drops although responding to the latter takes more time than responding to the former. This happens because the DAA uses past interblock times as empirical evidence to adjust difficulty. The number of blocks required to impact difficulty is approximately the same for sudden hash rate increases and decreases. However, when the hash rate drops, this number of blocks is produced much slower.

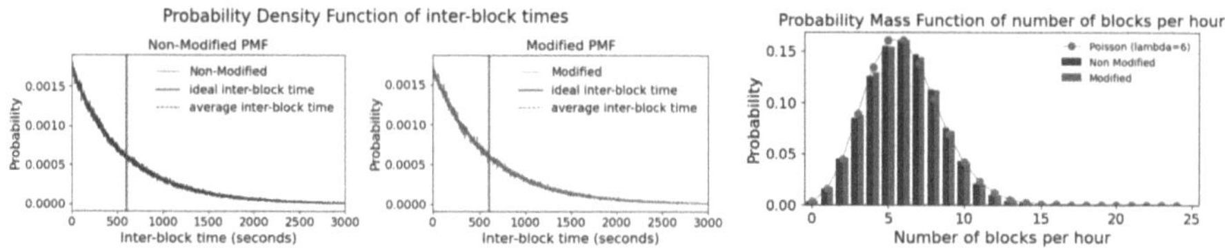

Fig. 6. Block time distributions for non-adaptive staircase hash function.

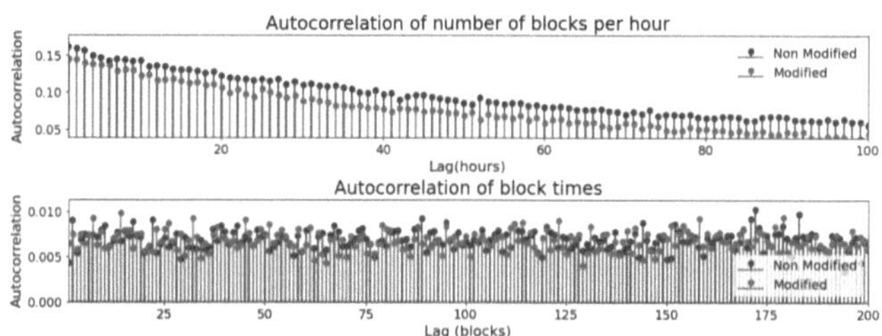

Fig. 7. Autocorrelations for non-adaptive staircase hash function.

6.2 Adaptive Hash Rate

In the real world, miners are sensitive to difficulty and changes in coin value. To simulate this behaviour, we developed an adaptive hash rate function. More specifically, we consider three different classes of miners: *loyal miners*, *variable miners*, and *greedy miners* with hash rates H_l, H_v, and H_g respectively. The total maximum available hash rate is controlled by a predetermined hash rate function but at any given moment, the network's current hash rate is given by:

$$H = H_l + H_v + H_g \tag{6}$$

$$H_v = \begin{cases} 4 \cdot H_l, & \text{if } R_D \leq 1 - \epsilon \\ \dfrac{4 \cdot H_l}{1 + e^{-\frac{1 - R_D}{\epsilon^2}}} & \text{if } 1 - \epsilon < R_D \leq 1 + \epsilon \\ 0, & \text{otherwise} \end{cases} \tag{7}$$

$$H_g = \begin{cases} 4 \cdot H_l, & \text{if } R_D \leq 1 - \epsilon/3 \\ 0, & \text{otherwise} \end{cases} \tag{8}$$

where:

- R_D is the ratio of the average difficulty of the latest 6 blocks divided by the average difficulty of the 6 previous.
- H_l is following a predetermined function similar to the hash rate function of the previous section.
- $\epsilon = 0.05$

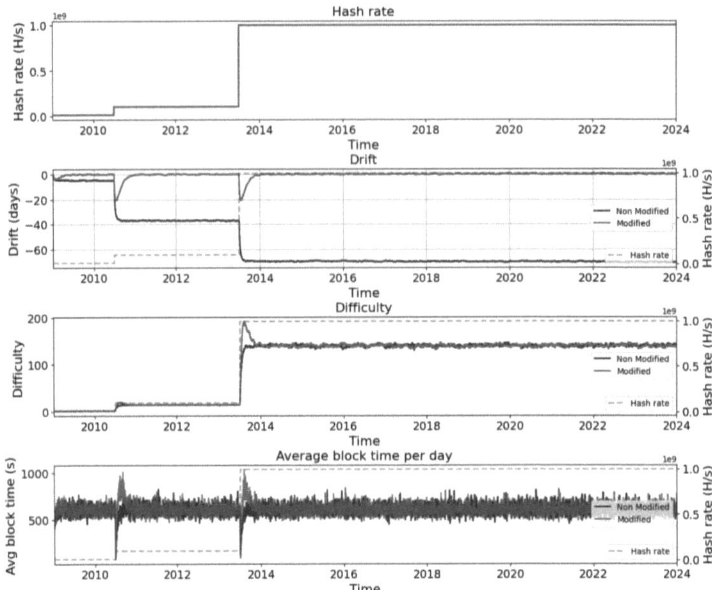

Fig. 8. Comparison for non-adaptive staircase hash rate function.

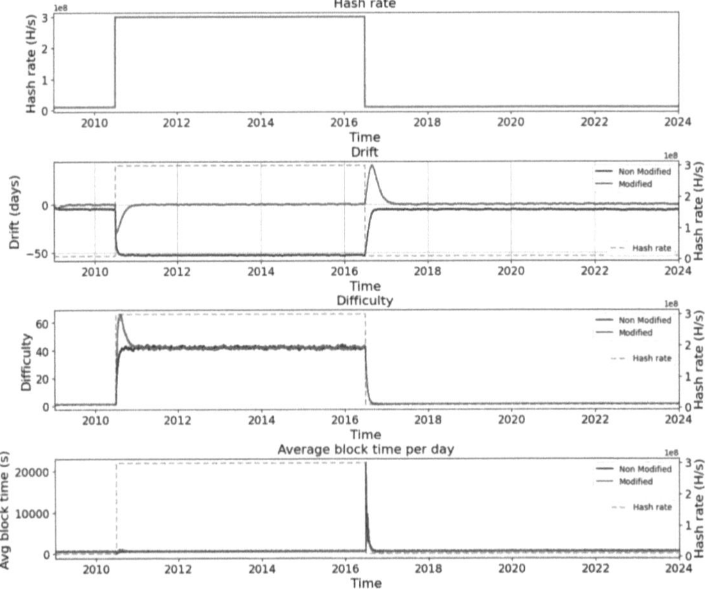

Fig. 9. Comparison for non-adaptive rectangular hash rate function.

This hash function is much more representative of real mining behaviour and it provides important information about the similarities between the two algorithms in terms of block-time distribution and autocorrelation (see Figs. 10–12). It also complements the mathematical proofs, as many of the findings here cannot be directly derived from the equations of Sect. 5. As shown in Fig. 11, both DAAs show a large negative autocorrelation to the recent blocks and no autocorrelation to the earlier ones. This is expected as DAAs need to rapidly adjust to interblock times that deviate a lot from ideal but should not have any direct dependencies to any old interblock times.

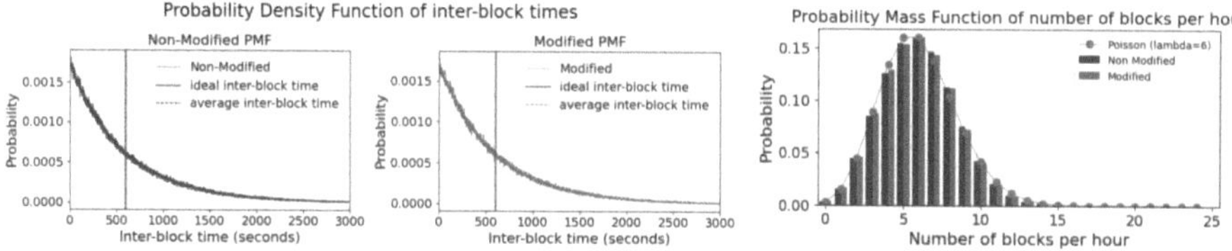

Fig. 10. Block time distributions for adaptive staircase hash function.

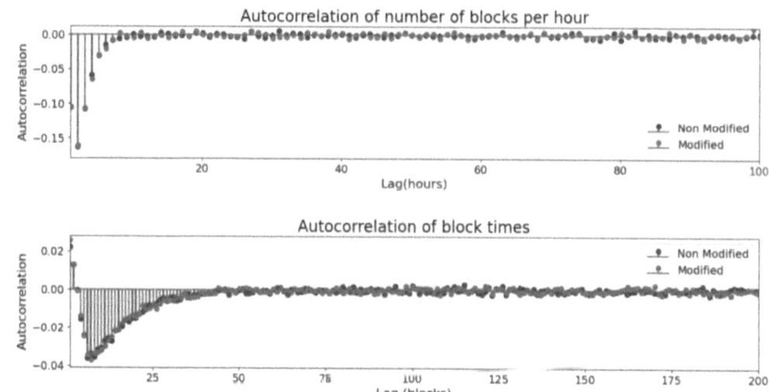

Fig. 11. Autocorrelations for adaptive staircase hash function.

6.3 Smoothing Factor Effect

The smoothing factor controls DAA's responsiveness. The larger it is, the longer it takes to eliminate drift, but at the same time, difficulty adjustment is smoother, and daily average interblock time does not deviate that far from the ideal of 10 min. For the simulations, we used a smoothing factor $S = 14$ days.

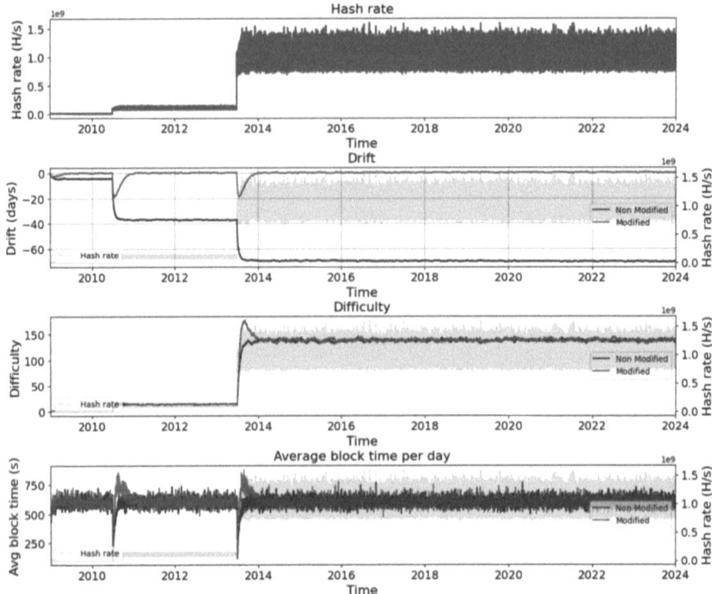

Fig. 12. Comparison for adaptive hash rate function.

7 Future Work

We are currently working on a generalised DAA that can potentially exterminate drift even for super-exponentially increasing hash rate functions. This DAA will introduce the meaning of drift-resistance level. NEFDA and $\mathrm{NEF(DA)}^2$ can be categorised as special cases of the general DAA. Furthermore, core ideas introduced in this paper could be used to develop a similar BTC-compatible DAA.

8 Conclusion

Through this paper, we analysed the behaviour of present and past DAAs of BCH and revealed flaws in their designs. Moreover, we proposed $\mathrm{NEF(DA)}^2$, a novel yet simple DAA that successfully eliminates drift while inheriting the desired properties of the existing BCH DAA. We believe that the incredible simplicity of the new algorithm and the way it can be seemingly added to the existing DAA are its main strengths. Accordingly, our algorithm, immaculately and essentially without increasing computational complexity, ensures long-term stability, dependability, and predictability in block-production rate. We have also supported our claims with mathematical proof and robust open-source simulations. Overall, we provided a complete and substantiated proposal of a Difficulty Adjustment Algorithm compatible with most Proof-Of-Work blockchains.

A Comparison Table of BTC/BCH Halvings to the Ideal

Table 1. Comparison of BTC/BCH halvings to the ideal

	Ideal	BTC	BCH
Genesis Block (block #0 - reward 50 BTC)			
Date		2009-01-09	2009-01-09
Halving 1 (block #210000 - reward 25.0 BTC)			
Date		2013-01-06	2012-11-28
Days since last halving (deviation)	1458 (0)	1419 (-39)	
Days since genesis (deviation)	1458 (0)	1419 (-39)	
Halving 2 (block #420000 - reward 12.5 BTC)			
Date		2017-01-03	2016-07-09
Days since last halving (deviation)	1458 (0)	1319 (-139)	
Days since genesis (deviation)	2916 (0)	2738 (-178)	
Halving 3 (block #630000 - reward 6.25 BTC)			
Date		2020-12-31	2020-05-11	2020-04-08
Days since last halving (deviation)	1458 (0)	1402 (-56)	1369 (-89)
Days since genesis (deviation)	4374 (0)	4140 (-234)	4107 (-267)
Halving 4 (block #840000 - reward 3.125 BTC)			
Date		2024-12-28	2024-04-20	2024-04-03
Days since last halving (deviation)	1458 (0)	1440 (-18)	1456 (-2)
Days since genesis (deviation)	5832 (0)	5580 (-252)	5563 (-269)

B   Analysis for NEF(DA)^2

Recursive Formula We have:

$$\widehat{H}_n = \frac{1}{S}\left[\sum_{i=0}^{n-1} D_i e^{\frac{t_i - t_n}{S}}\right]$$

$$T_n = T \cdot \exp\left(\frac{t_0 - t_n + nT}{S}\right)$$

Thus:

$$D_n = \widehat{H}_n \times T_n$$

$$= \frac{T}{S}\left[\sum_{i=0}^{n-1} D_i \exp\left(\frac{t_i - t_n}{S}\right)\right] \cdot \exp\left(\frac{t_0 - t_n + nT}{S}\right)$$

We make t_{n-1} appear in the sum, and the exponential factor:

$$= \frac{T}{S}\left[\sum_{i=0}^{n-1} D_i \exp\left(\frac{t_i - t_{n-1}}{S}\right)\right] \exp\left(\frac{t_{n-1} - t_n}{S}\right) \cdot \exp\left(\frac{t_0 - t_n + nT)}{S}\right)$$

$$= \frac{T}{S}\left[\sum_{i=0}^{n-1} D_i \exp\left(\frac{t_i - t_{n-1}}{S}\right)\right] \cdot \exp\left(\frac{t_0 - t_{n-1} + (n-1)T}{S}\right) \exp\left(\frac{t_{n-1} - t_n}{S}\right) \exp\left(\frac{t_{n-1} - t_n + T}{S}\right)$$

We simplify:

$$= \frac{T}{S} \left[\sum_{i=0}^{n-1} D_i \exp\left(\frac{t_i - t_{n-1}}{S} \right) \right] \cdot \exp\left(\frac{t_0 - t_{n-1} + (n-1)T}{S} \right) \exp\left(\frac{2(t_{n-1} - t_n) + T}{S} \right)$$

We develop the sum

$$= \frac{T}{S} \left[\sum_{i=0}^{n-2} D_i \exp\left(\frac{t_i - t_{n-1}}{S} \right) + D_{n-1} \right] \cdot \exp\left(\frac{t_0 - t_{n-1} + (n-1)T}{S} \right) \exp\left(\frac{2(t_{n-1} - t_n) + T}{S} \right)$$

Thus we have

$$= \left[D_{n-1} + \frac{T}{S} D_{n-1} \cdot \exp\left(\frac{t_0 - t_{n-1} + (n-1)T}{S} \right) \right] \cdot \exp\left(\frac{2(t_{n-1} - t_n) + T}{S} \right)$$

Which gives us the final formula:

$$D_n = D_{n-1} \left[1 + \frac{T}{S} \cdot \exp\left(\frac{t_0 - t_{n-1} + (n-1)T}{S} \right) \right] \cdot \exp\left(\frac{2(t_{n-1} - t_n) + T}{S} \right)$$

Non Recursive Formula Let us with:

$$D_n = D_{n-1} \left[1 + \frac{T}{S} \cdot \exp\left(\frac{t_0 - t_{n-1} + (n-1)T}{S} \right) \right] \cdot \exp\left(\frac{2(t_{n-1} - t_n) + T}{S} \right)$$

Using the following hypothesis: $x = \frac{T}{S} \times \exp\left(\frac{t_0 - t_{n-1} + (n-1)T}{S} \right) \ll 1$, we have $1 + x \approx e^x$, thus giving us:

$$D_n = D_{n-1} \exp\left(\frac{T}{S} \exp\left(\frac{t_0 - t_{n-1} + (n-1)T}{S} \right) \right) \cdot \exp\left(\frac{2(t_{n-1} - t_n) + T}{S} \right)$$

$$D_n = D_{n-1} \exp\left(\frac{T}{S} \exp\left(\frac{t_0 - t_{n-1} + (n-1)T}{S} \right) + \frac{2(t_{n-1} - t_n) + T}{S} \right)$$

We finally have:

$$D_n = D_0 \exp\left[\sum_{i=0}^{n-1} \left(\frac{T}{S} \exp\left(\frac{t_0 - t_i + iT}{S} \right) + \frac{2(t_i - t_{i+1}) + T}{S} \right) \right]$$

$$D_n = D_0 \exp\left[\frac{T}{S} \left(\sum_{i=0}^{n-1} \exp\left(\frac{t_0 - t_i + iT}{S} \right) \right) + \frac{2(t_0 - t_n) + nT}{S} \right]$$

C   Additional Simulations

Figures 13 and 14

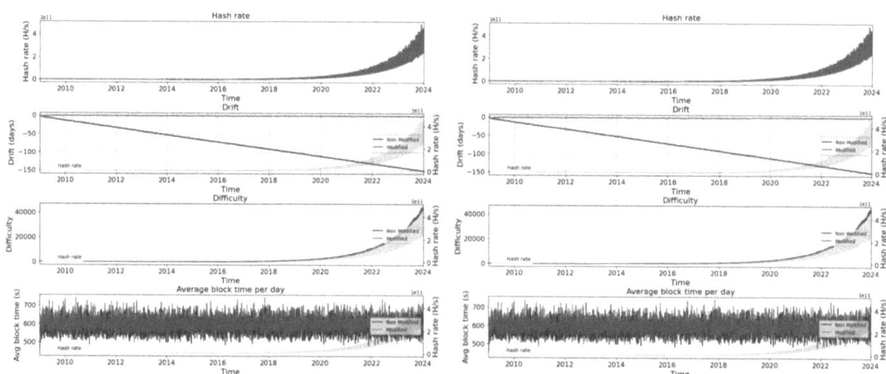

Fig. 13. Comparison for non-adaptive and adaptive exponential hash rate function.

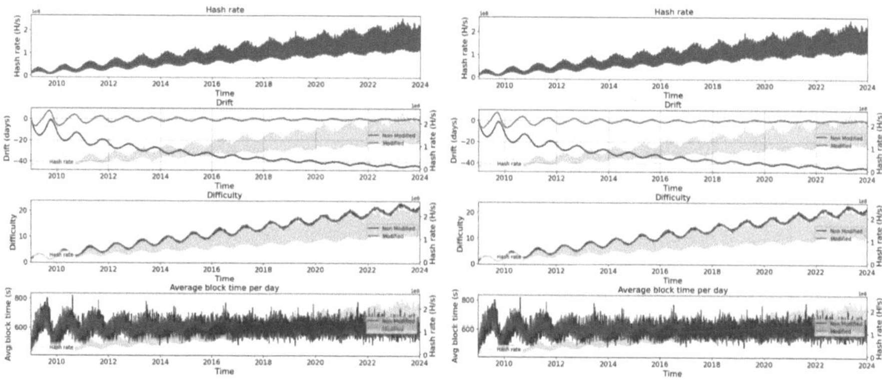

Fig. 14. Comparison for non-adaptive and adaptive sinusoidal and linearly increasing hash rate function.

References

1. Amaury Sechet: Announcing the grasberg DAA. https://read.cash/@deadalnix/announcing-the-grasberg-daa-ff52e96d
2. Zegers, A.: Bringing stability to bitcoin cash difficulty adjustments. https://mengerian.medium.com/bringing-stability-to-bitcoin-cash-difficulty-adjustments-eae8def0efa4
3. Arena, L., Oriol, N., Veryzhenko, I.: Too fast, too furious? trading algorithmique et instabilité des marchés financiers. Systèmes d'information & Manage. **23**, 81–106 (2018). https://doi.org/10.3917/sim.182.0081, https://shs.cairn.info/revue-systemes-d-information-et-management-2018-2-page-81?lang=fr
4. Bashir, I.: Mastering Blockchain: Distributed Ledger Technology, Decentralization, and Smart Contracts Explained, 2nd edn. Packt Publishing Ltd., Birmingham (2018)
5. Bitcoin ABC: Difficulty Adjustment algorithm update. https://www.bitcoinabc.org/2017-11-01-DAA/
6. Bitcoin Cash: Bitcoin Cash – Peer-to-Peer Electronic Cash. https://bitcoincash.org/
7. Bitcoin SV: The original bitcoin blockchain: bitcoin SV (BSV). https://bitcoinsv.com/
8. Buterin, V.: Ethereum: a next-generation smart contract and decentralized application platform (2014)
9. CoinDesk: Bitcoin Cash Price – BCH price index and live chart. https://www.coindesk.com/price/bitcoin-cash/
10. Ethereum: Proof-of-work (PoW). https://ethereum.org/en/developers/docs/consensus-mechanisms/pow/
11. Freetrader: On drift correction. https://read.cash/@freetrader/on-drift-correction-39974f66
12. freetrader, Toomim, J., Culianu, C., Lundeberg, M.: 2020-NOV-15 ASERT difficulty adjustment algorithm (aserti3-2d). https://upgradespecs.bitcoincashnode.org/2020-11-15-asert/
13. Ilie, D.I., Werner, S.M., Stewart, I.D., Knottenbelt, W.J.: Unstable throughput: when the difficulty algorithm breaks. In: Proceedings of the IEEE International Conference on Blockchain and Cryptocurrency, ICBC 2021. Institute of Electrical and Electronics Engineers Inc. (2021). https://doi.org/10.1109/ICBC51069.2021.9461086
14. Wade, J.: Hash Rate: How it works and how to measure. https://www.investopedia.com/hash-rate-6746261
15. Toomim, J.: Dark secrets of the grasberg DAA. https://read.cash/@jtoomim/dark-secrets-of-the-grasberg-daa-a9239fb6
16. Király, T., Lomoschitz, L.: Protability of the coin-hopping strategy. Tech. rep, Egervary Research Group, Budapest (2018)
17. Wuckert, Jr., K.: History on hash war. https://coingeek.com/hash-war-history/
18. Conway, L.: Bitcoin halving: what it is and why it matters for crypto investors. https://www.investopedia.com/bitcoin-halving-4843769
19. Lundeberg, M.B.: Static difficulty adjustments, with absolutely scheduled exponentially rising targets (DA-ASERT)-v.2 (2020). https://www.bitcoinunlimited.info/nexa/da-asert.pdf
20. Lundeberg, M.: Thoughts on grasberg DAA. https://www.reddit.com/r/btc/comments/hx4kgz/thoughts_on_grasberg_daa/

21. Nakamoto, S.: Bitcoin: a peer-to-peer electronic cash system (2008). https://www.bitcoin.org/bitcoin.pdf
22. Reference Cash: Difficulty adjustment algorithm. https://reference.cash/protocol/blockchain/proof-of-work/difficulty-adjustment-algorithm
23. Reference Cash: Proof of work. https://reference.cash/protocol/blockchain/proof-of-work
24. Kejriwal, S: Bitcoin vs bitcoin cash: an in-depth look at BTC & BCH. https://coinbureau.com/analysis/bitcoin-vs-bitcoin-cash/
25. The Investopedia Team: What is bitcoin cash (BCH), and how does it work? https://www.investopedia.com/terms/b/bitcoin-cash.asp

VeriCert: SSL/TLS Certificate Verification Based on Self-sovereign Identity and Blockchain

Andrea Giuliani[1], Andrea De Salve[2], Paolo Mori[2], and Laura Ricci[1(✉)]

[1] Department of Computer Science, University of Pisa, Pisa, Italy
`andrea.giuliani12@gmail.com`, `laura.ricci@unipi.it`
[2] National Research Council (CNR), Rome, Italy
`andrea.desalve@isasi.cnr.it`, `paolo.mori@iit.cnr.it`

Abstract. The Public Key Infrastructure is a critical component of digital communication and it relies on the trustworthiness of Certification Authorities to sign digital certificates, binding a public key with an entity in the digital domain. However, recent incidents have shown that attackers can force Certification Authorities to sign fraudulent certificates, creating a single point of failure in digital communication security. This paper presents VeriCert, a novel solution that mitigates this vulnerability by leveraging the Self Sovereign Identity paradigm and the Blockchain.

VeriCert allows web service providers to demonstrate control over their digital certificate information, supporting the verification and management of certificate transparency. VeriCert ensures that the trust, integrity and authenticity of digital certificates are maintained by a blockchain-based registry, without relying on centralized authorities, thereby reducing the risk of fraudulent certificates. A prototype of VeriCert has been implemented using Solidity smart contracts and a dataset consisting of digital certificates from well-known providers has been used to simulate client and web server behaviour during a TLS handshake. Performance evaluations indicate that the overhead required to detect rogue certificates remains below 700 ms for the majority of service providers, even in the event of a compromised Certificate Authority.

Keywords: Digital Certificate Management · Public-Key Infrastructure · Self-Sovereign Identity · Blockchain

1 Introduction

From the birth of the World Wide Web a main challenge was authenticating and securing digital communications among unknown entities in the digital domain. This is achieved with the support of the Public-Key Infrastructure (PKI), i.e., a set of processes, technologies, and policies in which digital entities can authenticate themselves worldwide [12]. At the heart of Public-Key Infrastructure (PKI)

© ICST Institute for Computer Sciences, Social Informatics and Telecommunications Engineering 2026
Published by Springer Nature Switzerland AG 2026. All Rights Reserved
W. Knottenbelt et al. (Eds.): Blocktea 2025, LNICST 669, pp. 80–97, 2026.
https://doi.org/10.1007/978-3-032-12335-0_5

are Certificate Authorities (CAs), which act as trust anchors by signing digital certificates that bind public keys to entities. This process ensures that clients can trust the web service providers they are communicating with during an HTTPS session, as the certificates are issued by trusted CA. However, several security incidents in past years [4,6,13,15] demonstrate that such assumption may not hold true in real scenarios. Due to their role in PKI, CAs became an attractive target for attackers. The attackers exploit CA's vulnerabilities to obtain a rogue certificate, i.e., a valid certificate signed by a CA where the attacker can control its payload. Rogue certificates issued by a compromised CA can pose several security risks to both clients and web service providers. Indeed, such a certificate can be used by attackers to impersonate legitimate websites, intercept sensitive data, and conduct Man-in-the-Middle (MiTM) attacks, potentially leading to data breaches, financial losses, and damage to the trust and reputations of the affected entities.

Due to this vulnerability, many security mechanisms were proposed to ensure the integrity and authenticity of digital certificates. Centralized solutions, such as [1], suffer from the single-point of failure vulnerability and they are extremely unreliable in case of CA compromising, which can be bypassed by attackers [10,11]. Approaches based on Peer-to-Peer networks, such as [14], redesign the entire PKI, discarding the hierarchical CA's infrastructure and limiting the compatibility with the already used PKI. Recently, approaches exploiting blockchain-based solution, such as [18], have been proposed and designed for specific blockchain frameworks.

This paper presents VeriCert, a novel methodology that leverages the Self-Sovereign Identity (SSI) paradigm to mitigate the vulnerability of rogue certificates issued by a compromised CA. VeriCert exploits the SSI paradigm to uniquely identify web service providers and to prove control over their certificate information without relying on centralized intermediaries. The VeriCert protocol is supported by a verifiable data registry that provides a robust and transparent infrastructure for verifying digital certificates information and to recover from different attacks scenarios.

To validate our approach, a prototype of VeriCert has been implemented using public Ethereum testnet as verifiable data registry. In order to test the functionality and evaluate the performance with real world certificates, we collected real data on SSL/TLS certificates from different web service providers, including apple.com, ebay.com, linkedin.com, forbes.com, swiss.com and booking.com. Performance results indicate that the average time taken by a client in order to authenticate and establish a secure connection with VeriCert is about 750 ms. In summary, the key contributions presented in this work are the following:

- design of a solution that integrates the SSI paradigm to mitigate the threat of rogue certificates within the PKI ecosystem.
- comprehensive security evaluations of the proposed solution in order to demonstrate the robustness of the system against relevant security threats.

- implementation of the proposed solution to demonstrate its feasibility and extensive experimental evaluation based on real dataset of digital certificates.

The rest of this paper is arranged as follows. Section 2 introduces fundamental concepts related to SSI and digital certificates. Section 3 identifies design goals and potential threats of the system. The VeriCert solution is presented in Sect. 4, while the security of the proposed solution has been evaluated in Sect. 5. Performance results are presented in Sect. 6 and related works are summarized in Sect. 7. Finally, the conclusions of the work are summarized in Sect. 8.

2   Background

This section introduces fundamental concepts and technologies that are essential for the presented research.

2.1   Self-sovereign Identity

The Self-Sovereign Identity is a new model for digital identity on the Internet, empowering individuals with greater control over their identity information. At its core, SSI exploits Decentralized IDentity (DID) to identify and represent an entity. The following example shows a DID which exploits addresses of the Ethereum blockchain as identifiers, such as `did:ethr:0x0a7E7ba0565E6cfFcF1eB64c313`... Each DID is paired to a DID document that contains public keys, verification methods, and service endpoints. This document is retrieved through *DID resolution*, supported by trusted registries such as blockchains. The DID subject is the entity identified by a DID while the DID controller is the entity having the capability to make changes to a DID document.

A Verifiable Credential (VC) is a tamper-resistant set of attributes some authority (called the *issuer*) claims to be true about a *subject* of the credential. Typically, the *subject* of a credential is also the credential's *holder*, i.e., the entity that keeps secure in its digital wallet the VC and presents it to a *verifier* by using Verifiable Presentation (VP). A VP is a set of VCs signed by the credential's holder and it includes proofs and digital signatures to verify the authenticity and integrity of the data. The *verifier* will be able to check that a VP has been presented by the intended holder of the credential and that the presented credential has a valid signature proof of the *issuer*.

2.2   Digital Certificates

A digital certificate cryptographically binds an entity's identity (e.g., a user or service) to a set of information used to establish secure, authenticated communication. The widely adopted X.509 standard [5,8] defines certificates within a Public Key Infrastructure (PKI), where trusted entities called CAs issue and manage certificates.

To obtain a certificate, an entity submits a Certificate Signing Request (CSR) to a CA, which verifies the request and signs the certificate. However, identity verification is typically handled by a Registration Authority (RA), which confirms the requestor's identity and proves the domain ownership. CAs are organized hierarchically, i.e., each of them can delegate the issuing of certificates to intermediate CAs. CAs located at the upper level are named *root CAs* and their certificates are included by default in the *trust store* of each browser and operating system. When a client C connects to a server S, the server provides a certificate chain (from its own certificate up to the root CA), allowing C to verify the server's authenticity. If the chain is valid, C and S establish a session key for encrypted communication.

3 Threat Modeling

The main actors involved in the reference scenario are the CA, the RA, a web service provider and a client interested in establishing secure communication with the web service provider. The CA, the RA, and the web service provider are uniquely identified by digital certificates, each embedding the related public key, while the client could optionally have a certificate embedding its public key.

We denote CA and RA as different actors because they are responsible for carrying out different tasks, even though their roles can be embodied by a single entity in some case. The RA is a trusted entity which allows a web service provider to prove the ownership of a domain and its identity information. Instead, trust in the CA depends on the extent to which critical resources of the CA are protected and the robustness of the security measures implemented to prevent unauthorized access or breaches. For this reason, in this paper we assume that a CA can be compromised or deceived to issue certificates containing false or misleading claims (*rogue certificate*). Indeed, a compromised CA can be forced to issue certificates whose payload is controlled by attackers, obtaining a real advantage against the PKI security. Attack vectors used to acquire a rogue certificate from a CA includes:

Impersonation: attacker convinces the CA that it is someone else [6].
Compromised the CA: attacker compromises the systems used by CA and issues one or more rogue certificates [4,13].
CA private key theft: attacker steals the signing key of the CA generating one or more rogue certificates.
Forged a certificate: attacker exploits weaknesses in signing algorithms to forge one or more rogue certificates [15].

We assume also that the underlying hardware and software infrastructure of the web service provider is robustly secured and its private keys remain confidential within the web servers' domain. Indeed, the focus of the research is not related to securing communications among clients and servers, and in the case that the private key of a certificate is lost or compromised, the web service provider must request the CA to revoke the certificate and issue a new one.

We operate under the standard cryptographic assumptions that an attacker lacks the capability to forge digital signatures or discover collisions within cryptographic hash functions. In our study, the main goal of an attacker is to collude with a compromised CA in order to obtain a rogue certificate related to a web service provider on a public key $e_{s'}$, which is different from the original e_s and whose matching private key $d_{s'}$ is known to the attacker.

3.1 Problem Statement

In this research, we focused on mitigating the critical security threat introduced by rogue certificates, providing actors the capability to detect and isolate a rogue certificate in the PKI ecosystem. For this reason, we define a Certificate Authority/Registration Authority in the following way:

Definition 1 (Certificate Authority/Registration Authority). *A certificate authority/registration authority CA/RA is an entity identified by a certificate $Cert_{CA}/Cert_{RA}$ and a public key e_a/e_r, which is trusted by one or more users to create and manage certificates that identify web service providers.*

Even if the CA is trusted by one or more users to issue certificates, there is always a risk that it could be compromised or attacked by malicious users. Consequently, a compromised CA is introduced in the model as follows:

Definition 2 (Compromised Certificate Authority). *A Compromised Certificate Authority (CCA) is a CA which can be forced to issue a rogue certificate $Cert_S$, binding a public key $e_{s'}$ to the subject s.*

As a result, a rogue certificate closely resembles a legitimate certificate, except for the public key of the subject, which, instead, is under the control of the attacker. In order to enhance the accountability of CAs, a Certificate Transparency (CT) property based on [1] is defined on the issued certificate.

Definition 3 (Certificate Transparency). *A certificate $Cert_S$ related to a subject S provides Certificate Transparency (Certificate Transparency (CT)) if it is included in a decentralized, verifiable, and append-only log which allows S proving the issuance/existence of certificates.*

For this reason, including a certificate in an append-only log provides a way to demonstrate the existence and issuance of the certificate, but it does not guarantee that the information contained in the certificate is trusted and controlled by the subject s. In order to solve this issue, we empower the certificate owner with Self-Sovereign Identity capabilities, ensuring that the certificate owner can present verifiable credentials and presentations without relying on a central authority. This enables the subject s to countersign the certificate $Cert_S$, asserting control and trust over the information it contains.

4 VeriCert

In order to enhance the security of digital certificate management, we propose VeriCert, a solution based on the SSI model. The main idea behind the proposed approach is to enable each web service provider to demonstrate control over both a DID and its associated web domain. This is achieved by obtaining from RA a proof of domain ownership (see Sect. 2.2) that not only verifies the ownership of the domain, but also establishes a secure and verifiable link between the domain and the associated DID. Once the certificate is acquired from the CA through the traditional workflow, the web server then publishes a fingerprint of this certificate and the proof of domain ownership on a blockchain-based verifiable data registry via a transaction. In particular, the proof of domain ownership can be used to authenticate the domain in various interactions, while the certificate fingerprint is used to pair the DID of the web service provider with the certificate, thus establishing an additional trust guarantee and enhanced control of the information contained in the certificate through the revocation mechanism. Exploiting VeriCert, the clients verify the authenticity and the integrity of the information embedded in the certificate through the blockchain, thus ensuring a secure and transparent certificate verification process.

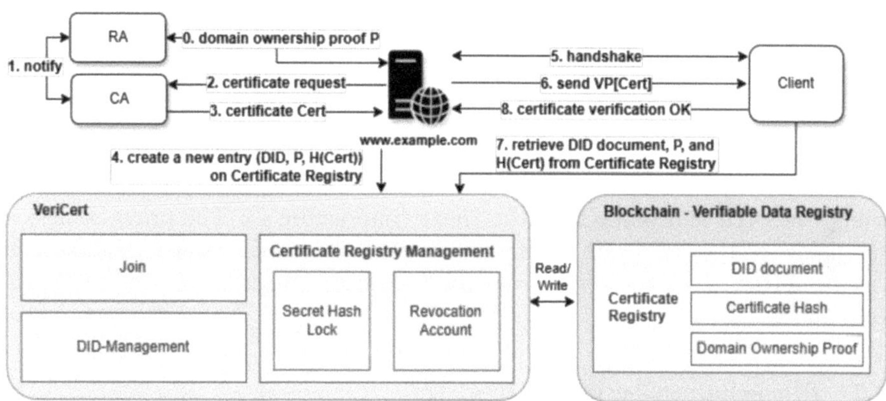

Fig. 1. Architecture of VeriCert.

4.1 Architecture and Entities Modelling

The main actors involved in the proposed system are: the CA and the RA, who are responsible for issuing certificates, a service provider (named *www.example.com*), and a client who wants to access the service. The logical architecture of our solution and the interactions between the various actors are depicted in Fig. 1. To have a clear understanding of how the protocol works, the entire process will be initially explained, composed by the traditional PKI integrating our solution, assuming that a web service provider has a valid domain name already registered and wants to request a certificate from a CA.

Actually, the architecture's workflow and messages exchanged among web service providers, RA and CA remain the same, as in the PKI (interactions 0–3 in Fig. 1). Indeed, the CA and RA behavior in certificate creation, as well as signature algorithms, remains unaltered, being outside of our model, guaranteeing that the solution adheres to the standard workflow and provides comparable functionalities to entities. The registration on VeriCert is managed by the *Join* component in Fig. 1 (described in Sect. 4.3), and it allows a web service provider S to be identified by using a DID and to be the controller of such DID. The proposed solution exploits a blockchain as a verifiable data registry to facilitate the exchange of cryptographic keys and the verification of the certificate information without involving central authorities (see Sect. 4.2). In particular, the *Certificate Registry* is a smart contract deployed in a blockchain and it is responsible for the management of DIDs and the respective information in the DID documents. Hence, after having received the certificate in the standard way from the CA, S invokes the *Certificate Registry* in order to publish on the blockchain the fingerprint $H(Cert_S)$ of such certificate $Cert_S$ and the domain ownership proof P (interaction 4 in Fig. 1). In this way, the web server pairs its DID with such certificate to assert control and trust over the certificate information. In addition, VeriCert provides to S a mechanism based on *secret hash lock* and *revocation account* to regain from the loss or the theft of the cryptographic keys used to control the DID (see Sect. 4.4).

When a client initiates a connection with a VeriCert-enabled web service provider, the enhanced handshake protocol is triggered to establish a secure communication (interaction 5 of Fig. 1). During this process, which is detailed in Sect. 4.5, the provider includes its certificate $Cert_S$ in a VP, signs the VP using the DID, and sends it to the client (interaction 6). The provider acts as the holder of the certificate credential, and the client as a verifier. Missing data can be retrieved by the client from the Certificate Registry on the blockchain (interaction 7).

4.2 Blockchain: Certificate Registry

A main component of the VeriCert architecture is the *Certificate Registry*, a smart contract designed to manage DIDs, supporting the exchange and verification of data about certificates and DID of the web service providers. The smart contract ensures that each DID is paired with a corresponding entry of associated attributes. The data in each entry belong to the following categories:

DID Resolution Data: each ledger entry stores the DID and the information needed to build the corresponding DID document.

Certification Data: consists of the information that allows a DID subject to assert control and trust over the attributes specified by the certificate. Such data include: *i)* a fingerprint $H(Cert_S)$ of the certificate $Cert_S$ (Certificate Hash in

Fig. 1) and *ii)* a proof P issued by the RA demonstrating that the web service provider is the owner of a specific domain and is in control of a specific DID (Domain Ownership Proof in Fig. 1).

Revocation Data: such data are used by access control mechanisms to empower the identity owner with secure and autonomous control over their identity information, even in the case of a compromised DID resulting from the unauthorized exposure of its cryptographic keys. This is achieved through a secure recovery process embedded within the contract, which allows the web service provider to revoke the compromised DID through a further DID, called revocation account, and by proving knowledge of a *secret hash lock.*

Furthermore, the smart contract incorporates mechanisms for DID operations and certificate management, as the update authentication method and the fingerprint of the certificate.

4.3   Join VeriCert

The first thing a web service provider has to do in order to join the VeriCert protocol is to create a DID. Each DID must be compliant with the W3C specification, and each web service provider is the subject and the controller of its DID. After the creation of a DID, the web service provider must prove to the RA the ownership over a specific web domain, as in the traditional PKI, where control over a domain must be verified from the RA before providing the certificate request to a CA (interaction 0 in Fig. 1). The approach used by RA to verify the ownership of a domain d exploits an extended version of the *challenge-response protocol*, by allowing web service provider to sign the secret in order to prove control over a DID. In the proposed approach, a secret k_S is shared by the RA with the web service provider S who claims to be the owner of d. The web service provider signs the secret k_S with its DID's private key to prove the control over the DID and modifies the DNS-TXT record of the domain d to include the signed secret. A DNS-TXT record is used by a domain owner to store text information associated with a domain and this record is typically obtained by querying the DNS server for the domain. As a result, the RA queries the DNS server of the domain d and checks if there is the secret value k_S signed by the DID of the web service provider S, being sure that requester can modify DNS-TXT records of this domain. Once RA has successfully verified the ownership of a domain, it sends the result of the verification to the CA to inform it that the web service provider is authorized to request a certificate (interaction 1 in Fig. 1), and returns to the web service provider a proof of domain ownership $P = (d, DID)_{Pr_{RA}}$ consisting of the domain name d and the DID of the web service provider signed by RA with its private key Pr_{RA}. As a result, the web service provider creates a CSR asking the CA to release a certificate. When CA releases the certificate $Cert_S$ to the web service provider S, the web server can publish a certificate fingerprint on the blockchain. This is achieved through the application of a cryptographic hash function $H()$ to the certificate $Cert_S$.

For this purpose, the VeriCert system allows the web service provider to interface with smart contract in order to register a new DID and resolve a DID to generate the DID document, necessary for the authentication of the DID subject and verification methods for VPs. The smart contract provides a method to update certificate fingerprint under a specific DID. Once recorded on the blockchain, any subsequent verification of the certificate can be performed by comparing the stored fingerprint against the hash computed of the provided certificate (see Sect. 4.5).

4.4 Secret Hash Lock and Revocation

In addition to vulnerabilities arising from rogue certificate, VeriCert is designed to take into account also possible treats related to the SSI paradigm, for instance the loss or the theft from the web service provider of cryptographic keys used to control a DID. As a countermeasure to this threat, VeriCert applies a mechanism to allow a web service provider to recover from a compromised DID, which is based on *secret hash lock* and *revocation account*. The *secret hash lock* is defined as the hash value $w = H(q)$ obtained by applying a hash function H to a random secret q known to the web service provider, while the *revocation account* is another DID under the control of the web service provider. The web service provider publishes the *secret hash lock* and the *revocation account* on the *Certificate Registry* smart contract, which checks if the provided secret hash lock and the revocation account are already used by someone else, and if the case, it reverts with an error. To effectively revoke a DID, a web service provider is required to execute a function of the *Certificate Registry* smart contract that meets the following criteria: *i)* The DID to be revoked exists and has not already been revoked; *ii)* The caller of the revocation function must be the DID revocation account specified during the registration phase by the web service provider; *ii)* The input value v provided by the caller must unlock the secret hash w specified by the web service provider, i.e., the hash value $H(v)$ computed on the input value v is equals to w. This ensures that only the entity that knows how to unlock the secret hash and has control of the revocation account is authorized to revoke a DID.

4.5 VeriCert Handshake

In particular, in the enhanced version of the handshake, the certificate of the web service provider is embedded into a VP along with the certificates chain and is sent to the client for verification (interaction 6 of Fig. 1). The client resolves the DID of the web service provider and generates the corresponding DID document in order to obtain the cryptographic materials to verify the authenticity and integrity of the VP (interaction 7 of Fig. 1). After confirming the authenticity of the VP, the client performs a common certificate verification process by using native system library (such as OpenSSL), involving the check of validity time, of the CA signature, of the potential revocation or expiration of the certificate and of the trust chain of CAs reaching a root CA inside the trust store of the browser. Finally, the client can evaluate certificate transparency by retrieving the certificate's fingerprint from the blockchain (interaction 7 of Fig. 1) as well and comparing it with the hash calculated on the certificate in the provided VP. If both fingerprints are the same, the VeriCert system ensures that the received certificate belongs to the real owner of the contacted domain.

5   Security Analysis

In this section, we analyze the security solution provided by the VeriCert system against different types of attack. We assume that an attacker is not able to break web service provider security and take control over its own services and data. The public keys of the RA and the CA are publicly known, allowing everyone to verify their signatures. However, the CA and the DID of the web service provider can be compromised. We identify three attack scenarios based on the state of the CA and DID (compromised or uncompromised), and demonstrate how the VeriCert solution can prevent or mitigate them.

5.1   Compromised CA

Let us assume that the CA is compromised and the DID is, instead, under the control of the real web service provider only (i.e., uncompromised). After that, the web service has been correctly set up with the VeriCert solution, the attacker can obtain a forged certificate from such a CA with the same common name of the targeted web service but with a public key under the control of the attacker. Since the CA is compromised, all clients, checking the signature on the rogue certificate, accept it as a valid one.

DoS Attack. Taking into account the previous assumptions, an attacker cannot modify blockchain data through the *Certificate Registry* on behalf of the DID owner, because it has no control on the web service provider DID. Indeed, the access control mechanism of the *Certificate Registry* allows only DID owner to modify data related to this DID. Consequently, although the attacker obtained a rogue certificate, the web service provider still holds the authentic certificate, presents it to the client, and the data on the blockchain confirms that such certificate is a good one and it is paired with the right DID. Hence, the DoS attack cannot be conducted.

Impersonation Attack. Exploiting the rogue certificate, the attacker could make a client believe that an ad-hoc built malicious web server is the targeted web server, thus breaking the PKI goal.

As a countermeasure to this attack, the VeriCert system requires the client to verify that the certificate received from the web service provider and embedded in the VP has been signed by using the DID of the authentic web service provider, that the hash of the provided certificate is equal to the certificate fingerprint specified by the DID on the blockchain, and that the proof of domain ownership signed by the RA. Since the DID of the web service provider has not been compromised, the attack fails, because the malicious web service cannot sign the VP sent to the Client with the private key of the DID specified in the proof of domain ownership released by the RA.

5.2 Compromised DID

In this scenario, the CA is honest but the DID is compromised because the attacker knows the private key associated with a DID of a web service provider. Consequently, the attacker can change some values stored in the blockchain through the *Certificate Registry* (such as, the certificate fingerprint or the proof of domain ownership) by sending a transaction on through the DID of the web service provider.

DoS Attack. The attacker can execute a DoS attack by storing random values as the RA signature or the certificate's fingerprint on the blockchain for the compromised DID, through *Certificate Registry*, in order to invalidate the verification mechanisms of VeriCert. In this way, the client is not able anymore to match the certificate fingerprint stored in the blockchain with the fingerprint computed on the certificate embedded in the VP sent by the web service provider, or to successfully verify the RA signature.

As a countermeasure, the VeriCert system allows the web service provider to revoke the compromised DID by sending a revocation transaction from a revocation account (see Sect. 4.4) in order to stop the potential misuse of the DID. The revocation operation makes the revoked DID unusable and the web service provider is required to join VeriCert by using a new DID.

Impersonation Attack. In this scenario, an attacker can manipulate data stored on the blockchain though the *Certificate Registry*, but it does not hold a rogue certificate targeting the web service provider, because CA is not compromised. To impersonate a web service provider, the attacker must have a rogue certificate with the same common name as the web service provider.

5.3 Compromised CA and DID

This last scenario is the most critical because it assumes that the attacker has compromised all the relevant components of VeriCert, i.e., both the DID of the target web service provider and the CA. For these reasons, the attacker can obtain a rogue certificate about the target web service provider from the compromised CA embedding a malicious public key. Since the attacker also knows the private key associated with a DID, it can update the certificate fingerprint in the *Certificate Registry* in order to make clients believe that the rogue certificate has been accepted by the web service provider. As a countermeasure to this attack, the VeriCert system allows the web service provider to revoke a (compromised) DID using the revocation account. In particular, if the *Certificate Registry* entry related to a DID is changed, the web service provider owner, as

DID owner, receives the event emitted by the smart contract. Consequently, if this event refers to an unwanted update of the entry related to its DID, the web service provider sends a revocation transaction signed by the revocation account (as explained in Sect. 4.4) in order to stop the potential misuse of the DID.

6 Performance Evaluation

To evaluate the proposed solution, the VeriCert system was implemented using the Ethereum blockchain and developed in JavaScript[1]. The *Certificate Registry* was created with Solidity smart contract language and deployed on both the local Ganache blockchain and the Sepolia testnet for functional and performance testing. The web service provider's DID method is based on the Ether DID method, while VC and VP are formatted as JSON Web Token (JWT). The OpenSSL library verifies the CA's signature on certificates, and the cryptographic hash function used for the secret hash lock in the *Certificate Registry* is SHA-256.

6.1 Testing Methodology

Testing was done using a real dataset of TLS certificates from 100 most popular domains obtained from ChatGPT [16]. For each certificate, we developed a web application that simulate server's behavior, accepting HTTPS communication from client. In particular, the server web application initializes a wallet and generates a DID for the server, publishing it to the *Certificate Registry* along with the secret hash lock, the revocation account, the RA signature, and the certificate fingerprint. Finally, the web server application, waits client connection and manages authentication and key exchange according to VeriCert.

The client connects to the server and initiates the VeriCert handshake (Sect. 4.5) by requesting the VP to the server. An interaction between a server and a client is initiated for each item of the dataset, and relevant measures about the time and the size consumed by the web service provider/client to perform the tasks required by VeriCert has been collected. A total of ten evaluations were conducted on each operation, and the resulting average value is considered to provide a reliable estimate of the operation's performance.

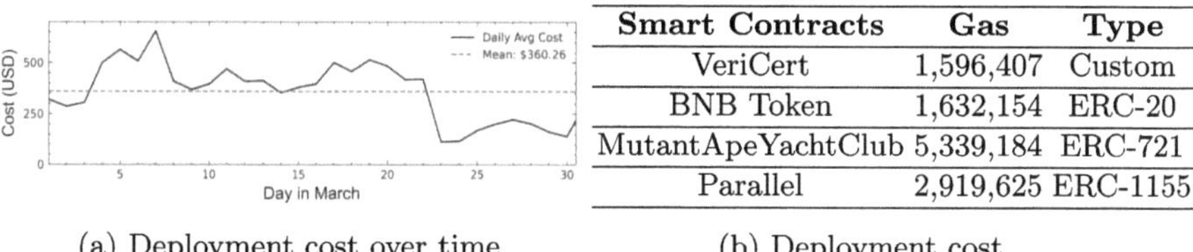

(a) Deployment cost over time

Smart Contracts	Gas	Type
VeriCert	1,596,407	Custom
BNB Token	1,632,154	ERC-20
MutantApeYachtClub	5,339,184	ERC-721
Parallel	2,919,625	ERC-1155

(b) Deployment cost

Fig. 2. Deployment phase.

---

[1] https://github.com/AndreaGiuliani-Git/VeriCert-Protocol.git.

6.2 Deployment

Table 2b shows the gas consumed for the deployment of the *Certificate Registry* and the gas consumed by the deployment of other popular smart contract registries utilized in token management. The used gas for deployment of the VeriCert solution is the same across all blockchains compatible with the Ethereum Virtual Machine (EVM) and it is comparable with gas units consumed for an ERC20 token contract deployment, e.g. for Binance Coin contract, while it is lower than the gas used for management of Not Fungible Token (NFT), such as ERC-721 and ERC-1155. Since the total price paid for deploying the *Certificate Registry* on the blockchain depends on the price per unit of gas (*gas unit price*) which changes every day, Fig. 2a shows the average daily deployment cost of VeriCert in March 2024 on Ethereum mainnet.

6.3 Server's Performance

The creation of a VP embedding the SSL/TLS certificate information is one of the main operations required to ensure CT. The average time taken by the web service provider for VP generation is shown in Fig. 3a. The plot illustrates the relationship between the size of a VP (x-axis) and the average time required for its creation (y-axis). The average generation time is 3.61 ms and a positive correlation can be observed, indicating that the average VP creation time increases as the size of the SSL/TLS certificate chain.

Another important evaluation is the assessment of the functionalities provided for the management of the SSL/TLS certificates, necessary to guarantee Certificate Transparency, and for the management of a DID. Since these operations are provided by the *Certificate Registry*, we show in Fig. 3b the gas used to execute each contract's method. The most expensive ones are those used by server to write into the *Certificate Registry*, i.e., the `newEntry()`, the `revokeDID()` and the `updEntry()` for both RA's signature and certificate's fingerprint. The *Certificate Registry* also provides the ability for clients to read the certificate information of a server (`infoCT()`) and to resolve a DID (`resolveDID()`).

The time between the transaction initiation and the contract's response received by a client is measured both on Ganache and Sepolia, and they are shown in Fig. 3d and 3c. The view functions, which are frequently used by all actors (i.e., the `infoCT` and the `resolveDID`), take 341 ms in Sepolia and about 12 ms in Ganache. Other functionalities are more time-consuming, but they are executed occasionally in VeriCert solution. For instance, the least frequently used is the DID revocation, which also coincides with the most time-consuming one.

6.4 Client's Performance

The steps performed by clients to initiate a connection to a web service provider can be summarized as follows:

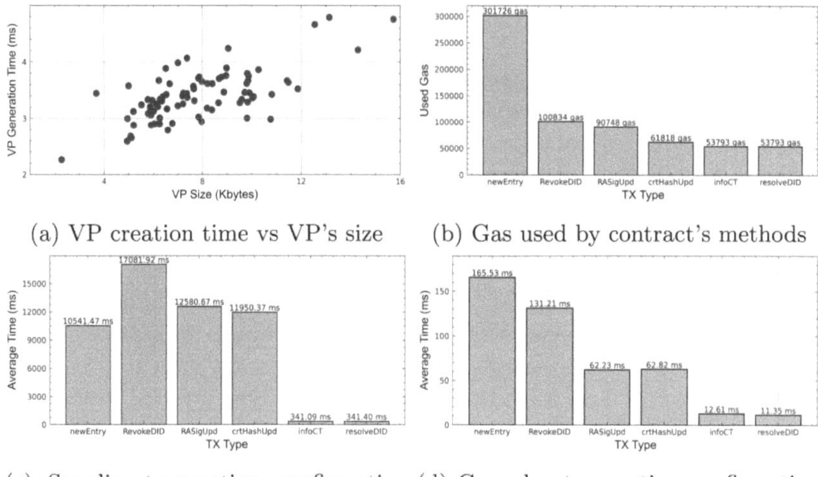

(a) VP creation time vs VP's size   (b) Gas used by contract's methods

(c) Sepolia: transaction confirmation (d) Ganache: transaction confirmation
time   time

Fig. 3. Performance results of the Server.

- *JWT Check*: time needed for VP verification, including the DID resolution.
- *Crt Transparency Check*: time needed by a client to check the certificate transparency by comparing certificate's fingerprint.
- *RA Signature Check*: time needed by a client to verify RA signature.
- *OpenSSL Check*: time needed by a client to check the validity of the certificates' chain (signatures and expiration dates).

Figure 4 shows the time required to conclude each step of the VeriCert's verification in Ganache and Sepolia, for each of the 100 domains in the database arranged in ascending order with respect to the certificate chain size, i.e., the number of certificates in the VP presented by the web service provider. Indeed, each certificate, from the web service provider to the last intermediate CA, contributes to the overall size of the VP.

In the local testing scenario depicted in Fig. 4b, the OpenSSL verification of certificates takes the longest time. This is attributed to the negligible delay in receiving local blockchain responses. Indeed, the latency introduced by the Ganache blockchain for *JWT Check* and *Crt Transparency Check* remains less than the time taken for OpenSSL verification.

In contrast to this, in Fig. 4a, the predominant components involve blockchain interactions: *JWT Check* and *Crt Transparency Check*, in this case, take more time to read the data from the Sepolia blockchain because the communication occurs with a remote node. In both testing environment, the *RA Signature Check* time is fixed because it depends only on a signature's verification without any executed blockchain transaction. As a result, the total average time to conclude all VeriCert's verifications is about 715 ms in Sepolia and 54 ms in Ganache while in both cases the average VP's size is 7.9 Kilobytes.

7   Related Work

This section explores related works that investigate similar approaches, methodologies, and findings within rogue certificates mitigation.

Authors of [18] propose a certificate transparency approach based on blockchain. Certificates and revocation information are published by the web server as a transaction in the certificate blockchain. Each web server has a publishing key pair to sign transactions that publish the certificate, to initiate or reset the publishing key. Once the publishing key is compromised, the web server cooperates with a set of trusted friends in order to update the publishing key. The main difference between VeriCert and the solution proposed in [18] lies in the use of a new methodology for managing personal information based on the SSI paradigm, which provides unique features that are not present in the existing solution. As for example, VeriCert allows individuals to selectively share information and to create verifiable credentials that are fraud-proof. In addition, unlike VeriCert, this solution is designed to be deployed on a specific blockchain architecture, having its own mining algorithm, and incentives mechanism.

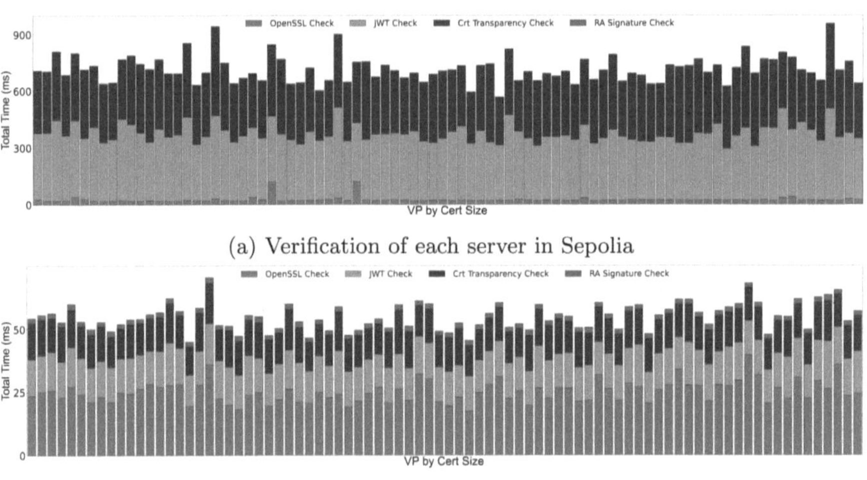

(a) Verification of each server in Sepolia

(b) Verification of each server in Ganache

Fig. 4. Performance results of the Client.

A Decentralizeed Public-Key Infrastructure (DPKI) based on DID and VC has been proposed by [2] for the X-Road ecosystem, a centrally-managed distributed data exchange layer [3]. This infrastructure is designed to replace X.509 certificates where VCs are issued by trusted authorities. However, the issuers of VC can issue rogue VC certificates and the member receiving such rogue VC certificates does not have the capacity to detect and isolate them.

In [7], authors studies the problem of rogue certificate on Facebook by deploying client-side applet in order to observe SSL connections on a large set of real-world clients. The study indicates that 0.2% over 3 million real-world Secure Socket Layer (SSL) connections were tampered with rogue certificates analyzing certificate content. In this report, the mitigation of rogue certificates is not provided, giving a detecting tool solution and acquiring useful information about rogue certificates.

Authors of [14] design a Peer-to-Peer network to detect local MiTM attacks against SSL/TLS. They check the certificate authenticity by retrieving them from different storage points on the network. Online Social Network is exploited to create Notary Groups that substitute the CA role in the PKI. The certificate will be signed not only by a single entity but the signature will be computed collaboratively.

Schlatt et al. [17] exploits SSI and blockchain to solve the know your customer (KYC) problem: a process used by financial institutions to verify the identity of a potential customer before establishing a business relationship.

A trust management system is proposed by K. Junaid et al. [9]. In particular, they proposed a ranking approach that assigns a trust score to each CA based on different features, e.g., the number of valid/invalid certificates issued by the CA.

Finally, the Internet Engineering Task Force (IETF) proposed the RFC-9162 [1] an experimental protocol that allows anyone to audit CA activity by publicly logging the issued certificates. However, the proposed approach does not provide a mechanism for certificate owners to assert control over their certificates. Instead, it relies on external monitors to observe public logs and detect rouge certificate. In contrast, VerCert allows a service provider to assert control of both a certificate and the corresponding domain name by using DID and VC.

8   Conclusion

In this paper, we address the critical issue of rogue certificate detection and prevention in the digital domain by proposing a novel approach based on a SSI paradigm compatible with traditional PKI. The proposed solution, VeriCert, exploits SSI paradigm to ensure web server authentication and certificate fingerprint publishing, enforcing the traditional role of CA with a blockchain-based system. This enhances security by eliminating single points of failure. VeriCert was tested on the Ethereum testnet, showing higher security levels compared to traditional SSL/TLS handshakes, despite increasing time overhead.

Acknowledgment. This work was partially supported by project SERICS (PE00000014) under the MUR National Recovery and Resilience Plan funded by the European Union - NextGenerationEU.

References

1. Laurie, B., Messeri, E., Stradling, R.: RFC 9162: Certificate Transparency Version 2.0. RFC 9162, Internet Engineering Task Force (IETF) (2021). https://www.rfc-editor.org/rfc/rfc9162
2. Bakhtina, M., Leung, K.L., Matulevičius, R., Awad, A., Švenda, P.: A decentralised public key infrastructure for x-road. In: Proceedings of the 18th International Conference on Availability, Reliability and Security. ARES '23, Association for Computing Machinery, New York, NY, USA (2023). https://doi.org/10.1145/3600160.3605092
3. Bakhtina, M., Matulevičius, R., Awad, A., Kivimäki, P.: On the shift to decentralised identity management in distributed data exchange systems. In: Proceedings of the 38th ACM/SIGAPP Symposium on Applied Computing, pp. 864–873. SAC '23, Association for Computing Machinery, New York, NY, USA (2023). https://doi.org/10.1145/3555776.3577678
4. Comodo CA: Ltd.: Comodo report of incident-comodo detected and thwarted an intrusion on 26-mar-2011. Tech. rep., Technical report (2011)
5. Cooper, D., Santesson, S., Farrell, S., Boeyen, S., Housley, R., Polk, W.: Internet X.509 Public Key Infrastructure Certificate and Certificate Revocation List (CRL) Profile. Tech. rep. (2008). https://www.rfc-editor.org/rfc/rfc5280.txt
6. Cory F. Cohen: Vulnerability Note VU#869360 - unauthentic "microsoft corporation" certificates issued by verisign to an unidentifed person (2001). https://www.kb.cert.org/vuls/id/869360
7. Huang, L.S., Rice, A., Ellingsen, E., Jackson, C.: Analyzing forged ssl certificates in the wild. In: IEEE Symposium on Security and Privacy, pp. 83–97. IEEE (2014)
8. International Telecommunication Union - Telecommunication Standardization Sector (ITU-T): The Directory: Public-key and attribute certificate frameworks. Tech. rep. (2019). https://www.itu.int/rec/T-REC-X.509/en
9. Junaid, K., Janjua, M.U., Qadir, J.: A compliance-based ranking of certificate authorities using probabilistic approaches. Int. J. Inform. Secur. 1–30 (2024)
10. Li, B., Chu, D., Lin, J., Cai, Q., Wang, C., Meng, L.: The weakest link of certificate transparency: Exploring the tls/https configurations of third-party monitors. In: 2019 18th IEEE International Conference on Trust, Security and Privacy in Computing and Communications/13th IEEE International Conference on Big Data Science And Engineering (TrustCom/BigDataSE), pp. 216–223 (2019)
11. Li, B., et al.: Certificate transparency in the wild: exploring the reliability of monitors. In: Proceedings of the 2019 ACM Conference on Computer and Communications Security, pp. 2505–2520 (2019)
12. Maurer, U.: Modelling a public-key infrastructure. In: Bertino, E., Kurth, H., Martella, G., Montolivo, E. (eds.) ESORICS 1996. LNCS, vol. 1146, pp. 325–350. Springer, Heidelberg (1996). https://doi.org/10.1007/3-540-61770-1_45
13. Van der Meulen, N.: Diginotar: dissecting the first Dutch digital disaster. J. Strategic Secur. **6**(2), 46–58 (2013)
14. Micheloni, A., Fuchs, K.P., Herrmann, D., Federrath, H.: Laribus: privacy-preserving detection of fake ssl certificates with a social p2p notary network. In: 2013 IEEE International Conference on Availability, Reliability and Security, pp. 1–10 (2013)
15. Microsoft Security Response Center (MSRC): MSRC Blog: Flame Malware Collision Attack Explained (2012). https://msrc.microsoft.com/blog/2012/06/flame-malware-collision-attack-explained/

16. OpenAI: Openai chat. https://chat.openai.com/
17. Schlatt, V., Sedlmeir, J., Feulner, S., Urbach, N.: Designing a framework for digital kyc processes built on blockchain-based self-sovereign identity. Information & Management **59**(7), 103553 (2022). https://doi.org/10.1016/j.im.2021.103553, blockchain Innovations: Business Opportunities and Management Challenges
18. Wang, Z., Lin, J., Cai, Q., Wang, Q., Zha, D., Jing, J.: Blockchain-based certificate transparency and revocation transparency. IEEE (2021)

IDook: Empowering Labor Unions
with Decentralized Digital Identities

Thabata Ganga, Breno C. Nakamura, and Arlindo F. da Conceição⁽⊠⁾

Institute of Science and Technology, Federal University of São Paulo,
São Paulo, Brazil
`{thabata.ganga,breno.nakamura,arlindo.conceicao}@unifesp.br`

Abstract. This article presents *IDook*, an innovative blockchain-based
solution designed to empower non-profit organizations and labor unions
through secure and verifiable self-sovereign identity (SSI). The project's
primary objective is to develop a technological framework that enables
these entities to create and manage decentralized digital identities on
the blockchain, thereby enhancing the trust and transparency of organizations. The results validated the technical viability of the blockchain
solution, employing open-source technologies including the VON network (based on Hyperledger Indy), with agent implementation using
Hyperledger Aries Cloud Agent Python (ACA-Py). Key results include
credential issuance by unions, blockchain network configuration, Aries
agent evaluation, and wallet integration. Notably, the blockchain works
as a decentralized repository, supporting the issuance and verification of
credentials. The IDook prototype, hosted on AWS, is compatible with
multiple digital identity wallets, reinforcing the principles of SSI.

Keywords: Blockchain · Self-sovereign Identity · Labor Union ·
Non-profit Organization · Decentralized Identities · Verifiable
Credentials

1 Introduction

Unions are institutions formed by workers from companies in the same sector,
with the aim of supporting their members in the field of labor law. These organizations negotiate with employers on behalf of employees, dealing with issues
such as working conditions, wages, and benefits [14,20].

Labor unions play roles in society's welfare, influencing policies and promoting collective action to tackle various challenges in their respective domains [5].
However, these institutions face challenges in retaining members due to persistent bureaucratic relations, lack of transparency, communication problems,
and representativeness, contributing to mistrust [2]. According to data from the
Brazilian Institute of Geography and Statistics, Brazilian unions lost more than

This research was partially funded by FAPESP under the project titled *"Digital Identities: Customization of Open-Source Wallets"*, grant number 2023/00783-7.

3.8 million members in nine years, experiencing a steep decline after the Labor Reform in 2017, which eliminated the mandatory annual union contribution [8]. Even with over 16,000 unions in the country, many have fragile structures, communication, mobilization, and security difficulties, affecting their ability to act [9].

The innovative proposition of integrating blockchain and self-sovereign identity (SSI) in these organizations aims to enhance trust, transparency, mobilization, and representativeness in the digital context [6,13]. Self-sovereign identity is a decentralized identity model that enables individuals and organizations to fully own, control, and selectively share their digital identities without relying on centralized authorities [21]. This approach is supported by standards such as Decentralized Identifiers (DIDs) [23] and Verifiable Credentials (VCs) [24], which provide secure, privacy-preserving, and interoperable digital identity solutions. Blockchain technology, recognized for its robust security features, operates as a decentralized and tamper-resistant ledger that securely records transactions across a network of computers [15]. The decentralized identifiers (DIDs) and credential registries are anchored on the blockchain as immutable and verifiable records, while personal data remains securely controlled off-chain by the identity holders [11]. While no system is entirely invulnerable, the distributed nature of blockchain significantly enhances resistance to unauthorized access or manipulation [16].

As an identity model, SSI complements blockchain by granting individuals and organizations complete control over their personal and professional data. Unlike traditional centralized systems, where third parties store and manage data, SSI enables entities to own, control, and selectively share their information. This approach allows sharing only necessary information for each interaction [1].

Despite the potential benefits of this solution, there is a knowledge gap in empowering unions with self-sovereign identities, using blockchain as a tool for technological innovation. *What is the demand within these organizations for technologies that enhance trust and transparency? What are the usability requirements? What is the best system architecture for developing such an application?* We tried to contribute to the advancement of SSI technologies in the context of labor unions, and similar Non-Governmental Organizations (NGOs).

The remainder of this article is structured as follows: we first review related work and provide the necessary technological background. We then describe the methodology employed and present the results. Finally, we conclude with a discussion of key findings and future work.

2 Related Work

To the best of our knowledge, no prior studies have explored the use of SSI and blockchain technology within the context of labor unions. However, existing literature sheds light on noteworthy social initiatives applying blockchain and digital identity, increasing transparency and accountability [12]. For instance, the Fairfood project provides decentralized digital identities for small coconut producers in the Philippines. These identities enable producers to register and verify information about their production, quality, origin, and traceability of products, facilitating access to markets and services and ensuring fair and transparent remuneration for sold products.

Another notable example of transparency and accountability in fund management is the project developed by the NGO BitGive in partnership with the Bitcoin blockchain network [18]. This project, called GiveTrack, aims to enhance transparency and accountability in managing funds donated to NGOs. The GiveTrack platform allows donors to track the flow and impact of their funds in real time, from the source to the destination. The platform also enables NGOs to demonstrate the efficient and ethical use of resources, thereby enhancing the trust and reputation of the organizations.

Additionally, projects that highlight the use of blockchain and digital identity to improve the motivation and management of volunteers in NGOs. One of the initiatives introduces a platform facilitating the issuance of verifiable credentials for volunteers, recognizing their skills, experiences, and contributions [10]. This project highlights the diverse applications of blockchain in the nonprofit sector, employing Hyperledger Fabric for tokenizing rewards and Hyperledger Indy for managing decentralized digital identities.

3   Technological Background

Various platforms, such as Ethereum, Corda, and Hyperledger, play a significant role in developing blockchain solutions, with Hyperledger being one of the most popular choices [3]. However, Hyperledger stands out for developing digital identity, mainly due to the Hyperledger Identity Stack. This stack aims to create and manage decentralized digital identities based on blockchain. Comprising four main open-source projects (Hyperledger Indy, Hyperledger Ursa, Hyperledger Aries, and Hyperledger Anoncreds), the Hyperledger ID Stack aims to facilitate the implementation of SSI. This approach empowers individuals and organizations to control their data, promoting secure and verifiable interactions in the digital environment.

Hyperledger is part of the Linux Foundation Decentralized Trust, an open-source initiative focused on advancing blockchain technologies to develop and promote solutions for various sectors and applications [22]. Despite their robustness, these technologies face challenges related to interoperability, scalability, and regulatory compliance, which require careful consideration in the development of practical solutions.

4   Methodology

The study employs Design Science Research (DSR) methodology. DSR is a systematic and iterative approach applied in information systems, computer science, and engineering to create and validate innovative artifacts, such as software systems, models, or processes, addressing real-world problems [4].

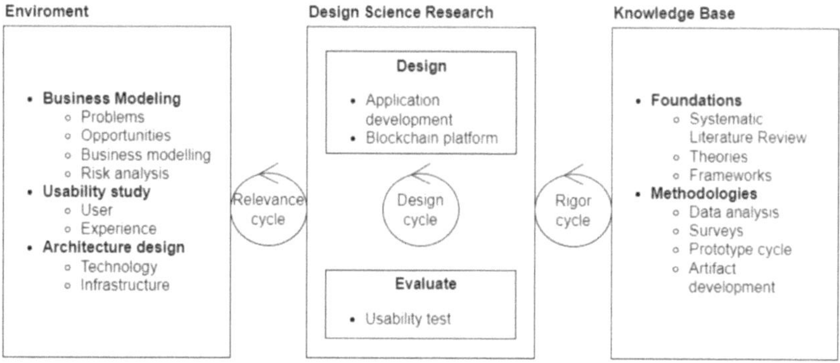

Fig. 1. Design Science Research (DSR) comprises three cyclic phases: Environment, Design, and Knowledge. Source: Author's Figure.

The methodology follows three cyclical phases: Environment, Design, and Knowledge. In the Environment phase, researchers identify and understand the problem context for nonprofits, unions, and political parties, exploring real-world relevance. The Design phase involves developing innovative solutions, emphasizing practical design considerations. Evaluation and validation of artifacts occur in the Knowledge phase. These phases iterate, ensuring real-world alignment and impactful results (Fig. 1).

4.1   User Experience (UX) Design

The UX Design process involved the creation of a prototype using Figma, which was informed by prior business modeling and a usability study conducted during the incubation phase at the São José dos Campos Technological Innovation Park (PIT). The prototype design focused on creating positive, intuitive, and satisfying user experiences across various platforms. It emphasized understanding user needs, conducting research, prototyping, and testing to enhance usability and accessibility. The final prototype illustrated the process using Sindpd as a practical case.

4.2   Architecture Design

The system's architecture was developed based on the prior business modeling and usability study. It is composed of four main components: the blockchain layer, digital wallet, cloud storage, and an Aries agent. The tools used were Node.js, MongoDB, React.js, and the Hyperledger ID stack. The choice of Node.js was due to its efficiency in handling asynchronous tasks and its vast ecosystem. MongoDB, a NoSQL database, was selected for flexibility and scalability, while React.js facilitated front-end development. The utilization of Hyperledger ID Stack, designed for digital identity applications, implemented the

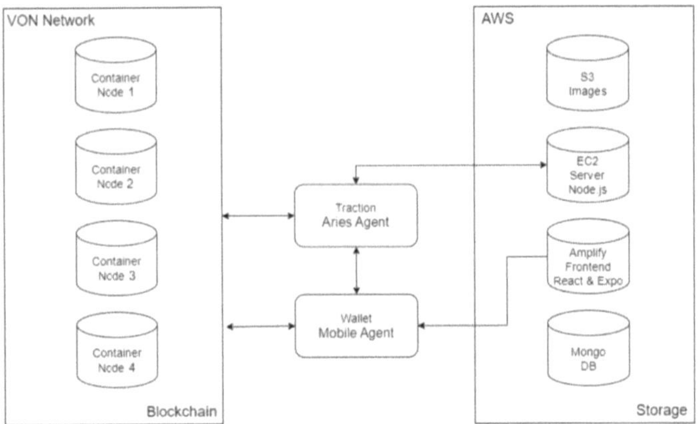

Fig. 2. The system's architecture comprises four main components: Blockchain, Digital Wallet, AWS Storage, and Aries Agent. Source: Author's Figure.

blockchain component, addressing specific use case limitations and ensuring secure SSI management (Fig. 2).

The blockchain component leverages the VON Network [17] based on Hyperledger Indy, which acts as the Verifiable Data Registry (VDR) responsible for anchoring DIDs and credential schemas. This ensures data immutability, tamper-resistance, and verifiability without exposing personal data on-chain.

The digital wallet layer supports credential issuance, storage, and presentation. The system is compatible with wallets like Lissi and BC Wallet, which adhere to DIDComm protocols, offering a user-centric experience for SSI interactions. These wallets manage private keys, DIDs, and verifiable credentials, enabling users to control and selectively share their identity attributes.

For backend and cloud infrastructure, the application utilizes AWS services: S3 for storing non-sensitive assets (e.g., images), EC2 instances for running the Node.js server and Aries Cloud Agent Python (ACA-Py), and AWS Amplify for front-end deployment based on React.js. MongoDB is employed as an off-chain database to handle application metadata that does not compromise user privacy.

The agent component, implemented with ACA-Py and the Traction framework, facilitates secure, encrypted communication between wallets, the blockchain (VDR), and the application. It handles credential issuance, revocation, and verification processes, following DIDComm messaging standards. Security is enhanced through the use of Hyperledger Ursa for cryptographic operations and AnonCreds for privacy-preserving credentials.

This modular architecture ensures compliance with SSI standards while providing scalability, high availability, and resilience suitable for nonprofit organizations and unions seeking privacy-preserving digital identity solutions.

4.3   System Development

The software development methodology adopted for this project follows a systematic and phased approach, ensuring the progressive evolution of the application from conceptualization to implementation. The development process has three distinct stages: Back-end, Front-end, and Integration, each serving a unique purpose and contributing to the comprehensive growth of the system.

  I. **Back-end:** In this phase, the initial focus is on back-end implementation, where the API is crafted based on the business rules. Node.js technology, renowned for its efficiency in handling asynchronous tasks, is chosen as the core technology, while the Express framework provides a robust foundation for application building and scalability. This phase involves translating abstract business rules into a functional API, establishing the groundwork for subsequent stages.

 II. **Front-end:** In this phase, the front-end development of the application occurs in two stages. The initial stage includes prototyping the system using the Figma interface design tool. The six entities that have been interviewed trial the prototype to evaluate its usability and collect possible improvements to the interface. The development of the prototype utilized the React.js framework after users had validated the design.

III. **Integration:** In the final stage, the back-end integrates with the front-end via the API and the Postman software. This meticulous integration process ensures the cohesive operation of the entire application, bringing together the complexities of back-end logic and user-visible elements into a functional whole.

4.4   Issue of Decentralized Verifiable Credentials

In this phase, the issuance and verification of verifiable credentials using a decentralized VDR are implemented. The Hyperledger ID Stack is utilized for this purpose, providing the necessary infrastructure and tools to enable secure and reliable credential management within the IDook system.

  I. **Wallet Selection:** The wallet selection process involved evaluating and choosing the most suitable wallets for the project. Testing was conducted on a Xiaomi POCO X3 with Android 12 and an iPhone 7 with iOS 15, ensuring compatibility and functionality across different mobile platforms. The selected wallets included BC Wallet, Lissi Wallet, Trinsic Wallet, Orbit Edge, and Esatus Wallet.

 II. **Blockchain Network:** The Indy prototyping network is established using a 4-node container within the Docker tool. It is enabled using the Von Network [17], developed by the Province of British Columbia, on a Ubuntu 16.04 LTS computer.

III. **Agent:** developed with the Hyperledger Aries Cloud Agent Python (ACA-Py) framework. ACA-Py serves as a platform for constructing Verifiable Credential (VC) ecosystems, leveraging DIDComm messaging and Hyperledger

Table 1. System specifications for development and production environments

Specification	Development Environment	Production Environment
Operating System	Ubuntu 22.04.4 LTS (Jammy Jellyfish)	Amazon Linux 2
Kernel Version	6.5.0–35-generic	5.10.214-202.855.amzn2.aarch64
Processor	Intel(R) Core(TM) i7-9750H CPU @ 2.60 GHz	AWS Graviton2 Processor ARM 64 Neoverse-N1 2.50 GHz
Memory	39 GiB	1.8 GiB
Disk	223.6 GB SSD (nvme0n1)	8 GB SSD (nvme0n1)

Aries protocols, designed to operate on servers rather than mobile devices. It supports essential Aries protocols for issuing, verifying, and holding VCs, incorporating W3C Standard Verifiable Credential Data Model formats.

IV. **Integration:** the DApp API was integrated into the backend of IDook to enable the issuance of verifiable credentials, integration with various wallets, and the issuance/verification of two digital certificates.

4.5   Performance Evaluation

To evaluate the system's responsiveness and scalability, a performance test was conducted focused on the proof verification process. This process is the most time consuming operation within SSI ecosystems, as identified in previous work [7,19]. Specifically, it requires interaction with the Aries Cloud Agent Python (ACA-Py) and involves complex cryptographic operations, including the decryption and validation of data anchored on the Hyperledger Indy blockchain network. We used two setups to run the tests (Table 1).

5   Results

The results show four stages: user experience (UX) design, system development, issue of decentralized verifiable credentials, and performance evaluation.

5.1   UX Design

I. The application development adhered to UX Design principles, that focuses on creating positive, intuitive, and satisfying user experiences across various platforms. The design phase involved creating an interactive prototype in Figma, refining it to create a more detailed version faithful to the final experience. This design was based on the Business Modeling and usability studies.

5.2   System Development

I. **Application Programming Interface (API):** The initial phase of API development involved creating a non-relational database using MongoDB. This database contains information about the institution, user types, users, alerts, news, and provisions for future integration of an events calendar, partners, and partner types. The API's backend was developed in Node.js using Axios and Express libraries.

II. **Interface:** Following database modeling and API development (Fig. 3). The tools React.js and Figma served to do this. Despite design changes due to CSS and HTML limitations, new features like the agenda, suggestion and complaint center, payment system (with Brazilian system PIX), and user activity ranking were added.

III. **Infrastructure:** AWS Brasil hosted the project's digital infrastructure. Three EC2 virtual machines hosted the back-end: one for the database, one for the application API, and one for the news scraping API. AWS Amplify hosted the two interfaces, while the S3 bucket stored images. The average monthly cost was R$33.29 or approximately US$6.75.

Fig. 3. Realistic prototypes using the Figma tool: a) the client interface b) the user interface.

5.3 Issue of Decentralized Verifiable Credentials

I. **Wallet Selection:** Five wallets were tested for verifiable credentials demonstration, yielding the following results:

    A. **BC Wallet:** Successful demo on Android, but with QR code reading slowness and response delays. Couldn't complete on iOS due to PIN creation issues. Appealing aesthetics, but doesn't allow custom ledger configuration.

    B. **Lissi Wallet:** Demo completed on both Android and iOS, with notification errors. Aesthetically pleasing and allows custom ledger configuration.

    C. **Trinsic Wallet:** Couldn't download on Android (version 12), but worked well on iOS. Good aesthetics, but recently shifted to only work with its own ledger.

    D. **Orbit Edge:** Demo completed smoothly on both Android and iOS, with fast interaction. Aesthetically pleasing but does not support DIDComm link communication.

    E. **Esatus Wallet:** Demo completed without issues on both Android and iOS, with fast interaction. Not aesthetically pleasing and doesn't support DIDComm link, but allows custom ledger configuration.

The Table 2 compares the evaluated digital identity wallet applications. Lissi and BC Wallets were chosen due to their compatibility, interoperability, DIDComm link, and performance, prioritizing project functionality over aesthetics.

II. **Blockchain Network:** The blockchain network was established using the VON-Network tool. VON implements a Docker network made up of four containers, each representing a different node, forming a test environment with an Indy blockchain. VON features a graphical interface for browsing the ledger and an API for direct manipulation.

III. **Aries Agent:** The Aries agent was created using Traction, necessitating a Docker instance comprising 13 containers, including databases, plugins, frontend, API, and wallet. Traction facilitates wallet creation, customized ledger configuration, and transaction endorser data recording. Its API offers documentation via Swagger, featuring functionalities such as invitation creation, credential schema creation, definition, issuance, proof solicitation, and submission. The IDook backend implemented services to interact with Traction's

Table 2. Comparison of digital wallet applications for identity. Source: Author's Table.

Wallet	Android	IOS	Performance	Aesthetics	Didcomm	Interoperability
BC Wallet	Yes	No	Average	Good	Yes	No
Lissi Wallet	Yes	Yes	Good	Good	Yes	Yes
Trinsic Wallet	No	Yes	Average	Good	No	Yes
Orbit Edge	Yes	Yes	Good	Good	No	No
Esatus Wallet	Yes	Yes	Good	Bad	No	Yes

API, employing JWT encryption with Bearer Token protection for endpoints. Functions were developed for invitation sending, credential issuance, proof solicitation and validation, and certificate issuance and verification. Additionally, a wallet and API access key were generated for the union, facilitating automated operations within IDook (Fig. 4).

IV. **Credentials issuing:** Through Traction, the credential schema (Fig. 5) for the affiliate was created and recorded in the ledger. Subsequently, specific credential and revocation definitions were established. These parameters stored in the blockchain were then configured in the IDook backend to enable automatic issuance and verification of credentials. This section of the administrative panel of IDook offers various methods for creating invitations, such as sending invitations via email, submitting a CSV file with email addresses and personal information, or integrating with an external API to access data directly. Users input their ID number (CPF) and birth-date, which are validated by the backend for authorization and accuracy. Upon validation, an email containing a six-digit access code is sent to the member. Users then update their personal information and capture a photograph before receiving a standard credential, which can also be issued to a digital wallet.

V. **Certificates Issuing:** After credential issuance to the wallet, users can request two certificate types via the IDook app: affiliation and collective agreement certificates. Clicking the corresponding button triggers a proof request that verifies the credentials expiration (Fig. 9) and, for the collective agreement, also validates union and company data (Fig. 10). Upon successful verification, a verifiable membership certificate is generated, containing the necessary data for authenticity verification on the ledger. The certificate includes options to share the link or print the document for further verification by third parties.

Through the IDook application, users request a new connection with the institution, receiving a QR code and a DIDComm link (Fig. 6). The QR code functioned well with all tested wallets except Trinity, while the DIDComm link worked only with Lissi and moderately with the BC Wallet.

Once the connection between the user's wallet and the institution's wallet is established, the user requests the issuance of the credential, which is received and stored in the wallet (Fig. 7). Subsequently, the user receives an SSI verified seal in the IDook wallet and a QR code for access to the user's public DID (Fig. 8). Proper functioning of push notifications on the wallet for accepting invitations and credentials is crucial at this stage. The Lissi Wallet encountered issues with push notifications, whereas the BC Wallet performed correctly.

5.4 Performance Evaluation

The methodology for performance evaluation was developed in a previous work [19]. It consisted in sending 100 consecutive requests for credential verification. Each request initiated the verification process through ACA-Py, simulating real-world interactions where users present credentials to verifiers. Figure 11

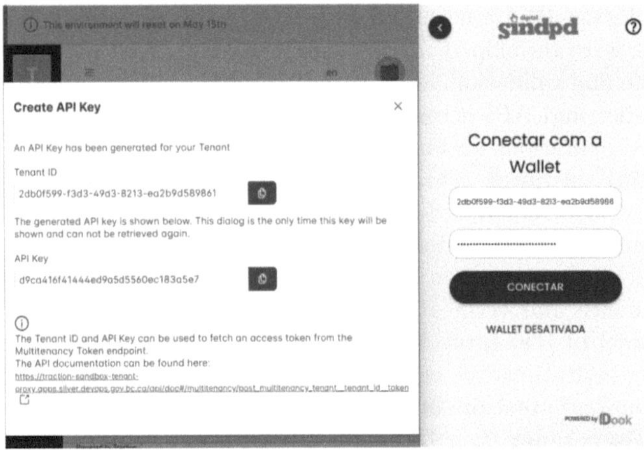

Fig. 4. The institution generates a connection key for the wallet's API using Traction and enters this data in the IDook admin panel. Source: Author's Figure.

```
{
    "refSchemaAttributes": [
        "DateOfExpiry",
        "Institution",
        "RegistrationNumber",
        "State",
        "CPF",
        "FullName",
        "Country",
        "City",
        "SocialName",
        "ZIP",
        "Photo",
        "DateOfBirth",
        "FiliationType",
        "Company"
    ]
}
```

Fig. 5. Filiation credential scheme. Source: Author's Figure.

and Table 3 summarizes the results in a desktop computer and a cloud virtual machine. The test script is available in: https://github.com/thabataganga/performance_api.

The results confirm that proof verification can consume several seconds. This analysis highlights the importance of optimizing proof verification, especially for use cases involving frequent credential checks, such as real-time membership validation in unions, nonprofits, and political organizations.

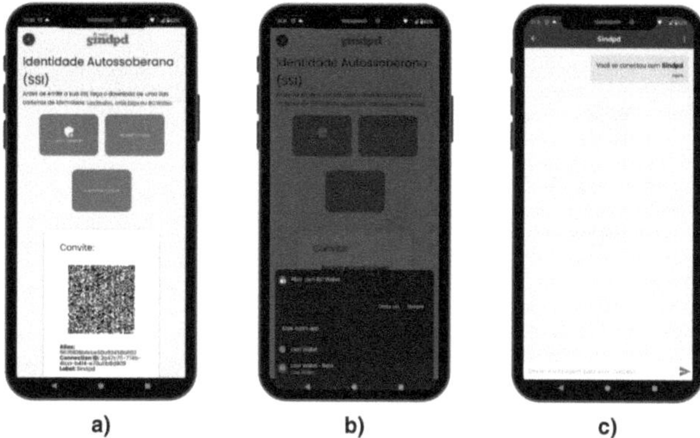

a)   b)   c)

Fig. 6. User requests a new connection and a QRCode and a DIDComm link are generated (a); the user can click directly on the link and choose the desired wallet (b); The connection between the union wallets and the user is established (c). Source: Author's Figure.

a)   b)   c)

Fig. 7. User can request the issuance of a verifiable credential (a). Wallet receives the credential and stores it locally (b). After accepting the credential, it is verified in the application (c). Source: Author's Figure.

Table 3. Send 100 sequential proof verification requisitions in development and production environments. Source: Author's Table.

Proof submission	Metric	Mean	Std. Dev.	Min.	Median	Max.
Development	Time (s)	1.363	0.026	1.322	1.358	1.453
	CPU (%)	1.461	0.998	0.100	1.300	5.200
	Memory (MB)	3177.790	14.399	3149.000	3176.000	3209.000
Production	Time (s)	5.006	0.615	4.368	4.696	7.722
	CPU (%)	1.432	1.252	0.200	1.000	8.800
	Memory (MB)	541.200	2.108	534.000	542.000	545.000

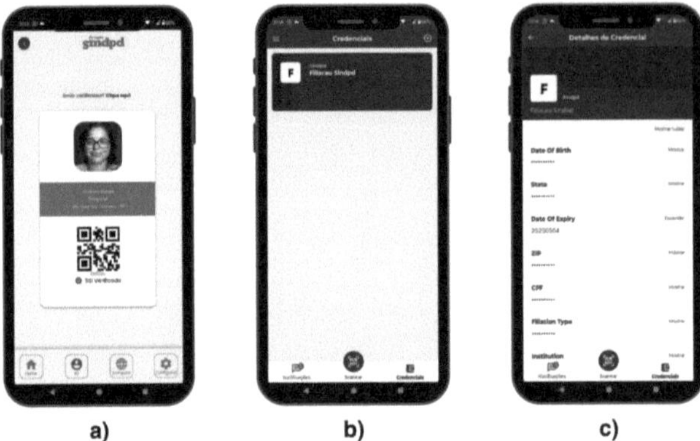

Fig. 8. The user has an access wallet with a public DID QRCode (a); the full credential is stored locally in the wallet (b) and the user can show and share only the desired data (c). Source: Author's Figure.

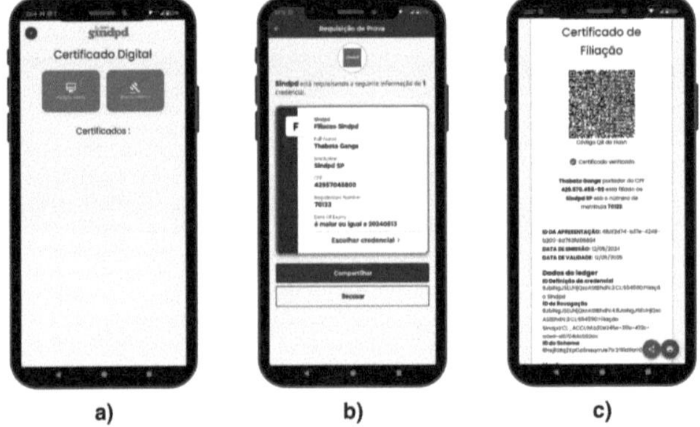

Fig. 9. User requests the issuance of an affiliation certificate (a) and receives a proof request where they share the credential data (b), with successful verification a verifiable membership certificate is issued (c). Source: Author's Figure.

5.5 Demonstration

To conduct the demonstration on mobile devices, it was necessary to set up a production environment on AWS. However, for the Blockchain and Traction components, we utilized the public test ledger and the BCovrin endorser. A video demonstrating the process of issuing the credential can be found in: https://tinyurl.com/idookdemo (in Portuguese).

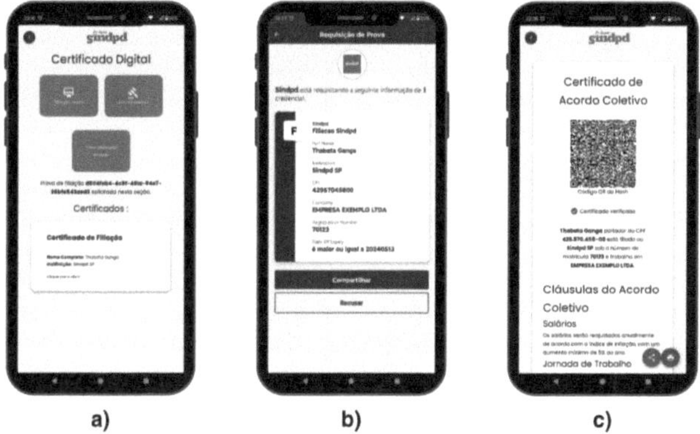

a)   b)   c)

Fig. 10. User requests the issuance of a collective agreement certificate (a) and receives a proof request where they share the credential data, where the expiration date, the union, and the company are automatically verified (b), with successful verification a verifiable membership certificate is issued (c). Source: Author's Figure.

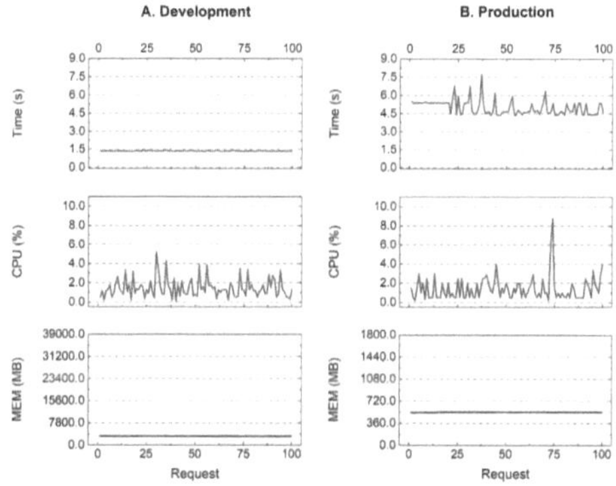

Fig. 11. Verification step performance.

6 Conclusion

The IDook prototype demonstrates strong potential to transform unions and the nonprofit sector by addressing critical challenges in digital identity management through SSI and blockchain technology. Feedback obtained from partner organizations confirms its usability and practical effectiveness in the real world.

This work identified key challenges in implementing blockchain-based decentralized identities within nonprofit organizations. The practical insights gained—spanning system architecture, usability, performance, and interoperability—demonstrate how SSI and blockchain technology can be integrated in labor union Apps. These findings have broader applicability and can be extended to a range of blockchain use cases in NGOs, including financial inclusion for small-scale producers [12], volunteer motivation and management [10], and promoting transparency and accountability in fund allocation [18].

Future research should investigate additional socially impactful applications and prioritize simplifying the technological framework to promote the widespread adoption of SSI solutions across diverse contexts.

References

1. Abid, A., Cheikhrouhou, S., Kallel, S., Jmaiel, M.: A blockchain-based self-sovereign identity approach for inter-organizational business processes. In: 2022 17th Conference on Computer Science and Intelligence Systems (FedCSIS), pp. 685–694. IEEE (2022)
2. Carneiro, B., Costa, H.A.: Digital unionism as a renewal strategy? social media use by trade union confederations. J. Ind. Relat. **64**(1), 26–51 (2022)
3. Decentralized identity: blockchain and self sovereign identity (2024). https://decentralized-id.com/blockchain/
4. Dresch, A., Lacerda, D.P., Antunes, J.A.V.J.: Design science research (1 2015)
5. Etchemendy, S.: The politics of popular coalitions: unions and territorial social movements in post-neoliberal latin america (2000–15). J. Lat. Am. Stud. **52**(1), 157–188 (2020)
6. Francis, E., et al.: Transparency, trust, and security needs for the design of digital news authentication tools. Proc. ACM Human-Comput. Int. **7**(CSCW1), 1–44 (2023)
7. Ganga, T.A.F.: Empowering nonprofit organizations with self-sovereign identities. Dissertação (mestrado profissional), Universidade Federal de Sao Paulo, Department of Science and Technology, Professional Master's Program in Technological Innovation, São José dos Campos, SP (2024)
8. IBGE: pesquisa nacional por amostra de domicílios contínua: características adicionais do mercado de trabalho 2019. IBGE - Instituto Brasileiro de Geografia e Estatística, Rio de Janeiro, Brasil (2019). https://biblioteca.ibge.gov.br/visualizacao/livros/liv101694_informativo.pdf
9. IPEA: sindicatos no brasil: O que esperar no futuro próximo. Ministério do Planejamento, Brasília (2016)
10. Korkmaz, U., Altunlu, H.I., Ozkan, A., Karaarslan, E.: Sustainable member motivation system proposal for ngos: Ngo-tr, pp. 1–5. IEEE (2019). https://doi.org/10.1109/UBMYK48245.2019.8965505, https://ieeexplore.ieee.org/document/8965505/
11. Kumar, S.R., Goyal, M.: Administration of digital identities using blockchain. In: 2022 5th International Conference on Contemporary Computing and Informatics (IC3I), pp. 2179–2183. IEEE (2022)
12. Lee, N.M., Varshney, L.R., Michelson, H.C., Goldsmith, P., Davis, A.: Digital trust substitution technologies to support smallholder livelihoods in sub-saharan africa. Global Food Secur. **32**, 100604 (2022). https://doi.org/10.1016/j.gfs.2021.100604, https://linkinghub.elsevier.com/retrieve/pii/S2211912421001127
13. Lim, S.Y., Musa, O.B., Al-Rimy, B.A.S., Almasri, A.: Trust models for blockchain-based self-sovereign identity management: a survey and research directions. Advances in Blockchain Technology for Cyber Physical Systems, pp. 277–302 (2022)

14. Mannrich, N.: The importance of trade unions and their role in social protection. Philosophical and Sociological Reflections on Labour Law in Times of Crisis, p. 177 (2022)
15. Nakamoto, S.: Bitcoin: a peer-to-peer electronic cash system (2008)
16. Pillai, A., Saraswat, V., Vasanthakumary Ramachandran, A.: Attacks on blockchain based digital identity. In: Blockchain and Applications: 3rd International Congress, pp. 329–338. Springer (2022)
17. Province of british columbia: Von network (2022). https://github.com/bcgov/von-network
18. Rehman, E., ET AL.: Using blockchain to ensure trust between donor agencies and ngos in under-developed countries. Computers **10**, 98 (2021). https://doi.org/10.3390/computers10080098, https://www.mdpi.com/2073-431X/10/8/98
19. Siqueira, A., Da Conceição, A.F., Rocha, V.: Performance evaluation of self-sovereign identity use cases. In: 2023 IEEE International Conference on Decentralized Applications and Infrastructures (DAPPS), pp. 135–144 (2023). https://doi.org/10.1109/DAPPS57946.2023.00026
20. Snell, D.: Trade unions and environmental justice. The Palgrave Handbook of Environmental Labour Studies, pp. 149–173 (2021)
21. Soltani, R., Nguyen, U.T., An, A.: A survey of self-sovereign identity ecosystem. Security and Communication Networks (2021)
22. The linux foundation: becoming a hyperledger aries developer (2022). https://www.edx.org/learn/computer-programming/the-linux-foundation-becoming-a-hyperledger-aries-developer
23. World wide web consortium (W3C): Decentralized identifiers (DIDs) v1.1 (2025). https://www.w3.org/TR/did-1.1/
24. World wide web consortium (W3C): verifiable credentials data model 2.0 (2025). https://www.w3.org/TR/vc-data-model-2.0/

Interlock Protocol: Interactive Cross-L2 Atomic Transactions via Stateless Shared Sequencer

Uri Lee[✉] and William J. Knottenbelt

Centre for Cryptocurrency Research and Engineering, Imperial College London,
London SW7 2AZ, UK
`{u.lee22,wjk}@imperial.ac.uk`

Abstract. Ethereum's scaling challenges have led to a proliferation of Layer 2 (L2) rollups, which now process more transactions than the underlying Layer 1 blockchain. As these rollups mature, there is growing demand for atomic cross-rollup transactions that maintain consistency across separate L2 chains. Interlock is a cross-Layer 2 atomic transaction protocol enabled by a stateless Shared Sequencer. The Sequencer coordinates atomic transactions to reach consensus via messaging between rollups and the sequencer. Interlock ensures atomicity while allowing continuous optimistic processing of transactions that do not depend on the pending atomic cross-chain transaction state. This approach combines atomicity guarantees with optimistic execution, ensuring transaction validity across independent rollup chains.

Keywords: Cross-rollup · Layer 2 · Atomic transactions

1 Introduction

Layer 2 chains have emerged as a response to the demand for scalability on low-throughput blockchains such as Ethereum [12]. As noted by Gudgeon et al. [9], L2 protocols "utilize the expensive and low-rate blockchain only as a recourse for disputes" while completing "off-chain transactions in sub-seconds rather than minutes or hours while retaining asset security, reducing fees and allowing blockchains to scale". This approach has driven significant user adoption, with recent research showing that trading activities have shifted substantially from Ethereum to rollups, with swaps on rollups occurring 2–3 times more frequently than on the base layer [8].

Asynchronous atomic crosschain transactions on independent distributed systems are possible as proposed by [10,13]. Though similar to the atomic commit problem in traditional distributed databases [5,11], cross-rollup transactions present a unique opportunity for synchronous atomic operations precisely because multiple rollups settle to the same underlying Layer 1 chain. This shared

© ICST Institute for Computer Sciences, Social Informatics and Telecommunications Engineering 2026
Published by Springer Nature Switzerland AG 2026. All Rights Reserved
W. Knottenbelt et al. (Eds.): Blocktea 2025, LNICST 669, pp. 114–130, 2026.
https://doi.org/10.1007/978-3-032-12335-0_7

settlement layer, combined with a shared sequencer, creates a natural coordination point for enforcing atomicity across Layer 2 chains. Enabling atomic cross-rollup transactions will unlock novel decentralized finance (DeFi) opportunities that are currently impossible, such as atomic swaps between assets on different rollups, cross-rollup collateralization, and complex multi-rollup financial products, all without requiring users to bridge assets.

We introduce Interlock, a protocol that enables consensus on cross-Layer 2 atomic transactions without the need to compute state at the sequencer layer and is designed specifically to be compatible with parallel execution such as Block-STM [7]. Interlock uses a shared sequencer that acts as a coordinator for atomic cross-chain transactions, allowing these transactions to reach an agreed outcome before any dependent state transitions are finalized. While consensus is being reached on atomic cross-chain transactions, Interlock continues to optimistically process transactions that are not dependent on the pending atomic transactions.

The interactive resolution of atomic cross-chain transactions provides two key benefits. First, unlike many protocols that require developers to predefine states modified and read, or necessitate state simulation to understand what will change, Interlock does not require pre-computation or simulation of transactions at the sequencer layer, as outcomes of atomic transactions are resolved during execution. Second, by interactively resolving the final state of atomic cross-chain transactions, we can reduce rollbacks by building only on agreed atomic cross-chain transaction states.

1.1 Contributions and Organization

Compared to existing approaches, Interlock demonstrates a novel architecture that eliminates the need for shared builders, thereby avoiding computational overhead at the sequencer level. The protocol enables rollups to maintain their own execution environments whilst coordinating atomic transactions through lightweight messaging via the sequencer. Furthermore, Interlock allows rollups to optimistically execute transactions that do not depend on pending atomic operations, thereby maintaining system performance during cross-chain coordination. In addition, unlike protocols that require state specifications prior to execution, Interlock processes atomic transactions dynamically during execution, providing greater flexibility and reducing the need for transaction pre-computation.

The remainder of this paper is organised as follows. Section 2 provides formal definitions of the key concepts underlying the protocol as well as background literature on similar atomic transaction protocols. Section 3 introduces the protocol and its specifications. Section 4 presents the protocol properties and formal proofs of correctness, atomicity, and liveness guarantees. Section 5 provides implementation details. Section 6 discusses the protocol's strengths, limitations, and security considerations under various threat models. Finally, Sect. 7 concludes with a summary of contributions.

2   Problem Background

As a result of Ethereum's scalability limitations, Layer 2's (L2s) have emerged as a solution [12] to offload computation off-chain whilst benefiting from the security and decentralisation of the Layer 1 (Ethereum). This has led to prolific growth of Layer 2 chains or rollups. Despite these rollups settling their transactions on the same Layer 1, there is no native interoperability between these L2 chains.

However, a shared settlement layer in addition to a shared sequencer presents a unique opportunity for built-in atomic interoperability between rollups. The common Layer 1 settlement layer, combined with coordinated transaction ordering, creates natural coordination points for enforcing atomicity across Layer 2 chains.

2.1   Definitions

We begin by defining key terms and assumptions underlying the protocol:

Definition 1 (Atomic Transaction Pair). *A pair of transactions (tx_i, tx_j), where tx_i is executed on chain A and tx_j is executed on chain B. Interlock ensures atomicity for such pairs: either both transactions are committed successfully on the L1 chain, or both fail (either reverted, failed or excluded).*

Definition 2 (Sequencer). *Given a mempool M containing a set of transactions $\{tx_1, tx_2, ..., tx_n\}$, a sequencer is defined as a function $S : M \rightarrow O$ that produces an ordered sequence $O = (tx_{i_1}, tx_{i_2}, ..., tx_{i_k})$ where $\{i_1, i_2, ..., i_k\} \subseteq \{1, 2, ..., n\}$ and each tx_{i_j} is unique. This ordering O is then committed to a data availability (DA) layer or Layer 1 (L1) blockchain to ensure the ordering is immutably preserved and adhered to before execution by the rollup's state transition function. A typical sequencer of a single L2 chain is a centralised entity [15] which takes the set of transactions submitted by users to the mempool and creates a deterministic ordering of the transactions to be executed.*

Definition 3 (Shared Sequencer). *A Shared Sequencer (SS) creates transaction orderings for multiple chains. In the case of Interlock, we assume 2 chains and hence the sequencer sequences for both chain A and B. SS issues ordered sequence of transactions $T_A = \{tx_1, tx_2, ...\}$ and $T_B = \{tx_1, tx_2, ...\}$ to chains A and B respectively.*

In Interlock, the Shared Sequencer ensures that atomic pairs (tx_i, tx_j) are globally ordered, i.e., if tx_i precedes tx_k in A's order, then tx_j precedes tx_l in B's order, where (tx_k, tx_l) is the next atomic pair. This is to prevent circular dependencies among the atomic transactions. In addition, we assume liveness of the Shared Sequencer. A malicious Shared Sequencer can prevent atomic transactions from succeeding but cannot break the atomicity guarantee (either both failing or both succeeding).

Definition 4 (Rollup). *A Layer 2 (L2) scaling solution that processes transactions off-chain and periodically submits compressed transaction data to a base layer chain (L1) [15]. Rollups maintain their own state while aiming to inherit the security guarantees of the underlying blockchain. They process transactions in batches and generate L2 blocks, which are collections of ordered transactions with state transition proofs that are eventually settled on Layer 1.*

Definition 5 (State Transition Function). *Each rollup or L2 chain implements its own state transition function, typically through a Virtual Machine (VM), which follows well-defined rules specific to that chain's protocol. A state transition function δ takes a current state s and a transaction tx as inputs, and produces a new state s' and a receipt r as outputs:*

$$\delta(s, tx) = (s', r)$$

where s' is the new state after executing transaction tx from initial state s and r is the execution receipt containing transaction execution outcomes such as success/failure status, gas used, logs generated, and any return values.

Each L2 chain has its own execution layer which takes in the set of transactions ordered by the sequencer, and runs those transactions starting with an initial state.

Definition 6 (Layer 1). *In the context of cross-rollup atomic execution, L1 serves as the settlement layer where transaction batches from different rollups are finalized and where the cryptographic proofs or state roots are verified.*

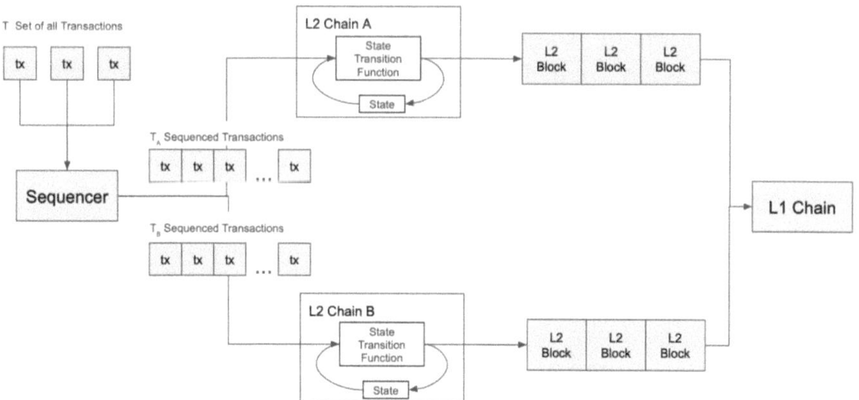

Fig. 1. Shared Sequencer and Two L2 Rollup Chains which settle to L1.

2.2 Environment Settings

In this work, we consider a cross-rollup environment (Fig. 1) where Layer 2 (L2) blocks from multiple rollups are settled to a base layer (Layer 1). In this setting, transactions from the mempool are sequenced and ordered for each chain. Each chain then executes its own state transition function or Virtual Machine (VM) on its transaction set, producing L2 blocks. A critical requirement in this environment is that transactions must not only be executed but also included and finalized on L1 while preserving atomicity across chains.

Atomicity across L2 blocks can be cryptographically enforced through an additional layer positioned between the rollups and L1. This intermediate layer, often referred to as an *aggregated proving layer* [6,14,16], acts as a buffer ensuring that L2 blocks containing cross-chain atomic transactions are committed to L1 in a single aggregated block. This layer creates an aggregated state root, and modifications to the L1 contract can ensure cross-chain atomic transaction validity, as demonstrated in Shared Validity Sequencing [16].

Shared Validity Sequencing, which is applicable to both ZK and optimistic rollups, ensures atomicity by requiring batches produced by each chain to be submitted to L1 in a single transaction. This approach verifies that the root of all transactions for a specified contract on Chain A matches the root of all transactions on Chain B, guaranteeing that for every atomic transaction, a corresponding counterpart exists and was executed successfully.

While stateless shared sequencing can guarantee atomic inclusion (ensuring atomic cross-chain transactions are included in the same batch), it cannot guarantee successful execution. Full nodes at the shared sequencer can simulate execution and allow only valid transactions to be sequenced, but this requires maintaining full nodes for every chain, introducing significant complexity and computational overhead. A stateless sequencer is one which does not maintain state nor perform any computation with regards to the state transition for a rollup or L2.

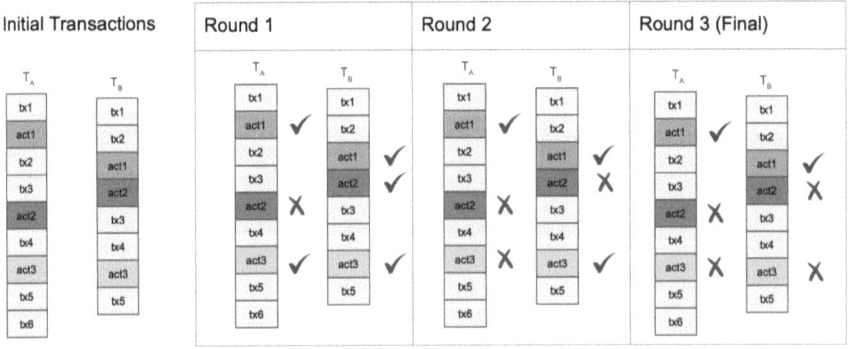

Fig. 2. Atomic Transactions and Dependency propagation.

2.3   Dependency Propagation

A further challenge arises when interdependencies exist between atomic transactions or between atomic and non-atomic transactions. In such cases, multiple re-computations may be necessary to reach a valid transaction batch. Figure 2 illustrates how separate computation of a transaction set consisting of intra-chain and inter-chain atomic transactions may require multiple re-computations. The initial computation shows a failure on Chain A of the second atomic transaction pair $act2$. In the second computation, $act2$ fails due to the atomicity condition, which causes $act3$ to fail due to dependencies. This failure must then propagate to Chain B, necessitating an additional round of computation.

Without re-computations or validity checking prior to block building, the system would produce invalid blocks that violate atomicity conditions, resulting in rollbacks. To address this, Interlock enables a shared sequencer and L2 chains to resolve atomic cross-chain transactions during execution sequentially, dynamically determining whether atomic transactions should revert. Despite this sequential resolution of atomic pairs, transaction computation continues optimistically for transactions not dependent on the atomic cross-chain transaction state. When the sequencer and rollups behave cooperatively, all produced blocks are valid (similar to the Final Round output shown in Fig. 2). However, malicious behaviour by the sequencer or rollups can result in invalid blocks, necessitating rollbacks.

2.4   Related Works

Many previous works exist on cross-chain asynchronous atomic transactions across heterogeneous chains [17] [13]. They typically involve multi-step commitment similar to Hash Time Locked Contracts (HTLCs) utilising a smart contract as an intermediary escrow.

Academic literature is more limited on synchronous cross-L2 atomic transactions. Early approaches focus on atomic inclusion protocols such as Astria [1] which guarantee transactions will be included at the same time (or same slot height) but provide no guarantees on whether those transactions are valid within the block and hence will be executed and eventually included on the L1.

To address this limitation and guarantee atomic execution and settlement to the L1, proposals such as Shared Validity Sequencing [16] and Polygon's AggLayer [6] introduce an intermediary buffer layer once the L2 blocks have been computed and prior to L1 settlement. Aggregated settlement involves "aggregating the settlement decisions across multiple L2s into a *single all-or-nothing* decision" that verifies both inter-rollup and intra-rollup validity [4]. This intermediary layer ensures atomicity and correctness of cross-rollup contract calls by settling a bundle of transactions with atomic transactions in a single L1 block. In Espresso's CIRC [3], the sequencer simulates execution of cross-chain contract calls and pre-populates communication between contracts using *inboxes* and *outboxes*. To ensure the shared sequencer's honesty and maintain atomicity, the system verifies that the inbox of one chain's contract equals the outbox of the other chain's contract and vice versa.

However, these approaches require a stateful sequencer where the sequencer runs full nodes of the rollup chains to check for transaction validity. Without a stateful sequencer, the rollups risk producing invalid blocks leading to rollback and recomputation from the latest valid state. Interlock, under the assumptions outlined in this paper, guarantees valid blocks without the need for a stateful sequencer. Interlock's approach allows rollups to maintain separate execution environments, enabling the sequencer to remain stateless, focusing solely on sequencing and managing atomic transactions through messaging.

3   Interlock Protocol

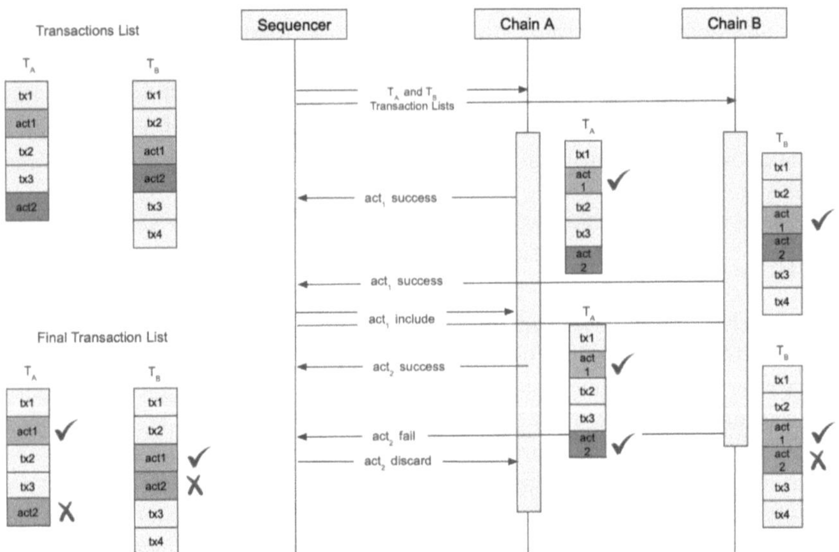

Fig. 3. Communication between Sequencer and Chain A for example transactions act_1 and act_2.

Figure 3 shows the communication between two chains, Chain A and B and two atomic cross-chain transaction pairs (act_1, act_1) and (act_2, act_2). The sequencer creates an ordering over the set of non cross-chain and cross-chain transactions. The sequencer ensures that the atomic cross-chain transactions or $acts$ maintain a global ordering across both chains such that act_i is always ordered before act_j in both transaction lists for Chain A and B where $i < j$ in the preset ordering. The Transaction List or preset ordering is the order to which the sequencer commits and the order in which transactions should be executed.

The L2 chains, which have their own execution environments, run the transaction lists up to the first atomic transaction. The chains then send a message regarding the outcome of the atomic transaction. The sequencer allows the atomic transactions to be included as successful transactions or to revert.

The sequence of communication is not dissimilar to the 2 Phase Commit protocol (2PC) with a few key differences. Firstly, the communication is trusted in that the "commitment" of the result is internally evaluated by the execution engine. A true commitment, similar to the role of a commitment (or locked intermediary state) in 2PC, would require a proof that all the computation up to a given atomic transaction act_i is correct, hence all transactions up to and including index i. Since sending intermediary proofs of correct computation is redundant computation, especially if the next layer can batch and aggregate to produce a single proof, Interlock trusts the rollups to send correct commitments to the sequencer.

High Level Overview on Consensus on Atomic Cross-Chain Transactions.

State Certainty A commitment of the result (*success* or *fail*) by the chain of an atomic cross-chain transaction, or *act*, only occurs once the resulting state of all previous transactions in the preset order have completed (or "committed"). The *act* transaction. Hence, consensus only begins when all *txs* with index $< i$, where i is the index of the *act*, have been committed. This is referred to as the Global Commit Index [7] - the index at which all transactions up to this index have been committed.

The transactions which follow the *act* transaction with index $> i$, are executed optimistically, and any transaction attempting to read from the *act*'s pending results are aborted and added as a dependency of the *act*. These dependent transactions will be placed in the dependencies queue, ready to be released after the resolution of the *act* transaction.

Outcome Commitment. Rollups send a signed message to the sequencer with the result of the atomic cross-chain transaction *act* (*success* or *fail*) along with the bundle ID.

– **Failed Transaction** If the outcome of an is *fail*, the rollup knows the outcome of the entire atomic cross-chain transaction bundle will also be *fail*. Hence, the rollup does not wait for a response from the sequencer, including the failed transaction and continuing with the processing of other transactions. Transactions dependent on this *act* are released into the execution queue E for execution.
– **Successful Transaction** If the transaction is executed successfully, the results are marked as pending and the rollup sends the *success* message regarding the transaction. The rollup must now wait for the response of the sequencer.

Sequencer. The sequencer sends *success* if messages received from all rollups regarding all parts of this bundle responded with *success*. The sequencer sends *fail* at the first *fail* message it receives regarding a cross-chain atomic transaction. Since a single failure in an atomic bundle leads to the *fail* of the entire bundle, the sequencer does not need to wait for all messages to order the failure of an *act* transaction.

Hence, there are two main outcomes which could occur during execution and the interaction between the rollups and the sequencer:

1. All *act*s are valid. Sequencer received the *success* messages and sends an include message to include all valid transactions in its current executed state.
2. One or more atomic cross-chain transactions in the bundle failed. Exclude all valid transactions in the bundle by executing the transaction in forced-fail mode, force reverting the transaction but still consuming gas.

Since Chain A executes an *act* which fails before Chain B gets to execute it, Chain B can use the *fail* message at execution and run the transaction in force revert mode, failing the transaction.

3.1 Background

We assume that both chains use an optimistic parallel execution engine such as Block-STM [7]. Block-STM is optimistic in nature, as it does not do any precomputations of the transactions and deals with dependencies during execution of the transactions. Block-STM optimistically assumes that, in the majority of cases, there will not be dependencies between the transactions and executes "optimistically" and has procedures in place to ensure correctness. Overall, the "final outcome is equivalent to the sequential execution of transactions in the preset order in which they appear in the block" [7].

In addition, we make the following assumptions:

Assumption 1 (Initial State Consistency). Chains A and B start in consistent and valid states.

Assumption 2 (Liveness of Shared Sequencer). We assume liveness of the Shared Sequencer, as the Shared Sequencer is required to coordinate the cross-chain transactions.

Assumption 3 (Liveness of Rollups). We also assume liveness and responsiveness of the rollups involved. Even with one chain experiencing downtime, atomic transactions cannot continue to be processed.

4 Protocol Properties and Proofs

4.1 Proof of Correctness of a Single Atomic Pair Bundle

Theorem 1 (Atomicity). *For any atomic pair (tx_i, tx_j), either both transactions are committed or both are reverted.*

Proof. Let tx_i and tx_j be an atomic transaction pair, where tx_i is executed on chain A and tx_j on chain B. We prove by case analysis:

- **Case 1: Both tx_i and tx_j succeed.** Chain A executes transactions up to tx_i and reports success to the sequencer. Similarly, chain B executes transactions up to tx_j and reports success. Upon receiving success messages from both chains, the sequencer sends a commit message to A and B, ensuring that both tx_i and tx_j are committed.
- **Case 2: tx_i fails on chain A.** Chain A executes transactions up to tx_i and detects a failure. It reports failure to the sequencer. Upon receiving the failure message, the sequencer sends a revert message to B. Chain B executes tx_j in revert mode, ensuring that no state changes occur. Thus, tx_i and tx_j are both reverted.
- **Case 3: tx_j fails on chain B.** Chain B executes transactions up to tx_j and detects a failure. It reports failure to the sequencer. Upon receiving the failure message, the sequencer sends a revert message to A. Chain A executes tx_i in revert mode, ensuring no state changes occur. Thus, tx_i and tx_j are both reverted.

In all cases, either tx_i *and* tx_j are committed, or both are reverted. Thus, atomicity is preserved.

Theorem 2 (Progress Guarantee). *Protocol will continue without deadlock due to circular dependencies.*

Proof. The sequencer provides a total order of transactions to both chains, including atomic pairs (tx_i, tx_j), (tx_k, tx_l), and so on. Chains A and B execute transactions in the sequencer's order. If tx_i on A precedes tx_k on A, then tx_j on B (paired with tx_i) precedes tx_l on B (paired with tx_k), as guaranteed by the sequencer's global ordering. This ensures that all chains observe the same relative order of atomic pairs, satisfying consistency.

Theorem 3 (Liveness). *If both transactions in an atomic pair can succeed, the protocol guarantees their commitment.*

Proof. If tx_i and tx_j both succeed, chains A and B send success messages to the sequencer. The sequencer waits for both success messages and then sends commit messages to both chains. Since the sequencer is live and all communication is reliable, the commit messages are delivered within a bounded time. Thus, both tx_i and tx_j are committed, satisfying liveness.

4.2   Correctness of Sequential Resolution of Atomic Transactions

We generalise the proof to show that resolving atomic transactions sequentially ensures correctness when there are dependencies between transactions across chains.

Setup and Generalised Notation. Consider two chains, A and B, each processing a batch of transactions. Let A have transactions $\langle tx_1^A, tx_2^A, \ldots, tx_n^A \rangle$, and B have transactions $\langle tx_1^B, tx_2^B, \ldots, tx_m^B \rangle$. Among these transactions are atomic pairs (tx_i^A, tx_j^B), which must be resolved atomically. Dependencies may exist between transactions such that the validity of later atomic pairs depends on the success of earlier ones.

Proof. We show that resolving atomic transactions sequentially ensures both atomicity and correctness of the final state across chains.

1. Sequential Resolution Process The Interlock protocol resolves atomic transactions one pair at a time in the order determined by the sequencer:

1. For each atomic pair (tx_i^A, tx_j^B):
   - Chain A processes transactions up to tx_{i-1}^A in sequence, producing state S_{i-1}^A. Chain A executes tx_i^A from state S_{i-1}^A and stores new tentative state S_i^A as a pending result. Chain A reports the execution outcome of tx_i^A as *success* or *failure* to the sequencer.
   - Chain B applies the same process reporting *success* or *failure* to the sequencer.
2. The sequencer waits for the results of both chains. If both succeed, the pair is committed. If either fails, the pair is reverted.

2. Dependency Handling and Propagation. Sequential resolution naturally handles dependencies:

- Later atomic pairs are only processed if all earlier pairs have been successfully resolved. This guarantees that dependencies are resolved in a valid order.
- If the outcome state of an earlier atomic pair (tx_i^A, tx_j^B) is unknown, the Interlock protocol does not attempt to resolve the later pair until the earlier pair's outcome is known.

3. Correctness Guarantee. Sequential resolution ensures correctness because:

- **Atomicity:** Atomicity is preserved in an atomic pair as both transactions reach either *succcess* or *failure* but never a combination of both outcomes.
- **Progress Guarantee:** The system will not encounter deadlocks or be unable to proceed due to circular dependencies, as the global ordering of atomic transactions provided by the shared sequencer ensures that all dependencies are resolved in a well-defined sequence.
- **Final State Validity:** Each atomic pair is resolved fully (committed or reverted) before moving to the next pair ensuring ensuring that only valid atomic transactions contribute to the final state across chains. Resolution is only attempted from known correct state transition of all previous transactions, preventing incorrect outcome due to the uncertain state of previous transactions.

Conclusion. By resolving atomic transactions sequentially, the protocol ensures the following. Firstly, all dependencies are respected, and failures propagate forward. Secondly, the final state across chains is correct, consistent, and valid, regardless of transaction dependencies or failures. This approach guarantees correctness in the presence of atomic transactions with dependencies.

5   Protocol Specification

We can modify the Block-STM implementation [7] as detailed in their pseudocode to allow processing of the *act* transactions. Interlock must ensure that the *act* execution occurs after the state of having executed all prior transactions is established. Hence, before the execution result of an *act* is sent to the sequencer, the Global Commit Index [7] must be equal to $i - 1$ where i is the index of the *act*.

During the consensus period, an *act* is treated as a transaction with a dependency, and hence the *act* aborts, and the write set of the *act* is noted as an *ESTIMATE*. Transactions with index $>$ *act* index attempting to read from this *ESTIMATE* location will also abort and be added as a dependency of the *act*. The validation of an *act* transaction also includes a check of the message from the sequencer of whether to force fail the transaction or to include the transaction as a success in its current form. If an *act* fails during execution due to the transaction being invalid, and the state of all prior transactions is confirmed and committed, the validation does not require a message from the sequencer and can continue to be committed as a failed transaction – as the outcome of the *act* transaction pair is known. The general outline of the pseudocode changes can be described as follows:

Execution Task: If the transaction is an atomic cross-chain transaction, check if an exclude message regarding this transaction exists. If excluded by the sequencer, run the transaction in *revert mode*.

If the exclude message does not exist, execute as normal. For non-cross-chain transactions, execute as normal.

Validation Task: If the transaction is an *act* transaction:

1. If there is a *fail* message from sequencer regarding this *tx*:
   - If the transaction was not run in *revert mode* and ran successfully, abort and reschedule *tx* for re-execution.
   - If *tx* failed or ran in *revert mode*, allow transaction to commit successfully
2. If validation succeeds and Global Commit Index $= i - 1$ where i is the index of the *act*:
   - If no message has been sent to the sequencer already sent regarding this *act*, notify sequencer of successful execution
   - Treat the *act* as if it has a dependency and the *act* must be aborted marking every write values as estimates.
   - Wait for response (without blocking other executions) and allow the validation to continue.

- If response is *fail*, reschedule *tx* to be executed in *revert mode*.
- If response is *success*, validation is successful. Allow *tx* to be committed as usual.

3. Else, if validation fails or the Global Commit Index < *tx* − 1
   - Abort as usual, marking write set as estimates and rescheduling *tx* for execution.

6   Discussion

One of *Interlock*'s strengths is that it does not require the sequencer to run full nodes of the chains involved, allowing the sequencer to remain state-blind and light in operation, maintaining responsibility for the sequencing only. In addition, Interlock is designed to be compatible with parallel execution models such as Block-STM [7] so that transactions can continue to be processed while awaiting the result of an atomic transaction. Interlock also allows rollups to run their own separate execution environment instead of a shared builder set up, using messages to reach consensus over shared state.

The communication in Interlock is trusted in that the "commitment" of the result is internally evaluated by the execution engine. Since the atomicity guarantee is cryptographically enforced via the next layer in the system (aggregation layer or L1 as discussed in Sect. 2), we believe assuming a trusted protocol with a way to trace malicious behaviour is an acceptable trade-off in this scenario, since having to prove the correct state output would entail multiple intermediary ZK-proofs of all transactions up until the atomic transaction. Repeated intermediary generation of ZK-proofs appears to be wasteful work, especially if the proofs can be generated all together over a batch across both chains after computation.

The atomic transactions require a special execution flag which allows the rollups to run the transaction in "revert" mode or to allow a transaction to gracefully fail. The Interlock protocol requires the rollup to have autonomy, which leads to non-deterministic outcome of atomic transactions (from a single chain perspective). This will likely require a flag that is dynamically adjustable at runtime by the rollup. Despite non-determinism of cross-chain atomic transactions from a single-chain perspective, across the chains, atomic transactions have a correct deterministic outcome. In the worst-case scenario, if the assumptions do not hold, the misuse of the revert mode will censor an atomic transaction but never allow a transaction to break atomicity. This is described in the following Sect. 6.1.

6.1   Liveness and Malicious Actors

Liveness. *Interlock* assumes liveness of both the sequencer and the participating rollups. However, mechanisms to deal with the potential downtime of rollups and the shared sequencer can be introduced. For example, should one of the two rollups experience downtime, the sequencer can wait for a fixed time period and then send a *fail* message to the waiting rollup so that the rollup can continue producing blocks.

Malicious Rollup. Firstly, a malicious rollup may send false results to the sequencer regarding a transaction. This will likely produce invalid blocks. Depending on the implementation of the aggregate proving layer, a malicious rollup may cause another rollup to recompute to produce valid blocks but be able to continue to get their blocks accepted. Ultimately, however, atomicity of cross-chain transactions will continue to be preserved due to the cryptographic checks on the next layer.

Secondly, a malicious rollup may execute an atomic transaction in revert mode when it should have been executed normally. This may cause an atomic transaction to fail. Although atomicity will be preserved by the next layer, this is similar to a censorship attack blocking a user's transaction while still exhausting fees and gas. In addition, two rollups may collude to censor an atomic transaction pair. However, this censorship is immediately recognizable if both transactions were run in revert mode when there was no transaction that reverted naturally due to invalidity, showing that there was malicious behaviour.

Malicious Sequencer. A malicious sequencer can also lead to false messages which cause the production of invalid blocks or certain rollups to produce invalid blocks. Both an honest sequencer experiencing downtime and a dishonest sequencer could lead to no messages being relayed, which would cause the inability to reach consensus on atomic transactions and the inability to process transactions. A decentralised shared sequencer network could mitigate both liveness and dishonesty in sequencers. However, this would introduce computational overhead compared to a centralised sequencer.

Malicious User. The user can create a Denial of Service type attack by submitting large amounts of atomic bundles which are invalid that block access to particular resources in the VM execution. If the fee for submitting an atomic transaction is zero (in the approach of excluding transactions versus running them in revert mode), the cost for the user for such an attack could be close to null. Hence, it is crucial to develop an appropriate fee system that bears a cost to the user if the transaction happens to be invalid.

6.2   Limitations

The current version of Interlock operates under several key assumptions that merit discussion. The protocol assumes honest behaviour and liveness from both the shared sequencer and participating rollups. Additionally, we assume a centralised sequencer, which introduces inherent limitations including potential censorship and dominance over transaction ordering. Whilst a decentralised sequencer would address these concerns [2], it would introduce additional computational overhead and latency compared to a centralised approach.

The protocol's liveness guarantees depend critically on the availability of both the sequencer and participating rollups. A more practical implementation could introduce timeout mechanisms whereby the sequencer mitigates risks from rollup downtime. However, sequencer availability remains essential - either through a centralised sequencer or through honest parties within a decentralised sequencer network - to ensure protocol progression and prevent transaction blocking.

A significant limitation arises from the interdependencies introduced by atomic composability. Malicious rollups can potentially create denial-of-service effects on other rollups, preventing their blocks from settling to Layer 1. This represents a novel risk that Interlock and similar systems introduce due to the interlinking required for atomic cross-chain operations. Even non-malicious rollups with slower execution speeds can adversely affect the settlement rate of faster rollups, creating performance bottlenecks across the system.

These limitations reflect unavoidable trade-offs inherent in achieving high levels of cross-rollup interoperability. Future work should address these challenges through robust timeout mechanisms, incentive structures to discourage malicious behaviour, and exploration of decentralised sequencer architectures [2] [15] that balance security with performance.

6.3 Future Works

Performance evaluations in a simulated setting of two parallel execution-based rollups should take place and be benchmarked against a single chain parallel execution setting. In addition, different experiments on the amount and type of cross-chain atomic transactions and the impact on performance should be measured.

To develop the protocol for a production setting, the liveness assumptions on the sequencer and rollups should be relaxed or removed, and mechanisms such as timeouts should be introduced to allow for such failures. In addition, incentive mechanisms must be investigated to create a model that deters misuse of the system. This includes both cryptoeconomic stake and slash models and potential reward fees for both the sequencer and the rollup. In addition, as cross-chain atomic transactions create additional complexity and computation for both rollups, appropriate fees paid by the user must also be investigated.

7   Conclusion

We present *Interlock*, a mechanism to achieve cross-L2 atomic transactions via coordination by the stateless Shared Sequencer without a shared builder. Interlock sequentially resolves the outcome of atomic transactions while optimistically continuing to build on state that does not overlap with the pending state. Interlock is designed to operate with parallel execution models such as Block-STM. Interlock only begins consensus on atomic transactions when state is known to give an accurate guarantee that the pending outcome of the transaction is correct. Transactions which are impacted by the result of atomic transactions are placed in a dependent queue ready to be executed once the atomic transaction is resolved.

Interlock allows atomic cross-chain transactions to run in "revert mode", which allows for state non-determinism (*success* or *fail*) of an individual atomic transaction but determinism across two chains' batches of transactions. The resulting outcome of Interlock, given that the assumption conditions are valid, is the correct production of blocks of intra-chain transactions and atomic inter-chain transactions. If the production of invalid blocks is acceptable (along with a need for rollback), some assumptions can be loosened to make it more robust in a practical setting.

References

1. Astria: Astria: The shared sequencer network (2024). https://www.astria.org/blog/astria-the-shared-sequencer-network. Accessed 01 Nov 2024
2. Charbonneau, J.: Rollups aren't real (2024). https://joncharbonneau.substack.com/p/rollups-arent-real. Accessed 24 July 2025
3. Espresso Systems: Circ: Coordinated inter-rollup communication (2025). https://espresso.discourse.group/t/circ-coordinated-inter-rollup-communication/43. Accessed 03 Jan 2025
4. Espresso Systems: Composability and circ: Differences between synchronous and asynchronous composability (2025). https://hackmd.io/@EspressoSystems/composability-circ?utm_source=preview-mode&utm_medium=rec#Differences-between-synchronous-and-asynchronous-composability. Accessed 03 Jan 2025
5. Ezhilchelvan, P., Aldweesh, A., van Moorsel, A.: Non-blocking two phase commit using blockchain. In: Proceedings of the 1st Workshop on Cryptocurrencies and Blockchains for Distributed Systems, pp. 36–41 (2018)
6. Farmer, B.: Aggregated blockchains (2 2024). https://mirror.xyz/0xfa892B19c72c2D2C6B10dFce8Ff8E7a955b58A61/TXMyZhhRFa-bjr7YHwmJpKBwt2-_ysirbh_VpNy3qZY. Accessed 02 Sept 2024
7. Gelashvili, R., et al.: Block-STM: scaling blockchain execution by turning ordering curse to a performance blessing. In: Proceedings of the 28th ACM SIGPLAN Annual Symposium on Principles and Practice of Parallel Programming, pp. 232–244 (2023)
8. Gogol, K., Messias, J., Miori, D., Tessone, C., Livshits, B.: Cross-rollup mev: Non-atomic arbitrage across l2 blockchains. arXiv preprint arXiv:2406.02172 (2024)
9. Gudgeon, L., Moreno-Sanchez, P., Roos, S., McCorry, P., Gervais, A.: SoK: layer-two blockchain protocols. In: Bonneau, J., Heninger, N. (eds.) FC 2020. LNCS, vol. 12059, pp. 201–226. Springer, Cham (2020). https://doi.org/10.1007/978-3-030-51280-4_12
10. Guerraoui, R.: Non-blocking atomic commit in asynchronous distributed systems with failure detectors. Distrib. Comput. **15**(1), 17–25 (2002)
11. Hadzilacos, V.: On the relationship between the atomic commitment and consensus problems. In: Fault-Tolerant Distributed Computing, pp. 201–208. Springer (1990)
12. Han, H., Wang, M., Yang, F., Jia, L., Sun, Y., Zhang, R.: A layer-2 expansion shared sequencer model for blockchain scalability. Blockchain: Research and Applications, p. 100292 (2025)

13. Herlihy, M.: Atomic cross-chain swaps. In: Proceedings of the 2018 ACM Symposium on Principles of Distributed Computing, pp. 245–254 (2018)
14. Ko, H., Ju, C., Radius: Cross-rollup synchronous atomic execution (2024). https://ethresear.ch/t/cross-rollup-synchronous-atomic-execution/20193. Accessed 19 Dec 2024
15. Motepalli, S., Freitas, L., Livshits, B.: Sok: decentralized sequencers for rollups. arXiv preprint arXiv:2310.03616 (2023)
16. Umbra Research: Shared validity sequencing (6 2023). https://www.umbraresearch.xyz/writings/shared-validity-sequencing. Accessed 02 Spet 2024
17. Zakhary, V., Agrawal, D., Abbadi, A.E.: Atomic commitment across blockchains. arXiv preprint arXiv:1905.02847 (2019)

Short papers

Can Blockchains Rebuild from a Financial Collapse?
Collapse?
The Case Study of Lebanon

Harry Halpin[1,2]([✉])

[1] Nym Technologies, Neuchâtel, Switzerland
[2] American University of Beirut, PO Box 11-0236, Riad El-Solh, Beirut, Lebanon
`harry@nymtech.net`

Abstract. The potential for blockchain technologies to help countries in the global South transform their economies is explored in this case study on Lebanon. Lebanon experienced hyperinflation due to the failure of its central bank. Based on these experiences, we sketch a possible deployment of blockchain technologies in Lebanon based on stablecoins that would enforce transparency for the central bank of Lebanon.

Keywords: Blockchain · Development · Inflation · Lebanon

1 Introduction

The promise of blockchain technologies is to modernize the world's archaic financial system using techniques from distributed systems and cryptography, allowing developing countries to liberate themselves from forms of colonialism and crisis. Although there has been a veritable revolutionary transformation due to digital systems throughout society at the turn of the millennium, national financial systems to a large extent have escaped unscathed these developments, and crucial functions, such as banking deposits and equity trading, run on top of proprietary code on nearly-dead programming languages like COBOL, a programming language that has remained relatively unchanged since the 1960s, with operations being centralized on large mainframes.[1] This sorry state of affairs prevents financial systems from upgrading to the latest digital technologies, including artificial intelligence (AI) and other methods of automation, and leaves gaping holes in their cybersecurity. So it should come as no surprise that blockchain technologies are viewed as one tempting path of development, as they promise to deliver a brave new world of secure payments built on top of modern programming languages and open source code. Yet the financial system consists of massive incumbents, with only a few commercial banks openly embracing blockchain for real-world financial usage for their customers. Likewise, most governments are also only tentatively exploring blockchain technologies, with their usage being

---

[1] https://www.electronicpaymentsinternational.com/news/cobol-a-ticking-time-bomb-in-the-financial-system-sliverflow-ceo/.

W. Knottenbelt et al. (Eds.): Blocktea 2025, LNICST 669, pp. 133–143, 2026.
https://doi.org/10.1007/978-3-032-12335-0_8

restricted to either stockpiling particular cryptocurrencies such as Bitcoin in strategic reserves or small-scale experiments with centrally-banked digital cryptocurrencies (CBDCs) where a blockchain is used as an accounting layer for the central bank [2]. These blockchain experiments are not consumer-facing, and tend to be focussed on interbanking clearance between the central bank and commercial banking [4].

Our generalized hypothesis is that blockchain-based systems could lead to more rational economic development by providing a secure digital infrastructure with lower adoption costs [7]. Currently the adoption of blockchain technologies is driven by private industry in a "bottom-up" fashion, but limited in scope to small and privileged parts of the population that seek to diversify their portfolios or "get rich quick" rather than enable widespread economic development. Simply put, most nation-states are not at the point of absolute crisis where they can throw off the yoke of financial neo-colonialism and in a "top-down" install a new blockchain-based financial system.

Empirical evidence in terms of data collection will then come from macroeconomics and history [5]. Our study will focus on Lebanon. The case of Lebanon is particularly tragic, as Lebanon has suffered one of the most disastrous cases of hyperinflation in the 21st century (although not as catastrophic as Zimbabwe and Venezuela), with their currency losing value (as of July 2025) of approximately 5900% since 2019. Worse, there seems to be no easy way out, as the situation has degenerated to such an extent that the Lebanese currency is effectively worthless. The once world-renown reputation of Lebanon as the banking hub of the Middle East is in tatters, with its place being overtaken by more cryptocurrency-friendly jurisdictions such as the United Arab Emirates, in particular Dubai, a process started before the rise of hyperinflation in Lebanon but accelerated since 2019. We hypothesize blockchain technologies – if deployed carefully – could spark a larger transition to economic stability and effective governance by empowering financial transparency via technology.

2   The Economic Crisis of Lebanon

Lebanon is a fairly young country, and its financial crisis of 2019 to the present day is difficult to understand without a grasp of its rather peculiar economy. To summarize, the economic crisis of Lebanon was characterized by the collapse of the dollar peg of the local currency, the Lebanese lira. Therefore, we will first explore the functions of currency pegs in general in Sect. 2.1 before going into how they worked in Lebanon in particular in Sect. 2.2.

2.1   Currency Pegs in Lebanon

A currency peg attempts to guarantee, via the actions of a central bank, that the domestic currency can be exchanged for the foreign currency (the "pegged" currency) at a fixed exchange rate (the "peg") as opposed to a flexible exchange rate driven by the market as is traditional in macroeconomics. The general function of a currency peg from the local currency of a typically less stable nation-state to the foreign currency of a more established nation-state is two-fold: The first function is to maintain confidence in the financial markets in terms of the stability of a local currency, with the less stable country also being allowed to sell its exports for less than it would otherwise due to its peg on a foreign currency, as importers rely on the stability of the pegged currency, with the second more insidious function to maintain some level of artificial financial control over the domestic currency. This control is directly exerted by the local central bank and indirectly asserted by the foreign central bank. The peg is maintained via the domestic central bank of the less stable nation buying foreign currency in periods of demand for the domestic currency, and in periods of demand for the foreign pegged currency, the same central bank must increase its reserves of the foreign currency. The central bank thus provides artificial market equilibrium at the peg.

This is not without dangers for the less stable state. The entire point of an autonomous currency produced by a central state bank is to accurately reflect the economic value of the state, so that the creation and withdrawal of this currency from the wider financial market can be used foster economic growth (via loans and so forth) in the local economy while also maintaining control over the rate of inflation, as per classical Keynesian economics. In an unpegged currency, currency can be effectively withdrawn from circulation if the economy is experiencing inflation by the raising of central bank interest rates. Vice versa, the economy can be stimulated by not only lowering interest rates (so encouraging existing money supplies to search for new investments) but by "printing" new currency via giving loans to local banks in order to encourage investment.

However, when a currency is pegged to another currency, this function of stimulating the local economy by the state bank is lost, as the movements of the local currency on the market must in effect "maintain" the value to the peg regardless of the stability of the local economy. This means that for import and exporters of commodities trust the local currency to be redeemable at the price of the peg, and the general gambit is that the relative advantages of the currency peg in terms of increasing the flows of commodities outweigh any explicit management the central bank of the less stable nation-state can do [9]. In effect, currency pegs allow less stable nation-states to avoid the natural volatility that their own local currency would have without a peg, and gain the advantages of the pegged currency on the global market, in return for sacrificing their own financial autonomy over monetary policy. However, if belief in the peg is lost and the reserves of the foreign currency are not maintained, a currency crisis is the result, usually with hyperinflation of the domestic currency.

As theorized by modern monetary theory, the core of financial autonomy for a nation-state is its ability to control the establishment of the state-backed status of legal tender for its own currency. Simply put, legal tender is a currency that a nation-state uses for the collection of taxes. For example, it is not impossible for a buyer and a seller to use the Russian ruble inside the United States for their financial transactions in a private contract. However, for the collection of taxes, the United States government will only accept dollars. Therefore, even if there are multiple competing alternative currencies in circulation at a given time within a given nation-state, any currency with the status of legal tender will be preferred over any other currency as one certainty is that taxes must be paid to the state, lest the state have to deploy its monopoly on violence to extract its chunk of flesh. A pegged currency may or may not be *de jure* legal tender, but establishing a state-backed peg creates a *de facto* legal tender out of the pegged currency, with people able to maintain both currencies in their bank account and exploit differences in their real-world purchasing power, which can undermine the peg.

2.2   The Destruction of the Dollar Peg

Due to a ticking time-bomb at the heart of the Lebanese economy, the good times did not last. In traditional economies, the central bank would distribute newly created funds to various commercial banks, and the commercial banks maintain reserves independently of the central bank. Two factors caused Lebanon's financial system to go in a particularly perverse direction. First, the Banque du Liban (BDL), Lebanon's central bank, could not seemingly just print Lebanese lira and change interest rates as it wanted in order to run the Lebanese monetary policy with some degree of autonomy due to the dollar peg and the need to maintain reserves. Second, the BDL's original loan to rebuild the war-shattered economy remained on its balance sheets as Hariri did not raise enough taxes to repay the loan. Yet as the lira was pegged to the dollar in order to restore confidence in the Lebanese lira and ease trade, Lebanon effectively had to maintain dollar reserves at all costs. To address this issue, the BDL needed the commercial banks to put part of their balances on the accounts of the central bank in the form of bonds. These were "eurobonds," which are simply bonds denominated in a currency other than that of the issuer of the bonds, and in the case of Lebanon were given as dollars despite the term "euro" being used. This explained how Lebanese banks were able to weather the financial crisis of 2008 relatively unscathed, as they were exposed more to the BDL than the international stock markets.

This situation got worse, as Lebanon had very few exports and a massive amount of imports, and these imports led to a tremendous demand for dollars. This allowed Lebanese residents to consume much more than they could afford if the peg was not there, as their income was given in Lebanese lira yet their expenses were given dollars, and the banks supported both. For example, someone could purchase a car in dollars and pay off the loan using Lebanese lira at a much cheaper price than if the exchange rate was floating. How could the central bank both continue to have the dollars needed to run the economy and pay back the massive debts that the Lebanese government continued to incur, as Lebanon had one of the highest debt-to-GDP ratios in the world? This was exacerbated as much of the public spending of the Lebanese government appeared also to be lost in various forms of corruption and clientelism.

In order to address this dire situation, the governor of the Banque du Liban, Riad Salameh, then created a Ponzi scheme that would last for decades to "plug the hole" of the lack of dollars in the economy needed to pay off Lebanon's debts: The central bank would set an astronomically high (thought to be more than 20%) interest rate on these dollar-denominated eurobonds to encourage Lebanese banks to put dollars in the central bank, far greater interest rates than those of the US Federal Reserve. The Lebanese commercial banks would pass the results of this high interest rate to their customers, who would then in turn be encouraged to put their dollars in local banks to get these impossibly high interest returns. This in turn enabled a distorted "zombie" economy that discouraged production inside Lebanon, as it was more profitable for people to move currency into a dollar-denominated savings account in a Lebanese bank than starting a business or investing in stocks. Constant remittances from overseas Lebanese continued the flow of dollars into the economy. And as long as new customers kept showing up at Lebanese banks with these "fresh" dollars, these dollars would paper over the debts and continue the pay-outs to previous round of customers who put their dollars in Lebanese banks. This Ponzi scheme was bound to explode [9].

During the protests against a new "WhatsApp" tax in 2019, commercial banks halted withdrawals for two weeks, leading to a run on the banks when they re-opened. The banks simply were unable to allow their customers to withdraw dollars from their own accounts, and customers found their dollar accounts had frozen or disappeared. This even led to Lebanese citizens taking up weapons in the style of a bank robbery, but with the intention to force the bank to return the dollars in their own bank accounts that were rightfully theirs. This led to a classic "bank run," and so the Ponzi scheme crumbled dramatically: Lebanon had its first-ever sovereign debt default when in March 2020 it missed a 1.2 billion eurobond payment. The entire Lebanese economy in 2018 was estimated to be $54 billion, but the amount of eurobonds was comparable to the size of the entire economy: With commercial banks holding $15 billion, the central bank holding $5 billion, and foreign investors holding $20 billion.[2] The central bank attempted to hold the situation together by inflating the monetary supply while pretending the currency peg still held, but the actual peg in the black market collapsed dramatically, with the official peg remaining 1,500 lira to a dollar while the black market peg went up to 120,000 lira to a dollar.

As the economy of Lebanon shrunk, the majority of the population fell into poverty, even as Riad Salameh was put in jail [9]. To add insult to injury, in 2020 the port of Beirut was destroyed by an explosion under mysterious circumstances and Israel invaded again in 2024. Belatedly, the Banque du Liban admitted that the dollar peg had collapsed. Only in early 2025 did a new government take power after two years of delay causing a vacancy, with promises to remove Lebanon from the FATF (Financial Action Task Force) grey list and restore the Lebanese economy with an IMF (International Monetary Fund) loan. As of 2025, the dollar peg holds on the black market at around 90,000 lira to a dollar. However,

---

[2] https://www.reuters.com/article/business/lebanons-crisis-needs-20-billion-25-billion-bailout-former-minister-says-idUSKBN1Z21JB/.

the question of how to restore trust in the Lebanese financial system appeared impossible to answer.

3   A Blockchain-Based Solution for Lebanon

As of 2025, with a new government in power and trust in the banking system at an all-time low in Lebanon, this moment of transition provides an ideal time to rebuild its financial system. As seen from our exploration, both countries have very open economies with high dollarization whereby standard monetary policy is subject to high leakage and low effectiveness. What could happen if Lebanon adopted cryptocurrency, and could it ameliorate the issues that Lebanon faces? Although one could consider that cryptocurrency would only further destabilize the Lebanese economy, our hypothesis in particular is that a blockchain-based system for both central and commercial banking based on digital US dollars is required to recreate trust in Lebanon due its technological enforcement of transparency. This would require rebuilding the Lebanese financial system on top of open-source and auditable blockchain software, and to extend this system to consumer finance. After we outline the drastic overhaul of infrastructure needed to implement blockchain technology nationally in Sect. 3.1, we will explore how stablecoin-based dollarization can reduce inflation in Sect. 3.2.

3.1   Putting the Banque Du Liban on a Blockchain

Currently, there is rightfully no trust in the Banque du Liban by the Lebanese consumer, with over nearly 10 billion USD in cash stored in homes in Lebanon.[3] As explained in Sect. 2, this is due to the Lebanese commercial banks having no way to prove their holdings of reserves. This is a problem that blockchain technologies can not simply solve, but can help ameliorate if the blockchain is publicly readable. Fiat currency systems and traditional central banking already rely on a system of ledgers, with the fiat assets on the ledger being central bank notes and reserves, and the ledger recording the sending of these assets to and from commercial banks. In traditional banking, these ledges may be altered, such as when BDL apparently hid the actual reserves from the public and possibly even Lebanese government itself. By moving its central banking system, including the issuance of new fiat currency via digital reserves (as is already done), to a public ledger, a level of trust could be restored in the flow of currency from the central bank to commercial banks. This would effectively re-create the BDL as a centrally-banked digital currency (CBDC), which ironically Salameh himself has advocated for since 2017.[4] In order to extend this trust to commercial banks, their reserves and transactions with the central bank would also have to be verifiable. Although the amount of reserves would be more difficult to

---

[3] https://today.lorientlejour.com/article/1337755/cash-economy-worth-10-billion-in-lebanon.html.

[4] https://finance.yahoo.com/news/lebanon-preparing-central-bank-digital-163219798.html.

prove, the monetary policy by BDL could then be publicly verifiable in terms of transactions and inflation. This simple move by itself would have helped prevent the 2019 Lebanese lira crisis.

Yet the actual amounts recorded on the ledgers will be via *oracles*, which effectively are trusted (usually non-digital) information from an external source. Thus, putting the amount of a transfer on a blockchain just moves the issue of trust to the bankers writing on the blockchain, and these bankers could easily place false information on the blockchain. To address this question of verification, the issuance of new currency, reserves, and transfers between central banks and commercial bankers will require third-party audits in order to verify that the amounts put on the ledger are correct. These third-party audits could be done via independent accounting firms, as is done today, or committees of neutral academic experts that share their results with the public. Their job would be to make sure the transfers and reserve amounts recorded on the blockchain were accurate. The public could then use this blockchain-based information to attempt to check the auditing bodies. Although far from perfect, simply putting this information on the blockchain with regular audits would be a vast increase in the transparency of BDL. Furthermore, making transparent the interface with commercial banks could also allow BDL to use its ledger-based system for new direct access to digital reserves. An increased variety of commercial banks could then service a wider variety of consumers with loans, leading to a more efficient credit allocation and so a stronger Lebanese economy [?]. Assuming adequate verification of the oracles, the cryptographic integrity of the blockchain would ensure the honesty and transparency of the central bank and its relationship with commercial banks.

In terms of concrete technology, there have been various studies of CBDCs and their relationships to commercial banking [3]. We would put forward a simple permissioned blockchain system based on a single unified ledger ran by the central bank for its operations of issuance and transfers to central banks that could be implemented on any modular blockchain such as Hyperledger[5] or Celestia,[6] with byzantine-fault tolerant consensus via 'proof of authority' between banks and nodes ran by independent auditors (rather than proof-of-work via electricity-driven mining, which could prove difficult in Lebanon due to its lack of consistent electricity). Smart contract functionality, such as code in the Ethereum Virtual Machine, could be used to automate issuance and clearance. Although access to the ledger would need to be verified and so the ledger would be permissioned, copies of the ledger could be held by any interested party and so the central bank ledger itself would be public to promote transparency [6].

3.2 Dollarization of Lebanon via Stablecoins

The dollarization of the Lebanese economy has already happened due to the hyperinflation of the lira [9]. However, this dollarization needs to be recognized

---

[5] https://hyperledger.org.
[6] https://celestia.org/.

and formalized, and yet again blockchain technologies can play an important role. As we outlined above, while blockchain technology can help enforce reserve and capital requirements, the BDL has failed to manage the monetary base and so cannot plausibly act via setting the interest rate and open market operations. However, the BDL could stabilize the economy by embracing dollarization for stable prices, i.e. the accepting of dollars as legal tender for all public and private debts, which would lead to both renewed trust in the currency in the bank and more stable imports, which is absolutely required for basic necessities such as petroleum in Lebanon. This does not mean that the lira has to disappear overnight: BDL could stop issuing lira. The absurd problem of the dollar peg for the lira, including contradictions between the "official" peg and "lollars" (USD denominated dollars in Lebanese bank accounts that could only be withdrawn as lira or as dollars at absurdly low variable quotes) would then disappear. The primary issue then would be that the amount of printed fiat dollars in Lebanon would not be sufficient to circulate throughout the economy.

Lebanon could simply print its own digital dollars to match the amount of dollars required for economic stability and growth. Although there would be concern that these would be "fake" dollars, with new stablecoin legislation forthcoming in the United States, the creation of USD-denominated stablecoins would not necessarily be illegal, as long as there were adequate reserves.[7] While one sensible move would be to collateralize these digital dollars with commodities, as explored by the Tradecoin proposal [8], Lebanon lacks much in the way of valuable exportable commodities (except perhaps fresh water in a region increasingly desertified by climate change). Therefore, an alternative would be to back these digital dollars with a basket of relatively uncorrelated currencies (similar to Keynes' "Bancor" proposal), as explored by Facebook's Libra [1]. These currencies would not just be fiat currency, but could also include Bitcoin as a hedge against inflation. In this manner, Lebanon could create a Bitcoin strategic reserve as part of a large reserve strategy, which could then be monitored on the blockchain. Reserve requirements could start relatively small and increase in size as Lebanon's economy recovered. There would be numerous other advantages of blockchain-based dollarization as Lebanon would benefit from the exposure to dollars "for free" while also making it more difficult for the United States to punish Lebanon for deviations from US-approved foreign policy choices (particularly important for a country neighbouring Israel). When a country normally goes against various forms of financial colonialism in order to preserve their own fiscal autonomy, institutions like the IMF and international credit rating agencies could drive the value of their fiat currency to the ground, but this political move becomes untenable if dollars themselves are the currency of Lebanon. Even sanctions become more difficult as well due to peer-to-peer broadcasting in blockchain-based dollars. Fiscal autonomy would normally be lost to the US under this arrangement, but the issuance and control of US-denominated stablecoins by an entity like BDL or even private actors like Tether in concert with the Lebanese government would preserve financial autonomy.

---

[7] https://steil.house.gov/media/press-releases/steil-and-hill-introduce-stable-act.

Various diverse stakeholders would have to be brought on board, including government officials, banks, and citizens. A harder problem is moving the actual economy to a blockchain-based infrastructure given the habit of the Lebanese population on relying on hard cash. First it must be noted how digital even traditional arrangements are: Normally, fiat currencies are distributed throughout the population via commercial bank deposits, where commercial banks simply provide a digital representation of deposits to the customer. A payment system is just a way to record entries on a ledger (and possibly amend them), thus authorizing, then clearing (transferring), and finally recording the settlement between the commercial bank of the consumer and the commercial bank of the merchant. The consumer uses a financial instrument given by an issuing bank over a network such as Visa (or ACH, Stripe, etc.) to move funds to a merchant bank account.

By moving to a digital dollar, this morass of complexity can be taken over by digital wallets that use the ledgers of their commercial banks to read and write value. Not only can ledgers help reduce costs and shorten the time to settlement, these new wallets can increase financial inclusion and operate as an "app," even using self-custody (where the user controls the key for spending and receiving, not a third-party server) that gives the consumer more autonomy from commercial banks, where trust is still at an all-time low. As hard cash in dollars becomes harder and harder to find, cash becomes a limit to economic growth rather than a way to escape, so a digital dollar-based stablecoin could become a very attractive alternative for citizens. The current flight of funds from Lebanon can only be stopped with a restoration of trust, and that should motivate government officials to reform the Lebanese banking system using blockchain technologies. In fact, if Lebanon can adopt these technologies to regain its position in the international financial markets, the banking sector would also be motivated by future profits from deposits to investigate these technologies. The banks would also need to be brought on board, as they would be required to help solve the problem of trusted "on and off-ramps" for conversion of digital currency to physical cash at scale, although it is possible private enterprise could provision some form of this service.

4   Conclusion

It must be noted that cryptocurrency in any form is not a silver-bullet for economic success. Indeed, what made the Lebanese economic crash of 2019 unusual was the fact that the ponzi scheme behind the crash was based on fiat currency by a globally-recognized central bank, rather than a cryptocurrency Ponzi scheme run by a dubious cast of crypto-influencers. There is a striking parallel to Lebanon's 2020 crash in the infamous crash in 2022 of the Terra algorithmic stablecoin. While traditional stablecoins like Tether are backed by at least the notional concept of reserves in cash equivalent money, algorithmic stablecoins print their own stablecoins by having their own collateral in cryptocurrency. For example, the Terra stablecoin dollars required its collateral to be held in another token called Luna, and using Luna as reserves promised incredible 20% yield, similar to how BDL offered outrageous yield for parking dollar assets at the central bank. Of course, such a scheme was bound to collapse if the underlying assets went down dramatically in price (or simply disappeared, as was the case with Lebanon). In 2022, the price of the Luna token collapsed due to a wider macro-economic downturn in the token markets, leading to the de-peg of the Terra "dollar" stablecoin from the actual US dollar. As the price of Terra's dollar stablecoin went to pennies, this in turn led to a contagion that eventually forced cryptocurrency exchanges like FTX to go bankrupt. While the collapse of the value of many altcoins finds a parallel in the lira, the reason is the same: A ponzi scheme can never last forever, regardless if a blockchain is involved.

This is not to underestimate the considerable barriers to the plan presented and the thorny problems inherent in blockchain technologies, such as regulatory and implementation challenges. Although blockchain technology is currently not illegal in Lebanon, they are not benefit from a clear legal framework. There were warnings from the now disgraced Riad Salameh on the dangers of using cybercurrencies, and while Salameh supported a CBDC for Lebanon, he warned against the use of Bitcoin, and in particular noted that "the platforms and networks used for the issuance and trading in such currencies are not subject to any laws or regulations." [8] So, one of the first steps that must be taken is to create a clear legal standing, and the lack of regulation of these technologies in Lebanon could be a boon rather than a burden. Some of the more controversial aspects of the plan, such as the complete dollarization of the Lebanese economy, would face significant legal hurdles. However, this part of the plan can be bypassed as dollars are already the *de facto* currency of Lebanon since its 2019 crisis. The complete disarray of the Lebanese economy and lack of trust in the government, as well as the increasing dollarization and digitization of the Lebanese economy on the ground, have actually created ideal times for drastic change via the adoption of blockchain technology.

Implementation of the plan in terms of coding would be best sourced to private enterprise, but via open market mechanisms based on open standards for accessing the blockchain of commercial banks rather than closed standards and calls-for-tender that could fall victim to clientelism. Of course, there is no guarantee for perfection, as has been seen in the problems facing many CBDCs that aim for financial inclusion.[9] Furthermore, out-sourcing some of the development could lead to many risks if private companies defrauded customers, which would be harder to prevent in countries such as Lebanon with relatively weak legal enforcement capabilities. Given much of the risks are from the underlying bad faith of the actors rather than the technology itself, blockchain technologies offer a way for Lebanon to re-invent itself as a financial hub.

---

[8] https://perma.cc/57JH-T5R8.

[9] (https://www.cgap.org/blog/inclusive-cbdcs-inflated-expectations-or-new-productivity.

References

1. Catalini, C., Gratry, O., Parasuraman, S., Wernerfelt, N.: The libra reserve, J Mark Hou (2019)
2. Danezis, G., Meiklejohn, S.: Centrally banked cryptocurrencies. In: NDSS (2016)
3. Dashkevich, N., Counsell, S., Destefanis, G.: Blockchain application for central banks: a systematic mapping study. IEEE Access **8**, 139918–139952 (2020)
4. Fernández-Villaverde, J., Sanches, D., Schilling, L., Uhlig, H.: Central bank digital currency: central banking for all? Rev. Econ. Dyn. **41**, 225–242 (2021)
5. George, A.L., Bennett, A.: Case studies and theory development in the social sciences. MIT Press (2005)
6. Guo, S., Kreitem, J., Moser, T.: DLT options for CBDC. J. Central Banking Theory Pract. **13**(1), 57–88 (2024)
7. Kshetri, N.: Will blockchain emerge as a tool to break the poverty chain in the global south? Third World Q. **38**(8), 1710–1732 (2017)
8. Lipton, A., Hardjono, T., Pentland, A.: Digital trade coin: towards a more stable digital currency. Roy. Soc. Open Sci. **5**(7), 180155 (2018)
9. Ponsot, J.-F., Rizkallah, S.: Dollarization in Lebanon. Int. J. Polit. Econ. **53**(4), 473–491 (2024)

Smart Social Contracts for Public Accountability: Blockchain Oracles and Verifiable Governance

Cristina Carata[1,2]([✉]), Kimberley Cheung[1], Adam Hamilton-Smith[1], and William J. Knottenbelt[1]

[1] Imperial College London, London, UK
{c.carata19,kimberley.cheung24,adam.hamilton-smith24,
w.knottenbelt}@imperial.ac.uk
[2] National Institute for Research & Development in Informatics - ICI Bucharest, Bucharest, Romania

Abstract. Since the emergence of bitcoin, cryptocurrencies and the blockchain technology that underpins these virtual currencies have experienced a rapid growth, with a plethora of applications emerging. While most popular applications of blockchain technology are in the business field, its main features, such as decentralization or enhanced security, make it suitable to redesign social, cultural and political realities such as the social contract that regulates the relationship between states and citizens. In blockchain economy, the concept of "trust" is redefined as a computable and verifiable property and not as a social assumption. The present paper extends the concept of smart social contracts— a hybrid instrument that encodes public sector obligations into programmable logic— by introducing the essential role of decentralized oracle networks, which enables these contracts to interact with real-world data. The aim of the article is to explore the way in which smart social contracts, powered by consensus-based oracles, can build a new architecture for public accountability by automatically allocating funds or enforcing conditions based on externally validated milestones. To illustrate the concept, we present CivicXChain, a case study involving enhancing environmental accountability in public governance through smart contracts, oracle networks, and citizen engagement. By bringing together formal social theory with decentralized computation, the present paper contributes to the mathematics of trust and proposes a framework for verifiable governance.

Keywords: smart social contract · blockchain oracles · public governance · e-government · digital transformation

1 Introduction

Over the past decades, public governance reform has taken place in different forms and at different paces around the globe. The stated purpose of these reforms was to improve the provision of public services by understanding and respecting the needs of citizens, which

W. Knottenbelt et al. (Eds.): Blocktea 2025, LNICST 669, pp. 144–154, 2026.
https://doi.org/10.1007/978-3-032-12335-0_9

are the ultimate beneficiaries of these public services. Increasingly, the term "reform in public administration" has involved the integration of technology in order to improve efficiency and service quality.

A key driver in the inclusion of technology in the modernization strategy is the rapid technological change experienced in their lives by citizens of all communities. However, digital transformation in terms of public governance is still an ambiguous term that is not used consistently, even by experts [1]. Government organizations have been incorporating technology in their activity for many decades, beginning in the 1970s. Currently, the digitization of government is a complex and dynamic process, with implications that will take decades to be fully understood and that is continuously adapting to external technological developments, reflecting successive changes from "e-government" to "digital government" and, finally, to "algorithmic governance" [2].

Recent cutting-edge technologies, such as artificial intelligence or blockchain, have proved high potential in supporting participatory governance, providing means for high transparency and inclusion in decision-making processes. Among these new technologies, blockchain is the one that stands out for the ability to redefine public administrations operations by providing a secure and decentralized framework for data management. Due to a DLT-type architecture, blockchain is considered to be a tool capable of improving trust in inter-institutional relations and optimizing the efficiency of administrative processes. This technology bases its transformative potential on three fundamental features: data sharing, direct data exchange between users (peer-to-peer), and immutable storage capacity, which ensures traceability and transparency of shared information. Thus, various scenarios are explored through which blockchain technology could reduce the intermediary role of public administrations, thus facilitating direct interactions between citizens and institutions. At the same time, blockchain can be used to implement efficient end-to-end processes that cross institutional boundaries and provide continuity in the delivery of public services [3]. As such, we can consider that technology is an unavoidable tool for government reform.

An additional step for development with the help of technology can be represented by the smart social contract [4]. In this context, blockchain oracles play a key role, being able to serve as a connector between real-world data and smart contracts, hence ensuring the accuracy of information. Thus, this article aims to analyze these challenges and argue why smart social contracts represent a necessary step in the modernization of public administration through the integration of emerging technologies.

The remainder of the paper is organized as follows: Sect. 2 presents a brief literature review, showing insights of all major works related to the subject of social contract and smart contracts as well as blockchain oracles. In Sect. 3, we explain how blockchain oracles, the "bridge" that adds real-life data to blockchain architectures, can enhance the novel concept of smart social contract, a concept that unifies the social contract and smart contract, resulting in a digital instrument for overseeing the convention between a government and its citizens. We also discuss the need of integrating real-life data in the smart social contract. As a case study, in Sect. 4, we present CivicXChain, a novel blockchain-based platform that addresses the challenge of environmental accountability in public governance systems. The final Sect. 5 concludes the paper.

2 Literature Review

2.1 Philosophical and Legal Origins of the Social Contract

The ideology behind the state as we know it today has its foundations on the philosophical concept of the "social contract". The relationship between the state, its citizens and the law has been intriguing since ancient times: among the first mentions of a "social contract" are found in Plato's "Criton" Dialogue and "The Republic" and Aristotle's works, like "Politics" or "Nicomachean Ethics". In Plato's work, the concept of a social contract was seen as a necessity for providing common good and securing order in society. Aristotle had a different view on the social contract: not a deliberate agreement between individuals and the state, but rather a natural consequence of relationships between individuals [4]. The modern social contract theory and the best description of the relationship between the state, its citizens and the laws began to emerge in the Renaissance period and is found in the works of Thomas Hobbes, John Locke or Jean-Jacques Rousseau. Thomas Hobbes's 1651 original work, "Leviathan," stands as a prime example of social contract theory, in which individuals surrender their freedoms to an absolute sovereign in exchange for security and order, thereby escaping the anarchic state of nature. John Locke's theory of the social contract can be found in his 1689 work and envisions a consensual agreement to form a government that protects natural rights (such as life, liberty, and property) and has the authority to rule deriving from the consent of the governed. Another theorist of the social contract – and perhaps the best known of all – was Jean Jacques Rousseau. His theory of the social contract can be best described as a vision of collective self-rule, in which individuals, by entering into a mutual agreement, subordinate their private wills to the general will and thereby constitute a sovereign body politic based on liberty, equality, and the common good [4].

2.2 Computational Trust, Blockchain Oracles, and Smart Contract Applications

In the digital context, trust is not presumed but enforced through technical mechanisms such as cryptographic proofs, verifiable computation, and decentralized consensus. Smart contracts operate in "trust-minimized" environments, where the credibility of contractual execution does not depend on institutional intermediaries but on deterministic code, as described by Szabo [5]. More recently, Goldfeder et al. [6] and Bonneau et al. [7] discuss how trust can be redistributed through cryptographic like zero-knowledge proofs, secure multi-party computation, and decentralized oracle networks, which ensure that external data is trustworthy without requiring a central authority. As such, trust becomes verifiable code and not an implicit belief in the moral authority of the state. One of the most recent theoreticians of the modern social contract, Primavera de Filippi, resumes in her work "Blockchain and the law" the interplay between blockchain technology, legal systems and social contracts in the Web3 era. The paper argues that blockchain has the potential to change the traditional social contract between individuals and institutions by providing a transparent platform for governance and the legal system [4].

Moving forward, the smart social contract concept merges the principle of the traditional social contract theory with the capabilities offered by smart contracts. This concept recently proposed in literature aims to redefine the relationship between governments and citizens by automating agreements, increasing transparency and increasing accountability. Carata et al. [4] define the smart social contract as a digital agreement that is automatically executed once the predetermined criteria are met and accepted by all the parties involved, namely citizens and representatives of the public authority. The digitization of these agreements allows both the fulfillment of obligations in a transparent and autonomous way and also the reduction of the need for manual supervision, minimizing in this way the risk of error or abuse.

The crossroad between the smart contracts and the field of public administration has been discussed also in the specialized literature, mainly due to the hypothetical potential to increase transparency, accountability and efficiency in public administration. Research has highlighted that these types of contracts can automate complex workflows, reduce administrative burdens and also ensure compliance with regulatory requirements. For example, Omohundro [8] shows how smart contracts can be used in digital government in order to optimize diverse processes such as tax collection, distribution of social benefits or voting. However, some challenges remain, particularly in ensuring the accuracy of external data and also addressing the legal and ethical implications of the automated decisions.

Regarding blockchain oracles, recent specialized literature is paying more and more attention to this topic, especially regarding their main role in facilitating the interaction between smart contracts and real-world events.

Oracles act as intermediaries that enable the integration of external data into blockchain systems, crucial to the operation of smart contracts. This feature makes them indispensable for the implementation of the "smart social contracts" as contracts that aim to improve public governance.

Blockchain oracles can be assimilated as tools for public administration reform, due to the increase of efficiency and reliability of various administrative processes. Blockchain technology and oracles have the potential to redefine the relationship between citizens and public institutions mainly due to their ability to provide secure, immutable and decentralized data management [9]. Thus, blockchain oracles are digital intermediaries that retrieve, authenticate, and transmit external data to blockchain networks. At the same time, they solve the inherent limitations of blockchains, which, by their intrinsec architecture, cannot access external data directly. Al-Breiki et al. [10] classify oracles according to their functionality, distinguishing between input oracles (which obtain external data) and output oracles (which transmit data from the blockchain to external systems). These mechanisms ensure the accuracy and reliability of the data used to trigger the execution of smart contracts, making oracles a mainstay of blockchain applications. Blockchain oracles are essential for the implementation of smart contracts and especially smart social contracts, especially in the field of governance and public administration due to the fact that they allow the automation of complex administrative workflows and improve the quality of public services. Examples may include verifying eligibility to vote, automating the distribution of social benefits and ensuring compliance with regulatory requirements [11]. Decentralized oracle networks do not eliminate trust but distribute it among multiple independent data providers. This contrasts with the traditional governance systems, where a single authority maintains data monopolies. Instead of replacing trust, smart social contracts diversify it. In specialized literature, ensuring trust in the data sources of blockchain oracles is considered a major challenge associated with oracles. Although blockchains inherently offer transparency and immutability, the reliability of oracles depends on the accuracy of the external data they transmit. Additionally to the above-mentioned, Hileman and Rauchs [12] emphasize the importance of robust data certification and governance mechanisms in order to ensure the credibility of the information provided by oracles. Different solutions for oracles were analyzed according to their applicability in various cases (Chainlink, Band Protocol and Oraclize). For example, Chainlink uses decentralized networks of oracles to aggregate data from multiple sources and ensure in this manner accuracy through consensus mechanisms. It has been proven highly effective in areas such as financial markets and supply chains, but their application in governance remains an emerging field [10].

3   Verifiable Governance: Smart Social Contracts and the Role of Blockchain Oracles

The concept of "smart social contract" was introduced in the specialized literature in 2023 [4] and it combines principles both from smart contracts and social contracts. The goal is to establish a new digital system that aims to automatically manage agreements between citizens and governments. In this type of digital setup, the new contract automatically activates once specific criteria, agreed by the citizens, are fulfilled. This system enhances transparency and efficiency, with the potential to build public trust in government services and reduce misconduct. One distinctive aspect of a smart social contract is the digitalization of its terms, which were previously implicit, allowing obligations to be met transparently and automatically, without the need for intermediaries. This setup boosts procedural efficiency by removing manual oversight and ensuring that standards are consistently followed [4].

3.1   The Oracle Layer: Connecting Blockchains to the Real World

Smart social contracts operate based on the principle of trust decentralization, not on the principle of trust elimination. In this context, the role of blockchain oracles is not removing the need for verification, but that of mitigating the power asymmetries by sourcing data from multiple and independent actors, rather than relying on a single authoritative entity. This shifts the governance model from a centralized control of data (where verification is monopolised by only one institution) to a distributed verification framework, where consensus is reached among diverse participants. In this way, oracles reduce the risk of unilateral manipulation and increase systemic resilience. Given that blockchain systems are, by design, isolated from the real world, smart social contracts depend on external data streams to reflect empirical realities. Decentralized oracle networks enable this integration by aggregating information from sources that are heterogeneous, ensuring that no single actor can distort the decision-making process without detection by other nodes in the verification ecosystem.

In other words, blockchain oracles are digital third-party agents that aim to bring information from the outside world into a blockchain, working as a bridge. Data from various sources (e.g., weather services, news, banking systems, political events etc.) is then sent to the blockchain as transactional data. It is important to note that a blockchain oracle is not the data source itself, but rather the layer that verifies, and authenticates external data sources and then relays that information. Smart contract execution depends on this fundamental information, where they are invoked when predetermined conditions are met. Conditions can include any kind of data, such as successful payments, temperature readings, or price fluctuations [9]. As such, a blockchain-oracle workflow is typically executed between three types of participants, namely: data providers, oracle nodes/network operators, and blockchain operators. Data flow providers enable various web APIs and communication interfaces to read and provide data from various online data sources. Node operators enable certification policies to transfer highly accurate, relevant and trusted data to blockchain systems [9].

3.2 The Role of Real-World Data Integration in Enabling Smart Social Contracts.

The need for real-world data integration is critical to the operational logic of smart social contracts, as it enables them to react to empirical events and conditions. Otherwise, without such data, they would be "isolated" in a closed system unable to engage with the systems they aim to govern [7]. The data entered through blockchain oracles lead to real-time automation of governance processes, such as monitoring government commitments. For example, smart social contracts can track the fulfillment of government promises by tying specific milestones, such as building schools or developing infrastructure, to pre-set contractual conditions [4]. This layer of verification is essential to maintain the reliability and legitimacy of automated public processes, especially in environments with limited institutional trust.

Enhanced transparency when it comes to public spending can be considered one of the most transformative applications of smart contracts that are powered by data provided by oracles. By encoding conditional fund releases into programmable logic, smart contracts can minimize discretionary corruption and delay. Thus, if public budgets are connected to social smart contracts, their funds can be released automatically upon completion of predefined terms. For example, the completion of a road construction project, verified by satellite data for example, can trigger payments to contractors or rewards to the public administration. Opposite to this, failing to complete in time can lead to fines or even resignation from public duties.

Another facility offered by blockchain oracles is the real-time tracking of government promises. For example, election promises to build schools or provide medical facilities can be integrated into smart social contracts. Project data (such as construction progress or availability of medical services) provided by independent oracles ensures that these promises are kept. This increases public trust and accountability in governance It can thus be stated that smart social contracts that are powered by data provided through oracles have the potential to revolutionize the decision-making process in public administration.

4 Case Study: CivicXChain

Traditional environmental governance systems suffer from significant accountability deficits, which undermine the effective implementation of public policies. More than once, public officials make ambitious environmental commitments during their electoral campaigns. The absence of transparent monitoring mechanisms and enforceable consequences and incentive rewards often leads to unfulfilled promises and damaging public trust. Moreover, citizens also have limited methods to hold officials accountable for specific targets. This accountability crisis is more serious in urban environments as environmental degradation directly impacts public health.When talking about public policies, fields such as urban environmental policy implementation often suffer from both limited data transparency and insufficient mechanisms for verification and accountability. Although public officials may define some quantifiable objectives (for example, lowering unhealthy PM2.5 levels or expanding green urban zones) citizens frequently lack the access to real-time and reliable data that track these declared goals. The monitoring infrastructures that do exist are either fragmented, resource-constrained, or not interoperable with public digital systems. All of the above result in a trust deficit that compromises an effective governance and the civic engagement.

CivicXChain is a case study for the present paper which consists of a novel blockchain-based platform that addresses the challenge of environmental accountability in public governance systems. The platform is a blockchain-based accountability framework that enforces environmental policy commitments through smart contracts and oracle-based verification [19, 20]. The platform involves three types of actors: the public officials (who stake funds against the measurable environmental commitments), citizens (who monitor the environmental initiatives), and adjudicators (the trusted third-party group responsible for dispute resolution and manual verification when the automation process is inconclusive). The smart contracts encode specific policy targets (e.g., a 10% increase in the urban canopy coverage until a given date). Then, the decentralized oracles collect and validate the supporting data. If the commitment is met, rewards are unlocked; if not, penalties are automatically triggered. CivicXChain uses a modular contract architecture, with functions for commitment creation, oracle validation, and conditional rewards. The implementation follows Solidity best practices using OpenZeppelin security libraries.

The operational workflow for CivicXChain follows a four-stage sequence. The first one regards commitment encoding. As such, a public official creates a smart contract on the Ethereum blockchain, staking ETH and defining a measurable target (e.g., maintain average PM2.5 levels below 35 µg/m3 for six consecutive months). The smart contract creation process involves the main CivicXChain Governance contract in which the officials call the "createCommitment" function with their environmental targets. The encoding process validates the input parameters using two require statements. The first one requires the deadline to be in the future and the second one requires that the stake amount must be more than zero.

The second stage regards data collection and verification. Decentralized oracle networks (e.g., Chainlink) collect environmental data from sources like OpenAQ or NASA satellite imagery [21]. After the collection, the oracles aggregate and submit the processed data to the smart social contract. Following this step, the system employs a custom EnvironmentalDataOracle contract that provides the blockchain oracle compatible data feeds for key environmental metrics that include PM2.5 air pollution level or Air Quality index values and forest coverage percentages. Also, a live oracle updater service retrieves real environmental data from external sources in a continuous action. The updater operates at regular intervals, processing the API responses before recording it to the blockchain oracle. The frontend implements a React hook that reads live data from oracle contracts through standard blockchain interfaces. Oracle data verification occurs through automated comparison of environmental values against commitment thresholds, enabling real-time fulfillment tracking for environmental commitments. Each metric is stored with timestamp and verification status for a comprehensive environmental monitoring.

In the third stage, if the contract terms are met by the deadline, the officials receive their staked ETH plus a bonus. If the target is not met, the funds are redistributed (e.g., to community environmental funds or returned to treasury). The resolution mechanism is implemented through the claimEnvironmentalReward function which includes validation checks: only commitment creators can claim: commitments must be active, rewards cannot be claimed twice, and deadlines must not have passed. Successful resolutions transfer ETH with a 150% return. The platform currently supports flexible staking, where public officials can commit any amount ≥ 0 ETH. This design choice reflects the early stage of the project and aims to remain inclusive. Determining optimal staking levels will require empirical testing with real users—an avenue we identify for future research. The 50% bonus reward is a design suggestion which is grounded in incentive compatibility principles from game theory. It aims to balance motivation and risk. However, this parameter is subject to empirical validation in future field deployments and may evolve based on stakeholder feedback.

The final stage consists of the manual arbitration (fallback) that takes place in the case of conflicting oracle data or unavailable metrics. In that case, an adjudication panel reviews evidence and resolves the dispute manually via multisig governance.

CivicXChain addresses the challenges through a blockchain platform that involves three participation levels in order to create a comprehensive environmental ecosystem. The first panel is for public officials in which officials stake ETH when creating measurable commitments. The ETH staking mechanism uses payable functions where officials send ETH direclty with their commitment creation. Chainlink oracles can automatically verify achievement through real-time environmental data. If it is successful then ETH can be returned with a 50% bonus, for example. In case of failure, the stake ammount will be forfeit. Another panel is for citizens; they can participate in environmental projects such as tree planting and waste cleanup. They need to submit proof of their actions and verified contributions in order to earn rewards. An independent judge panel is also created in order to manually review and verifiy both citizen project submissions and public official commitments when automated verification is not possible to ensure accurate assessment of environmental contributions.

CivicXChain consists of these three main components that work together: smart contracts, oracle network, and web interface. The smart contract is written in Solidity and deployed on Ethereum blockchain in order to handle commitments, ETH staking, and reward/penalty execution. Chainlink oracles fetch real-time environmental data from external sources and feed it to the smart contracts. Real-time air quality monitoring data are obtained from governmental agencies and open data platforms (e.g. OpenAQ) and forest coverage and land use data are obtained from satellite imagery providence (e.g. NASA) for tracking deforestation and reforestation commitments. The frontend user interface is built using Next.js 15 framework with React for UI components and TypeScript. Key technical components include wallet integration in which MetaMask connects through Wagmi hooks to enable seamless blockchain interaction with automatic network detection as well as transaction management, real-time data display in which react components fetch live environmental data from oracles and external APIs, role-based access control, rewards and penalty interface as well as transaction management.

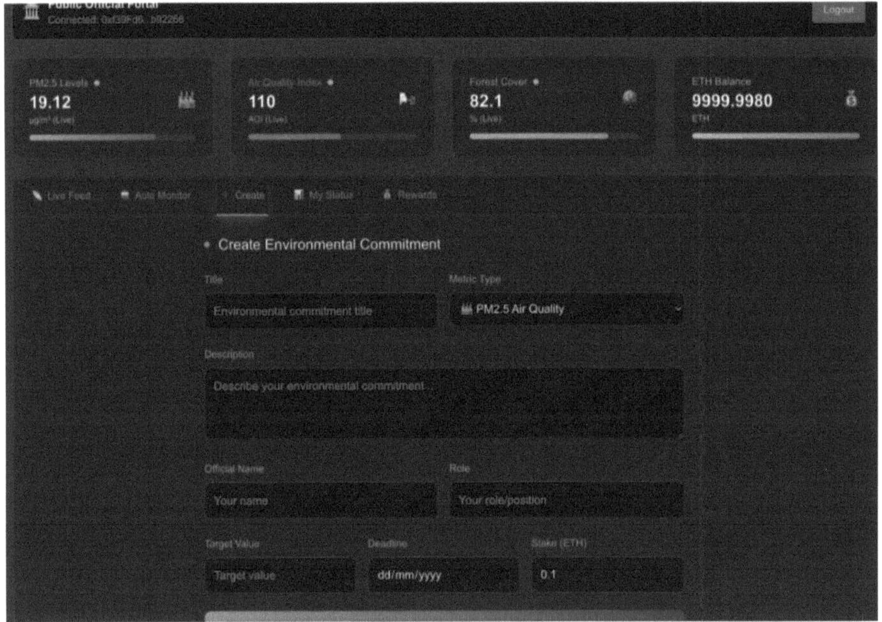

Fig. 1. CivicXChain Dashboard

In addition, the platform implements security measures including using OpenZeppelin's tested security patterns to prevent common attacks like reentrancy and unauthorized access. Access controls ensure only commitmentcreators can claim rewards or cancel their commitments. The contract inherits from OpenZeppelin contracts in which Ownable for access control and ReentrancyGuard for reentrancy protection. The system implements input validation through require statements checking deadline validity as well as ETH stake amount requirements. The contracts use Solidity mappings for efficient data storage in which commitments mapping stores all commitment data, oracleData tracks environmental measurements, and officialCommitments links addresses to their commitments. The system maintains commitment state through boolean flags (isActive, isFulfilled, rewardClaimed) ensuring proper ETH staking lifecycle management. These components work together to create a comprehensive security system that allow access control, state management, attack prevention, data integrity and user protection (Fig. 1).

CivicXChain demonstrates how blockchain technology can foster transparent, accountable governance especially in the area of environmental sustainability. This approach also demonstrates broader potential for blockchain-based governance beyond environmental policy. The same accountability mechanisms could address public infrastructure projects, education outcomes and other areas where traditional oversight has proven insufficient, and thus,this can transform governance across multiple sectors.

5 Conclusions

The concept of "smart social contract" is a novel one in literature regarding e-governance. It unifies concepts from both the social contract and the smart contract, resulting in an enhanced digital instrument that oversees the convention between public servants and citizens. Upon the achievement of predetermined conditions, such as the fulfillment of an obligation by a local government official, the smart social contract is capable of automatic execution. In this manner, the government-citizen agreement can be realized more efficient and transparent, and such, an elevated level of trust of citizens in public services can be reached. Smart social contracts that are enhanced with real-world data with the help of blockchain oracles can represent an even bigger step forward in modernizing public governance.

However, the widespread adoption of these contracts is not without its challenges. The reliability of the data sources, the scalability of the blockchain infrastructure or the interoperability between different platforms constitute aspects that require attention and must be analyzed in detail in future studies. In addition, we consider necessary a robust legal framework that addresses all the ethical and legal implications of automated decisions generated by such contracts.

References

1. Gasco Hernandez, M.: Reflections on three decades of digital transformation in local governments. Local Govern. Stud. **50**(6), 1028–1040 (2024). https://doi.org/10.1080/03003930.2024.2410830
2. Dunleavy, P., Margetts, H.: Data science, artificial intelligence and the third wave of digital era governance. Public Policy Admin. (2023). https://doi.org/10.1177/09520767231198737
3. Brinkmann, M., Heine, M.: The implementation of new public governance through blockchain: A Delphi-based analysis. In: Proceedings of the 15th International Conference on Theory and Practice of Electronic Governance (ICEGOV 2022), pp. 1–9. ACM (2022). https://doi.org/10.1145/3560107.3560108
4. Carata, C., Knottenbelt, W., Malinoiu, V.: Governance in the blockchain era: the smart social contract. In: Proceedings of the 25th Annual International Conference on Digital Government Research (2024)
5. Szabo, N.: The idea of smart contracts. Unpublished manuscript (1997). https://www.fon.hum.uva.nl/rob/Courses/InformationInSpeech/CDROM/Literature/LOTwinterschool2006/szabo.best.vwh.net/idea.html

6. Zhang, F., Maram, D., Malvai, H., Goldfeder, S., Juels, A.: DECO: liberating web data using decentralized oracles for TLS. In: Proceedings of the 2020 ACM SIGSAC Conference on Computer and Communications Security, pp. 1919–1938. ACM (2020). https://doi.org/10.1145/3372297.3417239
7. Bonneau, J., Miller, A., Clark, J., Narayanan, A., Kroll, J.A., Felten, E.W.: SoK: research perspectives and challenges for bitcoin and cryptocurrencies. In: 2015 IEEE Symposium on Security and Privacy, San Jose, 17–21 May 2015, pp. 104–121 (2015). https://doi.org/10.1109/SP.2015.14
8. Omohundro, S.M.: Cryptocurrencies, smart contracts, and artificial intelligence. AI Matters **1**(2), 19–21 (2014). https://doi.org/10.1145/2685328.2685334
9. Ezzat, S.K., Saleh, Y.N.M., Abdel-Hamid, A.A.: Blockchain oracles: state-of-the-art and research directions. IEEE Access **10**, 67551–67572 (2022). https://doi.org/10.1109/ACCESS.2022.3184726
10. Al-Breiki, H., Rehman, M.H.U., Salah, K., Svetinovic, D.: Trustworthy blockchain oracles: review, comparison, and open research challenges. IEEE Access **8**, 85675–85685 (2020). https://doi.org/10.1109/ACCESS.2020.2992698
11. Cardelli, L., Gordon, A.D., Paterson, G.: Digital social contracts (2020). arXiv preprint. https://arxiv.org/pdf/2005.06261
12. Hileman, G., Rauchs, M.: Global blockchain benchmarking study. SSRN Electron. J. (2017). https://ssrn.com/abstract=3040224
13. Polcumpally, A.T., Pandey, K.K., Kumar, A., Samadhiya, A.: Blockchain governance and trust: a multi-sector thematic systematic review and exploration of future research directions. Heliyon **10**, e32975 (2024). https://doi.org/10.1016/j.heliyon.2024.e32975
14. Naef, S., Wagner, S.M., Saur, C.: Blockchain and network governance: learning from applications in the supply chain sector. Prod. Plan. Control **35**(9), 932–946 (2024). https://doi.org/10.1080/09537287.2023.2229729
15. Rehman, E., Khan, M.A., Soomro, T.R., Taleb, N., Afifi, M.A., Ghazal, T.M.: Using blockchain to ensure trust between donor agencies and NGOs in under-developed countries. Computers **10**(1), 98 (2021). https://doi.org/10.3390/computers10010098
16. Ortega-Rodríguez, C., Licerán-Gutiérrez, A., Moreno-Albarracín, A.L.: Transparency as a key element in accountability in non-profit organizations: a systematic literature review. Sustainability **12**(14), 5834 (2020). https://doi.org/10.3390/su12145834
17. Nairi, C., Cicioğlu, M., Çalhan, A.: Smart blockchain networks: revolutionizing donation tracking in the Web 3.0. Comput. Commun. **228**, 107972 (2024). https://doi.org/10.1016/j.comcom.2023.107972
18. Mammadzada, K., Iqbal, M., Milani, F., García-Bañuelos, L., Matulevičius, R.: Blockchain oracles: a framework for blockchain-based applications. In: Asatiani, A., et al. (ed.) Business Process Management: Blockchain and Robotic Process Automation Forum. BPM 2020. Lecture Notes in Business Information Processing, vol. 393. Springer, Cham (2020). https://doi.org/10.1007/978-3-030-58779-6_2
19. Ethereum Foundation. Ethereum developer documentation. https://ethereum.org/en/developers/docs/. Accessed 20 July 2025
20. OpenZeppelin. OpenZeppelin Contracts: governance. https://docs.openzeppelin.com/contracts/5.x/governance/. Accessed 20 July 2025
21. Chainlink. Chainlink data feeds. https://docs.chain.link/data-feeds/. Accessed 20 July 2025

Applications

PolyIDns: A Blockchain-Based Solution for Decentralized Domain Management

Alessandro Marcelletti, Leonardo Migliorelli, and Andrea Morichetta[✉]

University of Camerino, Camerino, Italy
`{alessandro.marcelletti,andrea.morichetta}@unicam.it,`
`leonardo.migliorelli@studenti.unicam.it`

Abstract. The Domain Name System (DNS) is a key part of the Internet that translates human-readable domain names into numerical IP addresses, allowing computers to locate and communicate with each other. However, DNS systems have issues in multiple aspects. They suffer from security vulnerabilities, making them susceptible to various attacks. The hierarchical structure of DNS creates critical points of failure, while the use of centralized registrars introduces issues related to domain ownership and control. These limitations advocate for alternative approaches. The advent of blockchain enables the creation of novel systems, eliminating central authorities while providing direct and secure interactions. Integrating blockchain technology with DNS can address many of the shortcomings of traditional systems. The nature of blockchain can eliminate single points of failure and prevent unauthorized changes to domain information, allowing users to ensure their ownership of the domain. This paper proposes PolyIDns, a blockchain-based DNS system, offering a secure, decentralized, and user-owned solution. PolyIDns leverages blockchain to ensure secure storage and querying of domain names. By integrating smart contracts, it enables users to register, update, and transfer domains while maintaining full ownership, without relying on third parties. PolyIDns was implemented on the Polygon blockchain and evaluated in terms of costs.

Keywords: Blockchain · Domain Name System · Polygon · Decentralization · Smart Contracts · Web3

1 Introduction

The Domain Name System (DNS) is a critical Internet infrastructure that translates human-readable domain names (like example.com) into numerical IP addresses. Established in 1983, DNS operates as a hierarchical, distributed database managed by domain registrars and registry operators who control domain registration under specific Top-Level Domains (TLDs). Despite its importance, traditional DNS faces significant challenges. Security vulnerabilities plague DNS due to weak verification mechanisms, making it susceptible to

W. Knottenbelt et al. (Eds.): Blocktea 2025, LNICST 669, pp. 157–173, 2026.
https://doi.org/10.1007/978-3-032-12335-0_10

cache poisoning, DNS spoofing, and phishing attacks [23]. These vulnerabilities stem from limited encryption and authentication, creating security risks for users and organizations. Additionally, its hierarchical structure creates points of failure, with root and TLD servers vulnerable to DDoS attacks that can impact global internet accessibility, as demonstrated by previous incidents targeting root servers [26]. Another concerning aspect is the reliance on centralized registrars, which introduces issues related to domain user control. Registrars possess the authority to deny registration or seize existing domain names, enabling censorship. The subscription model requires ongoing payments to maintain ownership, while all domain updates must pass through these intermediaries, limiting users' direct control, raising questions about true domain ownership and creating potential conflicts between domain owners and registration authorities. These fundamental limitations have prompted researchers and developers to explore alternative approaches to preserve DNS functionalities while addressing its weaknesses.

In this context, blockchain technology offers critical improvements for DNS systems [14,15]. By distributing domain records across a network of nodes, it eliminates central points of failure, enhancing resilience against DDoS attacks and censorship [26]. Cryptographic verification mechanisms provide tamper-proof and verifiable domain records, reducing vulnerabilities like cache poisoning [15,24]. Smart contracts enable trustless domain management without intermediaries [18], while immutable ledgers create transparent audit trails of all domain-related transactions. Most importantly, blockchain enables novel ownership models where domains become permanent digital assets without ongoing fees or registrar dependencies [9,13]. While several blockchain-based DNS solutions have emerged, many face challenges with domain ownership, existing infrastructure integration, and registrar dependency. Some maintain centralized components or registrars, compromising decentralization; others struggle with scalability; and many fail to integrate with existing DNS infrastructure, creating adoption barriers [21,25].

For this reason, we propose PolyIDns, a blockchain-based DNS system for decentralized domain management. Our solution enables comprehensive domain lifecycle management while fundamentally shifting ownership from registrars to users through blockchain-secured smart contracts. This transforms domains from temporary leases into permanent digital assets that users own without recurring fees or third-party dependencies. Domain owners can directly create and modify DNS records, transfer ownership, and manage their digital presence, all cryptographically verified and secured on the blockchain. This approach offers significant benefits: by eliminating intermediaries, PolyIDns protects against censorship and arbitrary domain seizures, ensuring users maintain complete control over their online identities without fear of unexpected domain confiscation or content restrictions. The system bridges the gap with the traditional DNS standard by maintaining compatibility with existing DNS record types (A, AAAA, MX, CNAME, TXT) and integrating with traditional DNS infrastructure for seamless adoption. By distributing domain records across the blockchain network, PolyIDns eliminates central points of failure and provides resilience against DDoS attacks. We implemented this solution on the Polygon blockchain to leverage its performance and cost efficiency while maintaining Ethereum compatibility. The implemented solution was evaluated in terms of economic sustainability and practical feasibility for real-world deployment.

The remainder of the paper is organized as follows. Section 2 provides an overview of traditional DNS systems and blockchain. Section 3 examines existing blockchain-based DNS solutions. Sections 4 and 5 detail the design and implementation of PolyIDns, including smart contract design and query resolution mechanisms. Section 6 presents an evaluation of the system's costs. Finally, Sect. 7 summarizes our contributions and discusses future research directions.

2   Background

To introduce the main concepts behind PolyIDns, here we first give an overview of traditional DNS systems, focusing then on the Polygon blockchain.

2.1   Domain Name System

DNS employs a hierarchical architecture starting with the root domain (represented by ".."), where root servers direct queries to appropriate TLD servers (.com, .org), followed by Second-Level Domains and subdomains [27]. The system utilizes several essential record types to fulfill different networking needs, including: (I) A records for IPv4 addresses [28], (II) AAAA records for IPv6 addresses [29], (III) MX records for email routing [28], and (IV) CNAME (canonical name) records for domain aliases [28]. DNS allows for domain registration operations, where users obtain rights to specific domains through registrars that mediate between users and central registries. This process involves selecting a registration period, providing contact information, and maintaining ownership through periodic renewals to maintain ownership. DNS resolution begins when a stub resolver on a user's device queries a local DNS resolver. The resolver either returns cached information immediately or proceeds with resolution, either by providing addresses of higher-level servers (iterative resolution) or by completing the entire query process itself (recursive resolution), balancing efficiency with comprehensive name resolution.

2.2   Polygon: A Layer 2 Scaling Solution

Polygon [17] represents a comprehensive Layer 2 scaling solution designed to address Ethereum's limitations while preserving its security guarantees and ecosystem benefits. As a framework for building and connecting Ethereum-compatible blockchain networks, Polygon offers developers the tools to create scalable decentralized applications. **Polygon zkEVM** [1] is a Zero-Knowledge Ethereum Virtual Machine that leverages zero-knowledge proofs to validate transactions, enhancing privacy and reducing computational requirements while maintaining full compatibility with existing Ethereum smart contracts. As a Layer 2 solution, it processes transactions off the Ethereum mainnet while periodically committing transaction batches to Ethereum for security. This approach allows Polygon to address Ethereum's scalability challenges while maintaining security and compatibility with the Ethereum ecosystem. This architecture enables Polygon to achieve significant performance improvements over the Ethereum mainnet related to high throughput, low transaction costs, and fast finality.

Polygon zkEVM was chosen as the underlying implementation of PolyIDns for two main reasons. First, it ensures compatibility with EVM-based platforms, enabling the development of diverse custom implementations. Second, it offers optimized performance, addressing the scalability challenges inherent in blockchain infrastructure.

3   State of the Art

Blockchain-based DNS solutions aim to decentralize domain name management, offering alternatives to traditional DNS systems. This section provides an overview of existing solutions, highlighting their key features and limitations.

Namecoin [8] is the first blockchain-based DNS solution, relying on a Bitcoin fork to deal with scalability issues. It only manages '.bit' TLDs, providing functionalities for their registration, transfer, and update. It faces challenges, including using a custom fork, resulting in a small network and low adoption. Requires periodic renewals to maintain ownership, undermining direct control of the domain that could be removed. Blockstack Naming Service (BNS) [11], originally built on Bitcoin, employs virtualchains for scalability and an off-chain decentralized storage. In detail, the off-chain storage keeps DNS records while the blockchain provides all functionalities for their management (e.g., creation, transfer, and update). BNS allows for custom TLDs and relies on a two-phase commit process to prevent name stealing. However, it heavily relies on off-chain components and requires a 24-hour registration waiting period. Ethereum Name Service (ENS) [20] simplifies Ethereum wallet addresses into human-readable '.eth' names through a system of registry, resolvers, and registrar components. It fundamentally differs from DNS in both purpose and scope, functioning primarily as a naming service for blockchain resources rather than serving as a true DNS alternative. Handshake [12] is a proprietary PoW system focused on replacing Certificate Authorities. It uses Bitcoin-NG for improved throughput, offering custom TLD creation through auctions. Despite its innovative approach, Handshake faces significant challenges due to poor integration with existing DNS infrastructure, small network size, and security compromises from its Bitcoin-NG implementation. Unstoppable Domains [9,10], built on Polygon, offers an NFT-based solution providing permanent domain control. While it integrates with cryptocurrency wallets and supports IPFS-hosted websites, it lacks traditional DNS record support (A, AAAA, MX, CNAME) and uses proprietary TLDs like '.crypto'. With limited DNS integration, it functions more as an ENS alternative than a comprehensive DNS replacement, focusing primarily on decentralized applications rather than traditional web hosting. B-DNS [23] is a PoS-based system offering DNS services with traditional DNS compatibility. Despite B-DNS's reliance on registrars for domain management and potential revocation undermines decentralization. Also, it lacks custom TLD support. Blockzone [30] combines a proprietary PBFT consensus-based blockchain with external storage. While Blockzone aims at improving the system's security, it lacks custom TLD support and its external storage dependencies that introduce centralization and DDoS risks that compromise its decentralization purposes. D^{3}NS [16] combines Bitcoin with Distributed Hash Tables (DHT) for DNS record storage, offering DNS protocol compatibility with public key verification and domain direct management. However the system lacks custom TLD support and inherits Bitcoin's fundamental scalability limitations. 3DNS [3–6] operates on Ethereum's Optimism layer 2 solution. It implements NFT-based domains with lower fees than mainnet Ethereum and on-chain storage of domain information. However, it requires registrars like Superchain Identity [7] and restriction of third-levels to specific TLDs (.chain.box and .super.box) limits flexibility. DNSLedger [19] employs a multi-chain architecture for TLD management. It provides compatibility with legacy DNS systems and support for both blockchain-based and traditional DNS infrastructures. However, DNSLedger relies on external storage for DNS zone files, introducing significant off-chain data dependencies, leading to data integrity and availability risks.

Comparative Analysis. Here we provide a comparison of the described blockchain-based DNS solutions across key dimensions: support for custom TLDs, ownership[1] model, integration with traditional DNS, and employed blockchain. Table 1 reports the comparison, summarizing noteworthy aspects and limitations.

Table 1. Comparison of Blockchain-based DNS Solutions

Solution	Custom TLDs	Ownership Model	DNS Integration	Blockchain
Namecoin [8]	No (.bit only)	Requires renewals	Limited	Bitcoin (PoW)
Blockstack [13]	Yes	Direct	Limited to blockchain	Bitcoin (PoW)
ENS [20]	No (.eth only)	Requires renewals	Low	Ethereum (PoS)
Handshake [12]	Limited	Requires renewals	Low	Proprietary (PoW)
Unstoppable Domains [9]	No (proprietary)	Direct NFT-based	Low	Polygon (PoS)
B-DNS [23]	No	Requires registrars	Strong	Proprietary (PoS)
Blockzone [30]	No	Direct	Partial	Proprietary (PBFT)
D^{3}NS [16]	No	Direct	Strong	Bitcoin (PoW)
3DNS [3]	Limited	Requires renewals	Partial	Optimism L2 (PoS)
DNSLedger [19]	No	Direct	Strong	Multi-chain
PolyIDns	Yes	Direct	Strong	Polygon zkEVM (PoS)

---

[1] We refer to *ownership* as user direct control and exclusive rights over the domain.

The lack of **custom TLDs creation** capabilities across most systems severely restricts namespace flexibility, forcing users into predefined TLDs like ".eth", ".crypto", ".nft", and ".blockchain". Some solutions like [9,20] focus narrowly on cryptocurrency wallet address simplification rather than implementing comprehensive DNS properties, limiting their utility as true DNS alternatives. Among the solutions, only [9,13,19,30] provide **direct control** models, while others [3,8] rely on additional components and actors like registrars that limit a direct and exclusive management of the domain. Limited **integration** with traditional DNS standards remains a significant challenge, with only a few solutions [16,19,23] demonstrating interoperability with existing infrastructure. This compatibility gap creates potential adoption barriers for users and organizations who require transitions between traditional and blockchain-based systems. The choice of underlying **blockchain** platform impacts the security, scalability, and operational characteristics of DNS solutions. Most of the solutions rely on Bitcoin or proprietary blockchains, leading to scalability and performance issues or reducing security and trust guarantees due to the use of custom validator networks. Despite these innovations, each solution focuses on specific aspects, without managing all of them. With PolyIDns, we support all of the mentioned aspects to enable a widespread adoption of blockchain-based DNS as an alternative or complement to traditional DNS infrastructure. Unlike existing solutions, PolyIDns provides a balanced approach that combines custom TLD creation, direct control over DNS records, integration with traditional DNS standards, and an efficient implementation by leveraging Polygon zkEVM's Layer-2 infrastructure.

4   PolyIDns Architecture

In this section we introduce the PolyIDns architecture, focusing on its components and functionalities. PolyIDns is designed as a decentralized domain name system built as an EVM-compatible solution.

4.1   Components

The core architecture of PolyIDns relies on three main components implemented as smart contracts. These contracts allow users to create new namespaces, register domains within existing namespaces, and query domain information through both blockchain interfaces and standard DNS protocols. Specifically, those are depicted in Fig. 1 and consist of: the *NamespaceFactory* smart contract, the *Namespace* smart contract, and the *DNS Server*.

NamespaceFactory Contract. This smart contract is designed to manage namespace existence and addressing, allowing users to discover the appropriate contract address for any registered namespace. It manages the creation and discovery of namespaces, which are equivalent to TLDs in traditional DNS systems. In particular, when a user requests a new namespace, the factory deploys each

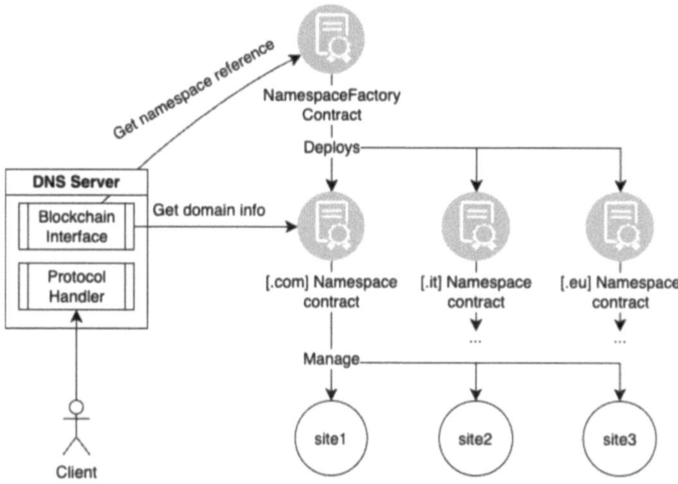

Fig. 1. PolyIDns Architecture Overview.

namespace as an individual smart contract. This is done by creating a new instance of the *Namespace contract* with the factory registering its address. This design choice enables separation of concerns by isolating the data and operations of namespaces, while preventing a single smart contract from becoming too large in size. Before creating a new namespace, the factory contract verifies that the requested namespace does not already exist and that it adheres to naming conventions. Indeed, PolyIDns enforces a simplified naming convention where namespaces cannot contain uppercase characters, spaces, or dots. Unlike traditional DNS with hierarchical TLDs like ".co.uk" [2], this approach eliminates ambiguity while maintaining compatibility with common TLD patterns.

Users can create custom namespaces at a fixed price, which serves both as an anti-spam measure and as a funding mechanism for the system's maintenance. While users pay to create namespaces, they do not gain exclusive ownership rights, therefore, any user can register domains within an existing namespace, preventing monopolization and ensuring system accessibility.

Namespace Contract. This smart contract manages the entire lifecycle of domains, exposing functionalities for registration, update, ownership transfer, and query. It represents a namespace in which users can register and manage multiple domains, maintaining references to ensure direct control. Each registered domain can also be associated with a different record type (e.g., A, AAAA, MX, CNAME) to detail its configuration. The smart contract also enforces rules such as unique domain names and ownership-based access control for updates. Additionally, when deployed, the smart contract stores a reference to its factory, used for verification of its creator.

DNS Server. This component bridges the blockchain-based domain registry with traditional DNS infrastructure, enabling resolution of blockchain-registered domains through standard DNS protocols. The DNS Server architecture consists of two primary subcomponents. The *DNS Protocol Handler* processes incoming DNS queries according to standard protocols (RFC 1035), constructs appropriate responses for various record types, and manages the communication with DNS clients. Meanwhile, the *Blockchain Interface* communicates directly with the blockchain to query the smart contracts, retrieving domain records stored on-chain. This hybrid resolver architecture allows the system to maintain compatibility with the existing DNS, lowering adoption barriers for decentralized domain names.

4.2   Functionalities

The PolyIDns system provides several functionalities divided into: namespace creation, domain Update, ownership transfer and domain resolution. These are reported in Fig. 2 and are described in the following.

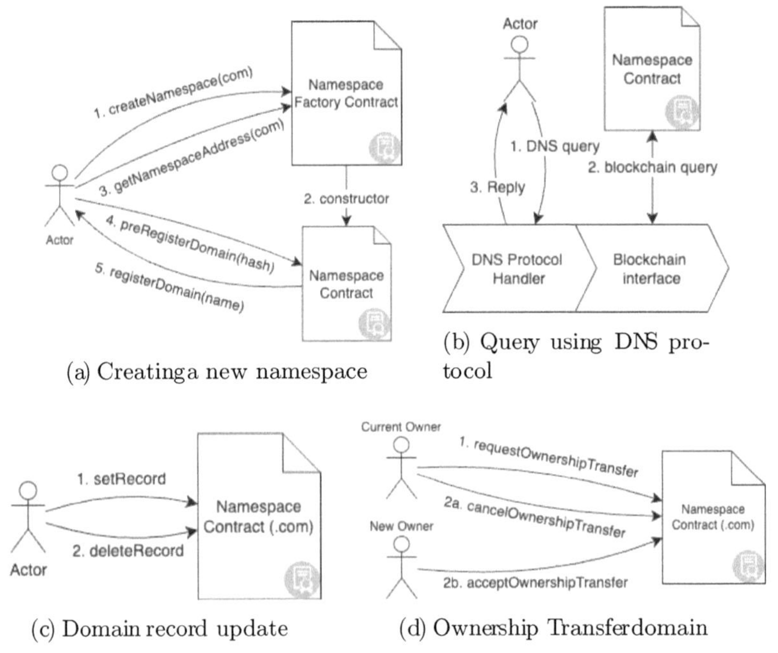

(a) Creating a new namespace

(b) Query using DNS protocol

(c) Domain record update

(d) Ownership Transfer domain

Fig. 2. Overview of PolyIDns functionalities.

Namespace Creation: This functionality includes the creation of a new namespace and a domain registration, which steps are reported in Fig. 2a. Users can create new namespaces (e.g., ".com") by invoking the NamespaceFactory contract (step 1) and paying a fixed fee. The factory contract deploys the new instance of the Namespace contract (step 2) and saves its address allowing for its retrieval (step 3). After creating a namespace, any user can interact with it to register domain names through a secure two-step process. The process begins from pre-registration with a commitment hash[2] (Step 4), where users submit the hash of the domain name instead of the actual domain name, preventing front-running attacks that try to steal domains by watching the mempool. After ensuring blockchain finality[3] through timestamp verification and verifying the caller's identity as the original pre-registrant, the actual registration (Step 5) completes the process, revealing the domain name. This two-phase registration sequence mitigates front-running attacks, ensuring legitimate ownership claims.

Domain Update: Domain owners can manage DNS records through access-controlled operations, as shown in Fig. 2c. This update can be done by interacting with the Namespace contract and setting or updating (Step 1) one of the available domain record types (with specific validation for A and AAAA address records) or deleting it (Step 2). This ownership-based access control ensures only verified domain owners can modify their domain's DNS configuration, protecting against unauthorized changes while supporting standard DNS record types.

Ownership Transfer: These functions enable secure domain transfers between users through a secure two-step process requiring explicit confirmation from both parties, according to the functionality, as depicted in Fig. 2d. Initially, the current owner requests a domain transfer to the Namespace contract (Step 1). Lastly, the new owner accepts the transfer request, receiving control over the domain (Step 2b). Before the domain acceptance, the current owner can revert the process (Step 2a) This design prevents accidental transfers to incorrect or inaccessible addresses by requiring active recipient confirmation, ensuring domains are never permanently lost due to transfer errors and maintaining strict ownership verification throughout the process.

Domain Resolution: Query functions provide read-only access to domain information stored in the contract, allowing any user, applications, and DNS resolvers to retrieve DNS records and verify domain ownership without requiring special permissions. The smart contract supports queries for both second-level (getRecord) and third-level (getSubdomainRecord) domains to retrieve specific record types. Moreover the DNS Server enables standard DNS resolution for blockchain-registered domains as shown in Fig. 2b. When a client sends a DNS query for a domain (step 1), the server parses the domain to identify the namespace and domain name, queries the appropriate smart contracts (step 2) through the blockchain interface, and returns the requested records in standard DNS for-

---

[2] Generated using a common hash algorithm.

[3] Blockchain finality refers to the guarantee that once a transaction is added to the blockchain, it cannot be altered or reversed. In the context of PolyIDns, finality ensures that the pre-registration commitment is permanently recorded before allowing the actual registration to proceed.

mat (step 3). This functionality allows users to access blockchain domains using conventional web browsers and tools without specialized software.

5   PolyIDns Implementation

This section details the technical implementation of the PolyIDns system, focusing on the smart contracts structure and their content. PolyIDns was implemented on the Polygon zkEVM platform due to its optimal balance of security, performance, and cost-effectiveness. It offers Ethereum equivalence while providing significantly lower transaction costs and higher throughput compared to the Ethereum mainnet. The zero-knowledge proof technology employed by zkEVM enhances privacy and security while maintaining the ability to verify transaction validity. PolyIDns smart contracts were developed using Solidity, the primary programming language for Ethereum-compatible smart contracts, ensuring compatibility with EVM-based platforms. The implementation is accessible online (Fig. 3)[4].

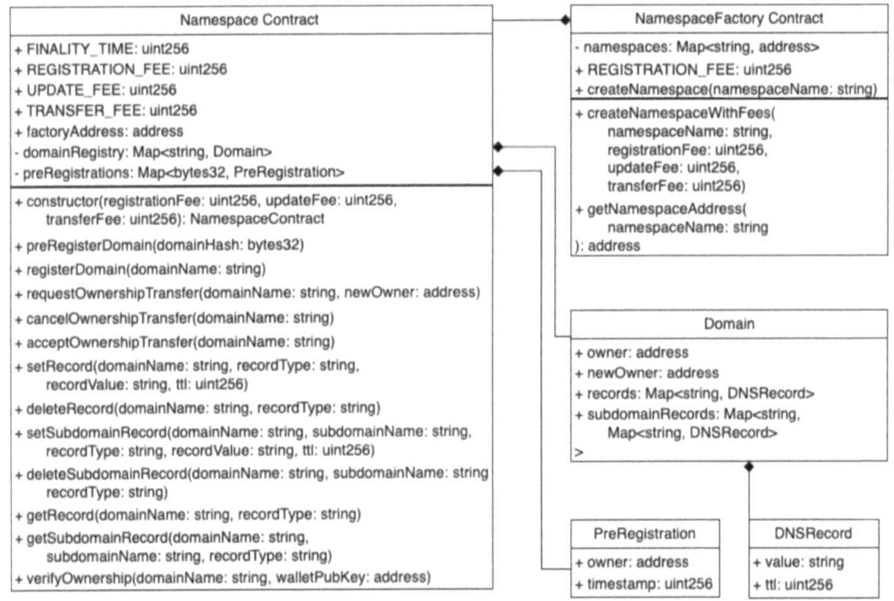

Fig. 3. PolyIDns Class Diagram.

---

[4] https://gitlab.com/Glydric/PolyIDns.

5.1   NamespaceFactory Smart Contract

The NamespaceFactory contract maintains two critical types of data. First, **namespaces** serves to keep references of namespace names, associating them with their corresponding contract addresses, enabling efficient lookup of namespace contracts. Second, **registration fee** stores the fee required to register a new namespace. The NamespaceFactory contract exposes two key functions. The **createNamespace** function allows users to create namespaces after verifying availability, deploying a new contract, and storing its reference. After registration **getNamespaceAddress** returns the contract address for a given namespace name.

5.2   Namespace Smart Contract

The Namespace contract stores several types of data to manage domains effectively. In first set of data serves for the definition of the price model. Indeed, the smart contract implements a configurable pricing model chosen during namespace creation that determines the cost of various domain operations. Stored as immutable parameters, these prices include **registration** fee (base cost for registering domains), record **update** fee (for modifying DNS records), and ownership **transfer** fee. This pricing structure serves as an anti-spam measure by imposing financial costs on domain operations, deterring malicious actors from registering large numbers of domains.

Domains are then managed through dedicated structures. **Pre-registrations** contain commitment data about pre-registered domains, including the registrant's address and timestamp, ensuring transaction finality before domain registration is completed. **Domain Registry** is a mapping that associates domain names with their metadata, also storing the owner's address, which has the authority to modify records or transfer ownership. Each domain is represented as a struct containing specific data. Resource **Records** stores domain record type, supported ones include A records (IPv4), AAAA records (IPv6), TXT, CNAME, and MX records. **Subdomain Records** data structure is used to maintain references for third-level domains (subdomains) under each second-level domain, enabling hierarchical domain management. This data model enables the Namespace contract to serve as a complete registry for its namespace, storing both ownership information and DNS records needed for domain resolution.

5.3   DNS Server Implementation

The PolyIDns system includes a custom DNS server implementation that serves as an additional component designed specifically for retro-compatibility with existing DNS clients and infrastructure. This component bridges blockchain-based domain registry with traditional off-chain DNS infrastructure, enabling resolution through standard protocols without requiring specialized software. Notably, the core PolyIDns system operates fully without this component, users have to directly interact with the smart contracts to register domains, manage records, and query domain information through blockchain interfaces. The DNS server exists purely to lower adoption barriers by allowing traditional DNS clients and web browsers to resolve blockchain-registered domains seamlessly.

This retro-compatibility approach cannot be replicated entirely on blockchain due to the fundamental differences between DNS protocol requirements and blockchain transaction models. Therefore, this hybrid resolver architecture represents a practical compromise that maintains the decentralized benefits of blockchain based domain ownership while providing familiar user experiences through traditional DNS protocols.

Implemented in Rust with Ethers.rs for blockchain interaction, the server ensures high performance and memory safety. The server functions as a hybrid resolver with a dual architecture. The Blockchain Interface component communicates directly with Polygon network to query the smart contracts, while the DNS Protocol Handler processes incoming queries and constructs appropriate responses for various record types. Together, these components create a seamless bridge between blockchain data and standard DNS protocols. When resolving domains, the server first parses the domain to extract the second-level domain and namespace, then queries the NamespaceFactory for the corresponding Namespace contract address. If the namespace exists, it retrieves the requested record from the appropriate smart contract and constructs a standard DNS response. When resolution fails, the server generates referrals to public DNS resolvers, maintaining compatibility with the existing DNS ecosystem. This implementation supports all standard DNS record types (A, AAAA, CNAME, TXT, NS, MX), ensuring blockchain domains can fulfill all traditional domain functions. By providing this additional DNS server component, PolyIDns combines blockchain's security and ownership benefits with universal accessibility. This architectural decision ensures that while the DNS server enhances usability, the fundamental security and decentralization properties of the system remain intact even if the DNS server component becomes unavailable.

6 Evaluation

This section presents an evaluation of PolyIDns, focusing on transaction costs to assess the feasibility of the proposed solution. To evaluate the performance and cost-effectiveness of PolyIDns, we deployed the smart contracts on the Polygon zkEVM Cardona testnet and conducted a series of transactions to measure gas consumption[5]. The conducted experiment involved creating a new namespace and registering a domain within it, then performing a domain record update. The following Table 2 summarizes the gas costs for the main operations in the system.

The most expensive operation is the initial contract creation, which is a one-time cost. Subsequent operations like namespace creation, domain registration,

---

[5] https://cardona-zkevm.polygonscan.com/address/0xF229888f411Ab401535da6b9c
2D469801fBaF289

Table 2. Costs for PolyIDns operations on Polygon zkEVM Cardona

Contract	Method	Gas Used (units)	Gas Cost (ETH)
Namespace Factory	Contract Creation	2,747,599	0.00002747167
	createNamespace	2,194,966	0.00002183855
Namespace Contract	preRegisterDomain	68,033	0.00000068033
	registerDomain	55,082	0.00000055082
	requestOwnershipTransfer	50,191	0.00000050191
	cancelOwnershipTransfer	32,282	0.00000017282
	acceptOwnershipTransfer	29,496	0.00000029099
	setRecord	77,675	0.00000077675
	deleteRecord	40,696	0.00000020348

and updates are significantly less expensive. When converted to USD, these costs are minimal due to Polygon's efficient fee structure, making the system economically viable for widespread adoption. Transaction fees never exceed 0.05 USD, with all normal operations costing less than 0.01 USD. These minimal transaction costs make the system practical for frequent use and accessible to a wide range of users. The two-step domain registration process (preRegisterDomain followed by registerDomain) adds only marginal gas costs while providing significant security benefits against front-running attacks.

The results of our evaluation demonstrate that PolyIDns represents a feasible and economically viable approach to decentralized DNS management. The cost analysis reveals that creating a decentralized namespace on Polygon zkEVM is affordable enough. Indeed, when compared to traditional DNS registration costs, which typically range from 10–30 USD annually [22] for domain registration alone, PolyIDns offers a competitive alternative with the added benefits of decentralization, censorship resistance, and enhanced security. The minimal transaction costs observed in our experiments indicate that the approach is practically implementable at scale. Furthermore, the performance characteristics of Polygon zkEVM, including fast transaction finality and high throughput, ensure that PolyIDns can handle the operational demands of a production-grade DNS system.

Testing Strategy. To ensure reliability and security, we implemented a comprehensive testing strategy for PolyIDns smart contracts using Hardhat's testing framework with TypeScript. Our test suite, available in the public repository[6], comprises over 60 individual test cases that systematically verify all system components and their interactions. The testing methodology follows a multi-layered approach. At the foundational level, unit tests validate the correct behavior of individual contract functions in isolation, ensuring each component works as designed. Building upon this, integration tests examine the complex interactions

---

[6] https://gitlab.com/Glydric/PolyIDns.

between contracts, particularly between the NamespaceFactory and Namespace-Contract instances, to verify seamless system operation.

Our test coverage encompasses the entire domain lifecycle, beginning with namespace creation and validation of parameters and ownership assignment. We thoroughly tested the complete domain registration workflow, including the two-step registration process that mitigates front-running attacks. The test suite also verifies record management operations for adding, updating, and removing DNS records, as well as ownership transfer protocols with request, acceptance, and cancellation scenarios. Special attention was given to access control enforcement to prevent unauthorized operations, along with edge cases and error handling to ensure system resilience under complex scenarios.

6.1 Discussion

With the current implementation of PolyIDns, we demonstrated the technical feasibility and evaluated the viability of blockchain-based DNS management. While the blockchain-based architecture of PolyIDns offers many core functionalities, the system currently lacks a user-friendly interface for end-users. Indeed, the presented work focuses on the core smart contract functionalities and the DNS server implementation. In its current form, the smart contracts deployed on the blockchain are publicly accessible and can be integrated with future Decentralized Application (DApp) implementations. The characteristics of blockchain ensure that contract interfaces remain stable and accessible, enabling developers to construct user-friendly front-end applications that interact with the existing deployed contracts without requiring modifications to the underlying infrastructure. Future development can focus on the creation of a comprehensive DApp, enhancing user experience, and utilizing established libraries and frameworks to deliver intuitive domain management capabilities. Such a DApp could incorporate features including visual domain portfolio management, streamlined record editing interfaces, ownership transfer workflows, and integration with wallets.

Layer 2 Architecture and Data Storage. PolyIDns operates on the Polygon zkEVM Layer 2 network, where domain data and smart contracts are deployed. This architectural decision prioritizes transaction cost efficiency and optimal query performance, as L2 operations provide significantly faster throughput and lower fees compared to Ethereum mainnet transactions.

The DNS resolver component must query the L2 network directly through RPC endpoints to retrieve domain information and DNS records via smart contract calls to the deployed NamespaceFactory and Namespace contracts. While Polygon zkEVM periodically commits zero-knowledge proofs to the Ethereum mainnet for security purposes, these proofs are not designed to enable straightforward queries directly from L1, creating a dependency on L2 infrastructure. The commitment process follows a unidirectional flow from L2 to L1, ensuring that inconsistencies or race conditions cannot occur since it is not possible to perform contract updates directly on L1. This design maintains the L2 network as the primary operational layer for all domain operations.

7 Conclusion and Future Work

The Domain Name System is a crucial part of the Internet, enabling users to access resources through human-readable domain names instead of numerical IP addresses. However, the traditional DNS faces several challenges related to security vulnerabilities and centralization.

These issues have spurred interest in alternative DNS solutions, with blockchain technology emerging as a promising approach. Blockchain offers decentralized, cryptographically verified records, eliminating central points of failure and enhancing data security. It ensures domain ownership without intermediaries, providing resistance to censorship and tamper-proof records. By using blockchain, DNS systems can maintain distributed domain records, making them more resilient to attacks. Blockchain also enables smart contracts for automated domain management, removing the need for intermediaries and allowing transparent audit trails. Moreover, blockchain-based DNS can offer novel ownership models, where users permanently own and transfer domains without relying on registrars or rental fees. Despite these advantages, many blockchain-based DNS solutions face challenges, such as domain ownership complexities, integration with existing infrastructure, and scalability issues. Some solutions still rely on centralized components, compromising decentralization and performance. To address these challenges, we proposed PolyIDns, a blockchain-based DNS system designed for decentralized domain management. PolyIDns offers permanent domain ownership, direct access to management functions, and full integration with existing DNS standards, while leveraging blockchain's security features. We implemented PolyIDns as an Ethereum-compatible solution and evaluated its performance for feasibility.

Future developments for PolyIDns include adding domain auctions with dynamic pricing to prevent squatting and set fair prices, supporting NFT standards to allow domain trading, and developing a comprehensive application that provides an intuitive web interface for domain management operations. Finally, creating user-friendly interfaces will also help make the system more accessible.

Acknowledgment. This work was partially supported by project SERICS (PE00000014) under the MUR National Recovery and Resilience Plan funded by the European Union - NextGenerationEU.

References

1. Ali, M., et al.: Blockstack: design and implementation of a global naming system with blockchains. Last visited on **25**(2) (2016)
2. Bagay, D.: Blockchain-based DNS building. Procedia Comput. Sci. **169**, 187–191 (2020)
3. Bansal, M.K., Sethumadhavan, M.: DNS security - prevent DNS cache poisoning attack using blockchain. Int. J. Innovative Technol. Explor. Eng. **9**, 2151–2162 (2020)

4. Benshoof, B., et al.: Distributed decentralized domain name service. In: IPDPSW, pp. 1279–1287. IEEE (2016)
5. Bjelic, M., et al.: POL: one token for all polygon chains. In: Polygon Technology (2021)
6. Buterin, V., et al.: A next-generation smart contract and decentralized application platform. White Paper **3**(37), 2–1 (2014)
7. Duan, X., et al.: DNSLedger: decentralized and distributed name resolution for ubiquitous IoT. In: ICCE, pp. 1–3. IEEE (2018)
8. Ethereum. Ethereum ENS. https://github.com/ethereum/ercs/blob/master/ERCS/erc-137.md
9. Giamouridis, G., Kang, B., Aniello, L.: Blockchainbased DNS: Current Solutions and Challenges to Adoption (2024)
10. handshake.org. https://handshake.org/files/handshake.txt
11. How To Register a Domain Name in 5 Simple Steps (Updated for 2023) — 3DNS — 3dns.box. https://3dns.box/blog/posts/register-domain-5-steps-2023/
12. Launch your own Namespace — docs.3dns.box. https://docs.3dns.box/docs/launch-your-own-namespace
13. Lehr, W., Clark, D.D., Bauer, S.: Changing markets for domain names: technical, economic, and policy challenges. In: Economic, and Policy Challenges (April 15, 2021). TPRC48: The 48th Research Conference on Communication, Information and Internet Policy (2021)
14. Li, Z., et al.: B-DNS: a secure and efficient DNS based on the blockchain technology. IEEE Trans. Netw. Sci. Eng. **8**(2), 1674–1686 (2021)
15. Liu, J., et al.: A Data Storage Method Based on Blockchain for Decentralization DNS, pp. 189–196 (2018)
16. Liu, Y., et al.: A comparative study of blockchain-based DNS design. In: Proceedings of the 2019 2nd International Conference on Blockchain Technology and Applications, pp. 86–92 (2019)
17. Moura, G.C.M., et al.: Anycast vs. DDoS: evaluating the November 2015 root DNS event. In: Proceedings of the 2016 Internet Measurement Conference, pp. 255–270 (2016)
18. Namecoin — namecoin.org. https://www.namecoin.org/
19. Polygon zkEVM — Scaling for the Ethereum Virtual Machine — polygon.technology. https://polygon.technology/polygon-zkevm. Accessed 08 Apr 2025
20. Shafranovich, Y.: Common Format and MIME Type for Comma-Separated Values (CSV) Files. RFC 1034. RFC Editor (2005). https://www.rfc-editor.org/rfc/rfc1034.txt
21. Shafranovich, Y.: Common Format and MIME Type for Comma-Separated Values (CSV) Files. RFC 1035. RFC Editor (2005). https://www.rfc-editor.org/rfc/rfc1035.txt
22. Shafranovich, Y.: Common Format and MIME Type for Comma-Separated Values (CSV) Files. RFC 3596. RFC Editor (2005). https://www.rfc-editor.org/rfc/rfc3596.txt
23. Stacks Cryptocurrency No Longer Treated as a US Security by Blockstack PBC — blog.blockstack.org. https://blog.blockstack.org/whyblockstack-is-migrating-to-the-bitcoin-blockchain
24. Superchain Identity — docs.3dns.box. https://docs.3dns.box/docs/superchain-identity
25. TLDs Listed Alphabetically — TLD-List — tld-list.com. https://tld-list.com/tlds-from-a-z

26. Unstoppable Domains — onchain domains for everyone — unstoppabledomains.com. https://unstoppabledomains.com/
27. Unstoppable Domains: Blockchain-Based Crypto Domain — Gemini — gemini.com. https://www.gemini.com/cryptopedia/unstoppable-domainszil-domain-crypto-domain#section-toward-a-more-decentralizedweb
28. Wang, W., Hu, N., Liu, X.: BlockZone: a blockchain-based DNS storage and retrieval scheme. In: Sun, X., Pan, Z., Bertino, E. (eds.) ICAIS 2019. LNCS, vol. 11635, pp. 155–166. Springer, Cham (2019). https://doi.org/10.1007/978-3-030-24268-8_15
29. What's the Difference Between 3DNS and Unstoppable Domains? — 3DNS — 3dns.box. https://3dns.box/blog/posts/difference-between-3dns-and-unstoppable-domains/
30. What's the difference between 3DNS, ENS, Unstoppable Domains, Handshake, and D3 — 3DNS — 3dns.box. https://3dns.box/blog/posts/comparing-decentralized-dns-providers/

Privacy-Preserving Auditable Hygiene Compliance Using Hyperledger Fabric in Hospital Environments

Pierluigi Gallo[1,2]([✉])(iD), Muhammad Rehan[1](iD), Francesco Saverio Cannizzaro[2], Gabriele Catalano[3], and Maria Timoshina[2]

[1] University of Palermo, Palermo, Italy
muhammad.rehan05@unipa.it
[2] SEEDS srl, Palermo, Italy
pierluigi.gallo@unipa.it,
{francesco.cannizzaro,maria.timoshina}@seedsbit.com
[3] Next Multiservice srl, Palermo, Italy
gabriele.catalano@nextmultiservice.it

Abstract. This research introduces a novel decentralized system designed to improve hand hygiene protocols in clinical environments, aiming to lower the incidence of hospital-acquired infections (HAIs). Monitoring techniques often fail to verify adherence or maintain secure, verifiable records, leading to audit challenges and increased infection risks. The proposed solution integrates a custom-trained YOLOv8 model to detect hand hygiene-related behaviors from real-time image and video streams, enhancing hygiene alerts for healthcare workers more accurate with a comprehensive tracking and tracing mechanism. Detected events are cryptographically anonymized and stored on a Hyperledger Fabric blockchain, ensuring immutable and transparent compliance records. Compared to traditional monitoring methods, recorded events are more accurate and practical for compliance checks and audit purposes to maintain hand hygiene practices. The proposed system ensures data integrity, preserves user privacy, and provides transparent audit trails.

Keywords: Blockchain · Computer vision · Immutable record · Healthcare infection control · Hospital-acquired infections

1 Introduction

Hospital-acquired infections (HAIs) remain a pervasive and costly burden for healthcare systems globally, affecting millions of patients annually and contributing to prolonged hospitalizations, increased antibiotic resistance, and elevated mortality rates. Despite widespread awareness and established hand hygiene protocols, ensuring consistent compliance remains challenging in real-world clinical settings. Contributing factors include high patient turnover, staff fatigue, time

W. Knottenbelt et al. (Eds.): Blocktea 2025, LNICST 669, pp. 174–193, 2026.
https://doi.org/10.1007/978-3-032-12335-0_11

pressure, and the presence of untrained or uninformed visitors, all of which can result in lapses in hand hygiene practices. This situation is further exacerbated by the presence of hospital-specific microbial strains, often more resistant and aggressive, which do not typically circulate in the community and can emerge due to the constant use of disinfectants and antibiotics in clinical environments.

Traditional hand hygiene compliance monitoring suffers from three fundamental limitations. First, it relies on manual observation and periodic audits by infection control personnel, which cannot ensure continuous and real-time surveillance, especially in dynamic and high-traffic clinical environments. Second, compliance assessments are often subjective, leading to inconsistent interpretation and partial adherence to protocols. Third, manual documentation is prone to omission, falsification, or human error, compromising both data integrity and traceability. Furthermore, the lack of immediate feedback reduces the likelihood that healthcare workers will adjust their behavior in real time. These limitations contribute to the underreporting of non-compliance and reduce opportunities for timely intervention to prevent infection transmission [2].

To overcome these limitations, this study presents an innovative automated compliance monitoring system that combines computer vision with blockchain technologies. At the core of the system lies a YOLOv8 deep learning model, trained on a customized dataset to recognize hand hygiene practices and personal protective equipment (PPE) usage from hospital surveillance videos. Unlike manual methods, this computer vision model offers real-time, non-intrusive monitoring with high accuracy. It can detect hand movements associated with hygiene procedures, such as rubbing gestures and handwashing duration, as well as recognize glove usage and the presence of hand or arm accessories like rings, bracelets, and watches, helping ensure compliance with hand hygiene protocols without interrupting medical workflows. The second major innovation lies in the secure and transparent recording of hand hygiene events using a permissioned blockchain platform—Hyperledger Fabric [14]. Every verified hand hygiene event is registered as a transaction on the blockchain, ensuring an immutable, verifiable audit trail that can be accessed by authorized personnel. This decentralized record-keeping approach overcomes the authenticity and reliability challenges commonly associated with conventional systems. The use of cryptographic anonymization ensures the protection of identities, preserving staff privacy while maintaining accountability [7].

Unlike existing solutions that focus solely on detection or logging, the proposed framework provides an end-to-end pipeline from real-time detection to tamper-proof compliance recording. The system also supports real-time analytics and alert generation, enabling hospital administrators to proactively identify hand hygiene lapses and take corrective action before infections occur. Over time, the data collected serves as a valuable resource for trend analysis, protocol optimization, and evaluation of hospital staff performance [12].

The experimental deployment of the system demonstrated a significant improvement in hand hygiene compliance compared to manual observation-based audits. This outcome highlights the potential of integrating artificial intelligence

(AI) and blockchain to create intelligent, resilient, and transparent systems that can transform infection control in healthcare settings [22]. Medical staff could be incentivized for consistent hygiene practices, and non-compliance could be monitored in an anonymized manner that still enables hospitals to identify trends and target areas for improvement. Real-time auditing and reporting of hygiene compliance can reduce human error and help ensure consistent adherence to hospital hand hygiene standards.

2   Related Works

The growing demand for effective infection prevention in clinical settings has led to increasing interest in technology-enhanced hand hygiene monitoring systems. In contrast to conventional methods, such as direct observation or manual auditing, recent approaches aim to deliver continuous, objective, and real-time compliance assessment. Research has explored various modalities, including computer vision, RFID-based tracking, wearable devices, and smart dispensers. While these systems show promise, they often encounter trade-offs in terms of scalability, accuracy, privacy, and auditability [23]. These limitations have driven a new wave of hybrid frameworks that integrate AI with secure data infrastructures, paving the way for more robust and trustworthy monitoring architectures.

Recent breakthroughs in AI and computer vision have enabled transformative approaches to hand hygiene monitoring, offering unprecedented precision and operational efficiency. The viability of multimodal imaging systems has been demonstrated through thermal and RGB sensor fusion, which achieved 93.5% accuracy in quantifying handrub coverage compliance [17]. Building on this foundation, recent research has leveraged skeletal hand-tracking algorithms to evaluate washing techniques in clinical settings, achieving near-perfect detection rates (99.5%) with sub-second latency—a critical advancement for real-time intervention.

Synergistic integration with healthcare informatics systems has moved beyond isolated monitoring, enabling predictive analytics for infection control. A recent hospital study correlated EHR-embedded hygiene compliance metrics with infection incidence using gradient-boosted decision trees (XGBoost), achieving a 93% area under the ROC curve (AUC) in forecasting HAI risk. These results validate the growing role of digital auditing as a proactive tool for infection prevention [3].

The adoption of blockchain technology in healthcare has gained significant traction due to its ability to enforce data immutability, auditability, and decentralized trust. Among permissioned blockchain platforms [16,19], Hyperledger Fabric has emerged as a preferred solution for medical applications, implemented its Identity Mixer (Idemix) protocol to achieve pseudonymous EHR access without compromising transactional verifiability [8]. This approach effectively addresses the critical trade-off between preserving the anonymity of both patients and healthcare personnel and ensuring regulatory compliance in the management of sensitive health data.

Recent architectural advancements have further enhanced the applicability of blockchain technology to clinical use cases [5]. An edge-computing hybrid model that integrates attribute-based encryption with Fabric's channel infrastructure, reducing latency by 40% while maintaining GDPR-grade data protection. Parallel advancements in IoT integration are evident in [12] SCALHEALTH framework, which leverages Fabric's private data collections to enable real-time vital sign monitoring from wearable devices with provable data provenance.

Collectively, these developments highlight transformative potential of blockchain in addressing three persistent challenges in healthcare: (i) Secure interoperability across fragmented medical systems (ii) Tamper-evident auditing for compliance-sensitive workflows (iii) Privacy-preserving analytics in environments with multiple stakeholders. Despite significant advances in the independent application of AI and blockchain in healthcare [20], synergistic integrations of both technologies remain in their early stages in both research and clinical practice. While AI-powered monitoring systems excel at real-time behavioral analysis, and blockchain provides robust solutions for data integrity, few studies have effectively converged these capabilities into unified frameworks, particularly for critical applications like hand hygiene compliance [9]. Current literature reveals a persistent disconnect between the detection accuracy achieved by computer vision systems and the security guarantees provided by distributed ledger technologies (DLTs), leaving healthcare systems without end-to-end solutions that simultaneously address real-time monitoring and immutable auditing needs.

3   System Design

To address the gap between computer vision performance and blockchain-based trust guarantees, the proposed system introduces a novel architecture that tightly integrates an optimized YOLOv8-based detection pipeline with Hyperledger Fabric's permissioned blockchain infrastructure. The proposed system achieves three transformative synergies:

- *Real-Time 'Monitoring:* The custom-trained YOLOv8 model detects hygiene events.
- *Provable Integrity:* Each detected event generates a cryptographic proof stored on-chain via Fabric's private data collections, creating an auditable trail resistant to retroactive modification.
- *Regulatory Alignment:* Zero-knowledge proofs (ZKPs) enable identity anonymization of healthcare workers while preserving auditability, thereby addressing both GDPR and HIPAA compliance requirements, an aspect not covered in previous works.

By unifying these technologies, the framework applies WHO-recommended hygiene standards through an accountable, AI-enhanced monitoring system in which detection triggers and audit records are seamlessly integrated rather than functioning as disconnected components. The system flow is illustrated in Fig. 1.

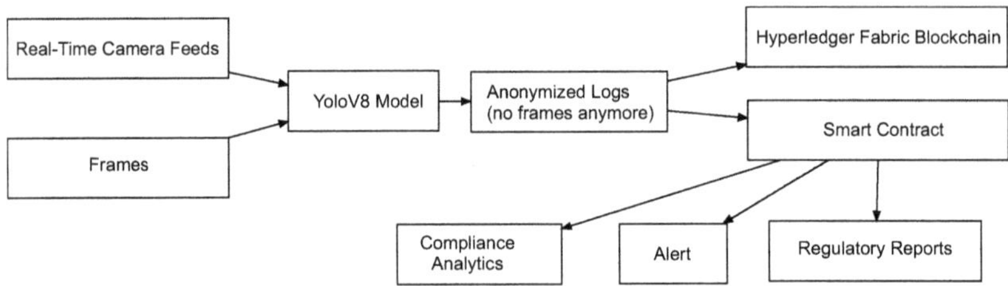

Fig. 1. System Flow Diagram.

3.1   Computer Vision Design

The proposed system employs a multi-module computer vision pipeline optimized for the detection and analysis of hand hygiene behavior in clinical environments. The pipeline integrates static marker recognition, hand pose estimation, accessory classification, and zone-based activity tracking, offering a comprehensive framework for hygiene compliance evaluation. The architecture is built on a YOLOv8-based object detection core, supplemented by custom-trained models and region-specific tracking logic. To establish spatial reference points, the system uses ArUco markers to tag each patient bed and gel dispenser within the monitored area. The cameras detect and track these markers in real-time, enabling automatic identification of their positions and monitoring of any movement (e.g., repositioning of beds). This spatial awareness is critical for assigning hygiene events to the correct patient context and for understanding the operator's proximity to hygienically sensitive zones.

The system employs a custom-trained hand-tracking model to detect and analyze hand movements within the monitored space. A key feature of the model is its ability to distinguish between healthcare workers or visitors, whose hand movements are subject to hygiene compliance evaluation, and patients, whose hand activity is deliberately excluded from analysis to avoid generating false positives. This differentiation is achieved through a combination of hand segmentation, full-body tracking, and contextual information, such as the direction of entry and the spatial trajectory of hands relative to the patient's bed. An exemplary hand recognition process in a controlled setting is shown in Fig. 2.

To assess hygiene behavior in context, the monitored environment is divided into three functional zones: the hygiene zone, where gel dispensers are installed; the proximity zone, which extends within one meter of the patient; and the contact zone, where direct interaction with the patient occurs. The movement trajectories of healthcare workers and visitors are continuously tracked using Deep SORT in combination with pose estimation. By identifying transitions between these zones, the system is able to infer hygiene-relevant events and opportunities, in alignment with the WHO's "5 Moments for Hand Hygiene" framework [15].

The system evaluates hand hygiene quality in accordance with the World Health Organization's "How to Handrub" protocol, which defines a standardized sequence of seven hand rubbing steps, preceded by the application of an adequate amount of alcohol-based handrub. The process begins with step (1), applying a palmful of alcohol-based formulation in a cupped hand and covering all surfaces. This is followed by step (2), rubbing hands palm to palm, and step (3), placing the right palm over the left dorsum (and vice versa) with interlaced fingers. Step (4) consists of rubbing palm to palm with fingers interlaced, followed by step (5), rubbing the backs of fingers against opposing palms with fingers interlocked. The sixth step (6) involves rotational rubbing of the left thumb clasped in the right palm and vice versa. Finally, step (7) consists of rotational rubbing backwards and forwards with clasped fingers of one hand in the other's palm.

Using pose estimation combined with temporal tracking, the system recognizes each of these distinct movements and estimates the duration of execution. Compliance is evaluated not only by the presence of the steps, but also by ensuring that the cumulative duration of the hand rubbing procedure meets the WHO's recommended range of 20 to 30 s. The system flags hygiene events as incomplete if one or more steps are missing or if the total time is insufficient, thereby enabling a more nuanced assessment of hand hygiene quality.

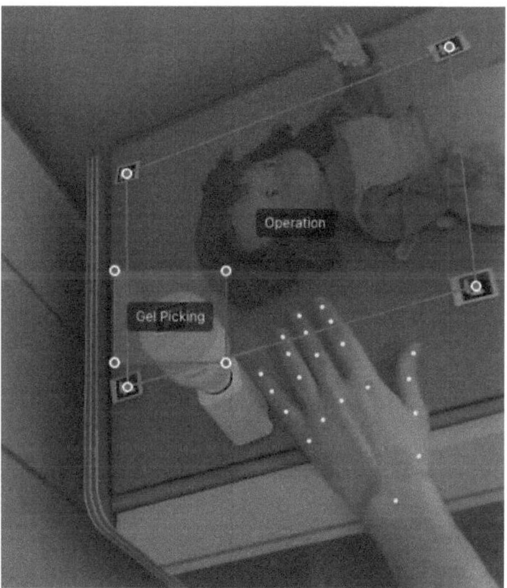

Fig. 2. Hand recognition and zone mapping during hand hygiene in a simulated clinical setting @ SEEDS srl.

In addition to behavioral tracking, the system includes a dedicated module for evaluating dress code compliance, focusing on the detection of items worn on hands and forearms. A custom dataset of 5,700 annotated images was used to train a YOLOv8 model on four relevant accessory classes: gloves, rings, bracelets, and watches. This model was chosen for its balance of high precision and speed, achieving 98.2% recall at 15 frames per second [21]. Detected accessories are cross-checked against institutional hygiene policies, which may prohibit certain items during patient interaction. Non-compliance is flagged as part of the overall hygiene assessment.

3.2 Hyperledger Fabric Design

Having captured and interpreted hygiene behavior through the computer vision pipeline, the system proceeds to securely record the resulting events using blockchain technology. In the proposed framework, Hyperledger Fabric serves as the backbone for secure and transparent logging of hygiene compliance data. The system performs pseudonymization of sensitive identifiers at the application level, before committing any data to the blockchain. As a result, all on-chain records are inherently privacy-preserving and contain no direct personal information. Only the resulting pseudonymous logs, which include timestamps, hygiene action types, compliance results, and location metadata, are submitted to the blockchain.

By anchoring these logs in a permissioned, tamper-resistant distributed ledger, the system guarantees data immutability, traceability, and institutional transparency. This is critical in hospital environments, where audits, incident tracking, and accountability must operate under strict regulatory constraints such as GDPR and HIPAA. Once hygiene events are stored on the blockchain, smart contracts are triggered to evaluate individual and group-level compliance against predefined thresholds. These contracts operate entirely on pseudonymized identifiers, ensuring privacy by design. If compliance scores meet or exceed certain criteria, the smart contract marks those pseudonymous IDs as eligible for an incentive.

To claim the incentive, the healthcare worker or a group of workers, such as a department team, can voluntarily submit their cryptographic key or token that links them to their on-chain pseudonym. This selective disclosure mechanism allows the system to maintain anonymity at rest while still enabling individual accountability when needed, aligning with modern self-sovereign identity principles. The immutable nature of blockchain records makes them well-suited for post-incident audits. In the event of an infection outbreak, pseudonymized logs can be analyzed to reconstruct hygiene patterns across patients, staff, and visitors, supporting forensic investigations without compromising privacy. This level of traceability enables rapid identification of potential negligence and supports targeted containment measures.

Moreover, the blockchain ledger accumulates longitudinal data that can be leveraged for predictive analytics. Trends in hygiene behavior, correlated with infection rates, can help identify high-risk zones and trigger proactive interventions. Over time, this contributes to more data-informed policies, resource allocation, and adaptive infection control strategies at the institutional level.

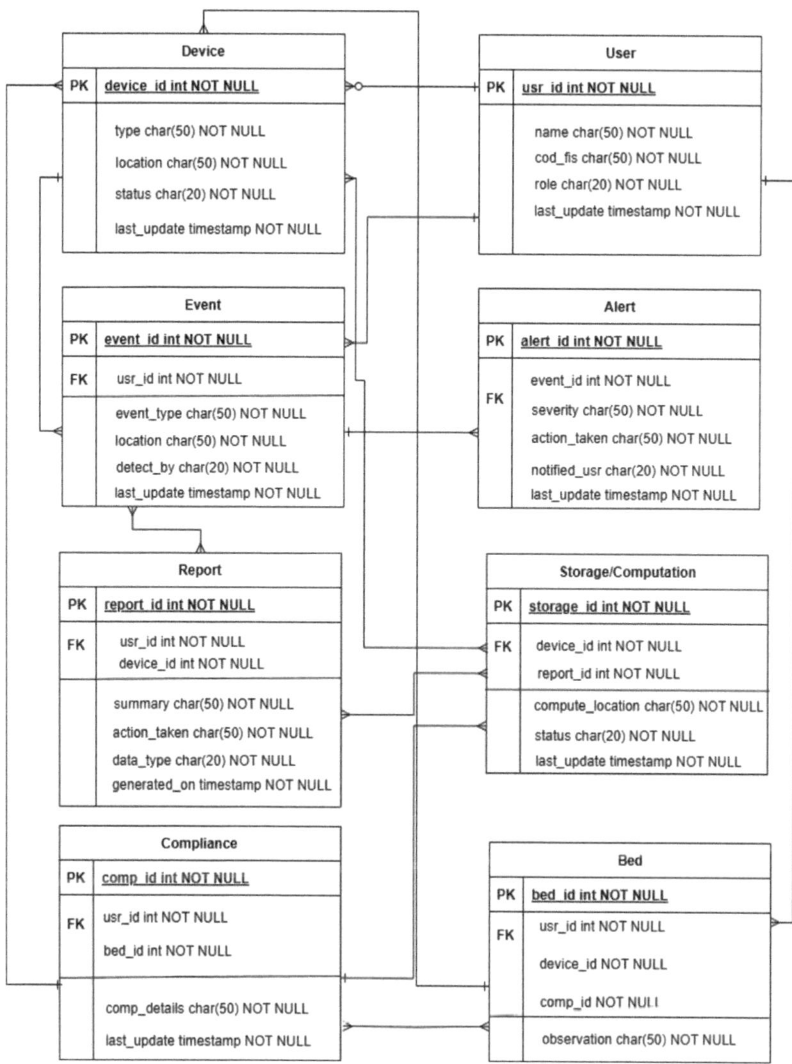

Fig. 3. Entity Relationship Diagram.

3.3 Privacy and Threat Model

The proposed system adopts a multi-layered privacy approach, integrating pseudonymization, minimal data exposure, and role-based access control. Each hygiene event is linked to a temporary, non-traceable pseudonymous ID, ensuring unlinkability unless voluntarily disclosed.

Threat Model. We consider an honest-but-curious institutional adversary capable of inspecting logs and inferring identities via metadata. Key threats include:

- *Linkage attacks*: Repeated pseudonymous events may be correlated to reveal identities.
- *Contextual inference*: Auxiliary data (e.g., schedules or room assignments) can compromise anonymity.
- *Inference tampering*: Off-chain CV results may be manipulated before blockchain entry.

Privacy Mitigations. The system mitigates privacy risks through:

- *Session-based pseudonymization*: Periodically refreshed identifiers prevent tracking across sessions.
- *Role-based visibility*: Smart contracts restrict access; department heads see only aggregated metrics unless voluntary disclosure occurs.
- *Access control*: Hyperledger Fabric's MSP enforces identity-bound query permissions.

Despite pseudonymization, quasi-identifiers (e.g., timestamp, bed ID, role) may still enable inference. To address this, we propose integrating the t-closeness model [10], which extends k-*anonymity* and ℓ-diversity by requiring that the distribution of sensitive attributes (e.g., compliance outcomes) in each equivalence class remains within a threshold t of the global distribution. This reduces the risk of attribute disclosure even in small or homogeneous groups.

In practice, equivalence classes can be formed by role, department, or shift time. Enforcing t-closeness ensures sensitive attributes (e.g., low compliance) remain statistically plausible and prevents behavioral patterns from revealing identities—particularly in cases like uniformly non-compliant night-shift groups.

t-Closeness is implemented as a pre-blockchain step, using generalization and suppression of quasi-identifiers. Earth Mover's Distance (EMD) is used to measure distributional divergence, enabling adaptive thresholds based on context sensitivity.

This integration aligns with GDPR's privacy-by-design principle and strengthens auditability without sacrificing analytical value for infection control.

3.4   Database Design

The database architecture supports the full operational scope of the proposed system platform, including real-time hygiene event tracking, user-role management, and privacy-preserving performance evaluation. Entities and relationships are designed to reflect the hospital's organizational structure, while ensuring compliance with privacy regulations and auditability requirements.

The system distinguishes among multiple actor roles: administrators, department heads, healthcare professionals (e.g., doctors, nurses, OSS), and patient relatives. Each actor interacts with the system through a role-specific interface with tailored access to data and functions. A complete overview of the database schema is shown in Fig. 3, which highlights the core tables and their interactions.

At the core of the schema is the Bed entity, which organizes a set of Beds, each linked to a specific Patient. Healthcare staff are assigned to departments and may be associated with one or more beds. The User entity manages the identity, role, and authentication credentials of each system user.

Healthcare workers access a personal interface where they can view their own hygiene compliance data, reports, and alerts using their real identity. In contrast, the Department Head interface provides an aggregated view of hygiene events across the entire department. In this view, individual operators are represented by pseudonymous identifiers to preserve anonymity. The Device table records camera and sensor endpoints used for inference. The Event table connects detections from the computer vision module with their corresponding hygiene actions, zone transitions, and timestamps. The Storage/Computation table stores serialized representations of detection events, including low-level outputs from the computer vision module (e.g., in JSON format), such as gesture classification, duration, and accessory detection results. It also includes metadata such as processing status and the location of the computational task, linked to both the device and the corresponding report. These records serve as the basis for generating system responses. The Alert and Report tables use this information to provide both real-time feedback and retrospective summaries, supporting compliance auditing and user notifications.

The Bed entity is associated with event-level metadata to support per-location compliance tracking. This enables the system to generate detailed statistics for each patient bed, useful for operational management and infection risk analysis. The Bed entity also stores metadata related to compliance checks and observational notes, enabling fine-grained traceability per patient location.

While all data are stored in the decentralized database location, compliance logs are also periodically recorded on the Hyperledger Fabric blockchain in pseudonymized form. This ensures data integrity and auditability for incentive eligibility calculation via smart contracts.

4 Methodology

Cameras equipped with AI-powered analytics are deployed to monitor **(i) compliance with hand hygiene protocols, (ii) the correct use of personal protective equipment (PPE), and (iii) adherence to institutional dress code policies** (e.g., absence of rings, bracelets, or watches). The proposed methodology addresses three key scenarios. First, it enables the identification and analysis of non-compliance patterns in critical hospital areas. Second, it ensures that only properly sanitized personnel can access high-risk zones such as isolation wards or neonatal intensive care units (NICUs). Third, it enables timely notifications for missed hand hygiene events following patient contact or contact with the surrounding environment.

The surveillance system leverages computer vision models to process image streams and video feeds in real time. These models analyze visual data to detect hygiene-relevant actions and contextual behavior. The system architecture is organized into three logical layers: *the computer vision layer*, which performs detection and analysis; *the blockchain layer*, which ensures immutable logging and incentive computation; and *the application layer*, which provides role-based interfaces for users, including feedback, statistics, and notifications. An overview of this layered architecture is shown in Fig. 4.

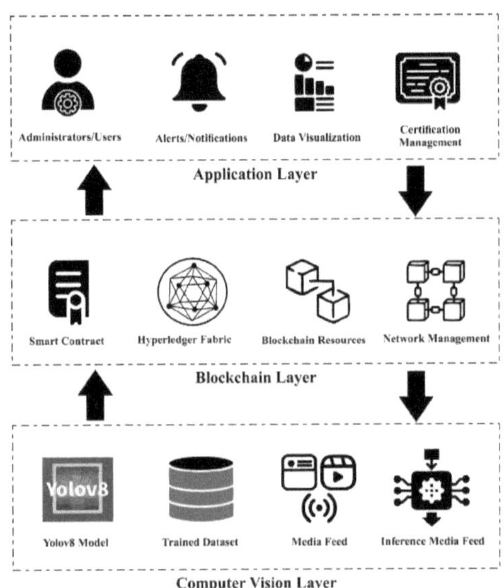

Fig. 4. System Architecture Diagram.

4.1   Computer Vision Layer

The computer vision layer processes inference images to detect compliance with hygiene-related actions and dress code standards. This includes the identification of gloves, rings, bracelets, and watches, as well as the recognition and evaluation of hand hygiene procedures. The system analyzes hand movements to determine whether proper hand rubbing steps have been performed and whether the total duration meets World Health Organization (WHO) guidelines. Training data was collected across different datasets:

- 5700 annotated hand hygiene images
- 3500 training usage instances
- 1500 validation usage instances
- 700 testing usage instances

The dataset reflects diverse clinical scenarios including surgical assessments, routine patient care, and equipment handling procedures. Training dataset graph is shown in Fig. 5.

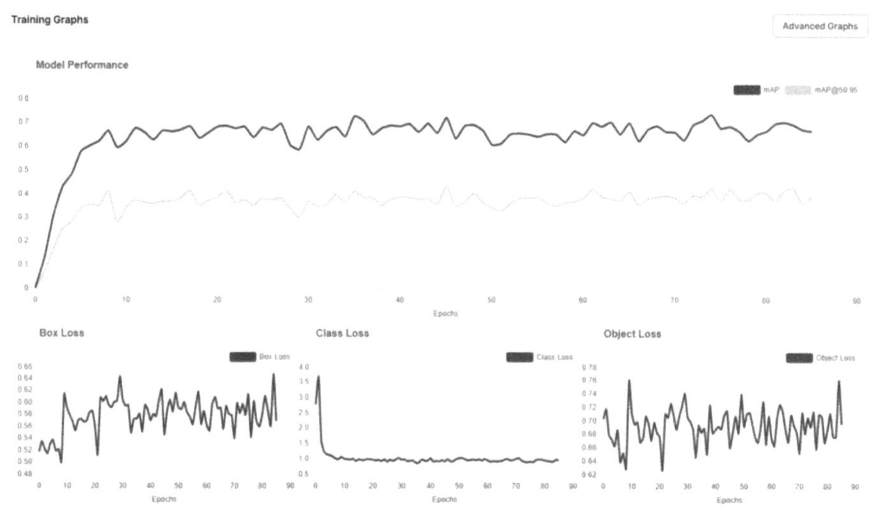

Fig. 5. Dataset Training Graph.

Computer vision part of the proposed model is really important because of the inference data feed. Starting from the image/video/live stream data feed to the dataset. Dataset images are passing through annotation, augmentation strategies to enhance the object detection. Cleaned dataset input to Yolov8 model for fine tuned training of inference images. Dataset divides into 65% training data, 25% validation data, and 10% testing data approximately. Inference model fine tuned with 100 epochs.

4.2 Blockchain Layer

The blockchain layer plays a central role in the proposed architecture by ensuring the integrity, transparency, and immutability of hygiene compliance records. The system leverages Hyperledger Fabric v2.5, selected for its modularity, performance improvements, and native support for peer load balancing—an advantage for real-time data ingestion and distributed deployments.

This version also simplifies the development and deployment of smart contracts (chaincode), providing a robust and flexible framework for implementing compliance logic and incentive calculation mechanisms within the network, as demonstrated in recent evaluations of Fabric v2.5 deployments [1]. The technology stack for the proposed blockchain layer is outlined below:

- Hyperledger Fabric v2.5
- Chaincode (Go)
- PyTorch (Python)
- FastAPI
- Docker

- CouchDB(v3.3)

Each component of the technology stack has a specific role and significance. Hyperledger Fabric is used to enable permissioned and secure transactions with high throughput and scalability. The Go programming language is employed for developing smart contracts (chaincode) that record inference-related events on the ledger. PyTorch is chosen for its seamless integration with the Ultralytics YOLOv8 inference model, facilitating efficient interaction with the computer vision layer [6]. FastAPI is adopted to support a lightweight microservice architecture and to facilitate blockchain-API interactions, particularly for storing detected images and metadata from the inference model. Administrative and application users are enrolled through the blockchain API, and their encrypted credentials are stored in the blockchain wallet infrastructure [4]. The platform uses Docker to containerize all core services, ensuring modularity and ease of deployment. For stateful storage of inference outputs in JSON format, CouchDB is used as the state database within the Hyperledger Fabric environment.

Blockchain layer is further based on three components. First network peers and organization nodes connect the hyperledger fabric network with the inference model. Second chaincode is the heart of the whole process which transforms the inference model detection into a recorded immutable record on the blockchain [18]. Inference images are stored in JSON format that can be used for further auditing purposes. Third blockchain resources includes the couchDB and network uptime that is required to smoothly process the application layer. In order to mantain modularity and secure access, custom blockchain-api access the enrolled admin and users of the system.

4.3 Application Layer

The application layer presents the output of the proposed system and serves as the interface between end users and the underlying architecture. A critical function of this layer is encrypted user management and secure access control. Security and traceability are enforced through Certificate Authorities (CAs), which authenticate system access. The Membership Service Provider (MSP) manages user identities and permissions based on encrypted enrollment data.

In the current implementation, the system is composed of two organizations with associated peers that handle transactions and data processing. Detection results from the inference model are serialized in JSON format and visualized in the user interface. These outputs also serve as the basis for real-time alerts and notifications, enabling immediate feedback and audit capabilities.

4.4 Identity Management

Proposed system adopts an identity model to balance traceability with privacy. At enrollment, each hospital staff member is assigned a public key and organizational role (e.g., nurse, doctor), registered through Hyperledger Fabric's Membership Service Provider (MSP). During operation, the computer vision module generates detection events tagged with session based pseudonymous identifiers. These identifiers are randomized per session and stored on the ledger without any persistent link to personally identifiable information. No direct mapping to individual users is maintained on chain unless voluntarily disclosed.

To support accountability at the organizational level, department heads are granted permission to view aggregated compliance data segmented by unit or staff role. Individual level tracing is only possible if a user chooses to participate in optional incentive schemes, such as receiving digital compliance certificates. In these cases, the user consents to disclose their ledger identity, enabling reward attribution while preserving default anonymity for all others.

4.5   FSM for Checking Hygienization Procedures

The monitoring procedure of hygiene compliance is modeled as a Finite State Machine (FSM) for hand hygiene procedures. This FSM functions as a real-time validator, continuously evaluating transitions based on spatial positioning, gesture classification, and time thresholds.

The process begins with an idle state, when no operator is present in the monitored area. Upon entry into the hygiene zone, the FSM transitions through successive states that track the initiation and execution of hand hygiene. Once the procedure is completed, the FSM continues tracking as the operator enters the patient proximity and contact zones. If an operator accesses these zones without having completed the required hygiene steps, the system registers the behavior as non-compliant and flags it accordingly for audit and alert purposes. After contact with the patient or with surrounding objects, the FSM also monitors whether a post-contact hand hygiene event occurs. Failure to perform hand disinfection after such interactions is similarly recorded as a non-compliance event and contributes to the operator's hygiene performance record. The FSM logic is implemented in Python and operates in close integration with the computer vision inference module, receiving continuous input from real-time detection pipelines. It not only triggers immediate alerts for hygiene failures but also produces structured compliance events for logging, blockchain registration, and incentive evaluation. The modular structure of the FSM supports future enhancements, such as the inclusion of aseptic procedures. A visual representation of the FSM logic is provided in Fig. 6, which illustrates the state transitions and corresponding hygiene events monitored during system operation.

4.6   Security Considerations for Inference Data

Since the detection of hygiene events is performed off chain by the computer vision (CV) module, this stage introduces potential attack vectors. An attacker with access to edge devices or system interfaces could attempt to inject false compliance data. To address these risks, the system incorporates several integrity-preserving mechanisms:

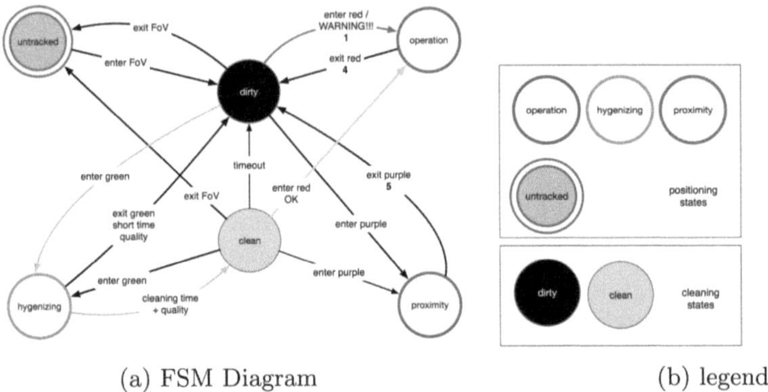

(a) FSM Diagram   (b) legend

Fig. 6. Extended Finite State Machine for hand hygienization checking and their legend about the states.

- *Digital signatures from edge devices:* Each detection event is signed using device specific cryptographic keys prior to being forwarded to the blockchain gateway, establishing a verifiable source of origin.
- *Timestamp verification:* Smart contracts validate event timestamps to ensure sequential consistency and detect anomalies such as out of order or replayed entries.
- Side ledger logging: A parallel tamper evident log is maintained off chain, recording signed events for redundancy. This log can be periodically cross checked by an auditing chaincode to ensure consistency.

Although performing inference entirely on chain is currently impractical due to resource constraints, the proposed architecture relies on a semi trusted edge model, where all inputs to the blockchain are verifiable and traceable.

4.7   Data Analysis

Our solution uses computer vision, AI and Hyperledger Fabric for monitoring and alerting hand hygiene practices in hospitals. The computer vision system provides real-time, accurate monitoring of hand hygiene compliance, while the blockchain ensures transparency, accountability, and traceability. This approach will not only reduce hospital-acquired infections but also streamline hospital operations and improve patient outcomes [13].

All data gathered through computer vision (e.g., hand hygiene), can be stored on Hyperledger Fabric [11]. This ensures data is tamper-proof, providing hospitals with reliable data for audits and decision-making.

Reports are generated on hygiene practices using compliance practices, identify patterns of non-compliance, and even predict areas with higher infection risks based on observed behavior. This could be further enhanced by correlating hygiene data with infection rates or patient outcomes.

4.8   Performance Evaluation

We assess system effectiveness through three metrics:

$$\text{Compliance Rate} = \frac{N_{\text{correct}}}{N_{\text{opportunities}}} \times 100\% \tag{1}$$

$$\text{Detection Latency} = t_{\text{alert}} - t_{\text{event}} \tag{2}$$

$$\text{System Accuracy} = 1 - \frac{\text{FP} + \text{FN}}{N_{\text{total}}} \tag{3}$$

5   Experimental Results

The novel decentralized hygiene monitoring system underwent comprehensive testing through a four-week evaluation using cross-examined dataset images from different hospital environment sections. This controlled assessment specifically examined three critical system aspects:

- The precision and reliability of computer vision detection
- The data security and operational efficiency of the blockchain infrastructure
- The practical utility and responsiveness of user alerts

Additionally, performance comparisons have been conducted against conventional observation techniques to quantify improvements as shown in Fig. 7.

The YOLOv8 model, fine-tuned on a custom clinical hygiene dataset, demonstrated strong performance in detecting hand hygiene-related features. Evaluation metrics were derived from the testing subset (700 images) and cross-validated with human-labeled ground truth; the testing results are reported in (Table 1). The blockchain layer built on Hyperledger Fabric v2.5 demonstrated robust performance in terms of immutability, fault tolerance, and throughput with the following performance:

- Average transaction throughput was 250 TPS (transactions per second) under load, sufficient for high-traffic clinical environments.
- Latency from inference event to ledger confirmation averaged 1.2 s.
- All detection events were successfully recorded in immutable JSON format, verified across two peer organizations with fault-tolerant redundancy.
- The chaincode (smart contract) logged compliance violations and normal behavior separately, facilitating audit filtering.

Table 1. Inference Model Testing Results

Detected Element	Precision	Recall	F1-Score
Gloves	0.81	0.91	0.75
Bracelet	0.78	0.81	0.75
Watch	0.85	0.86	0.71
Ring	0.81	0.85	0.78

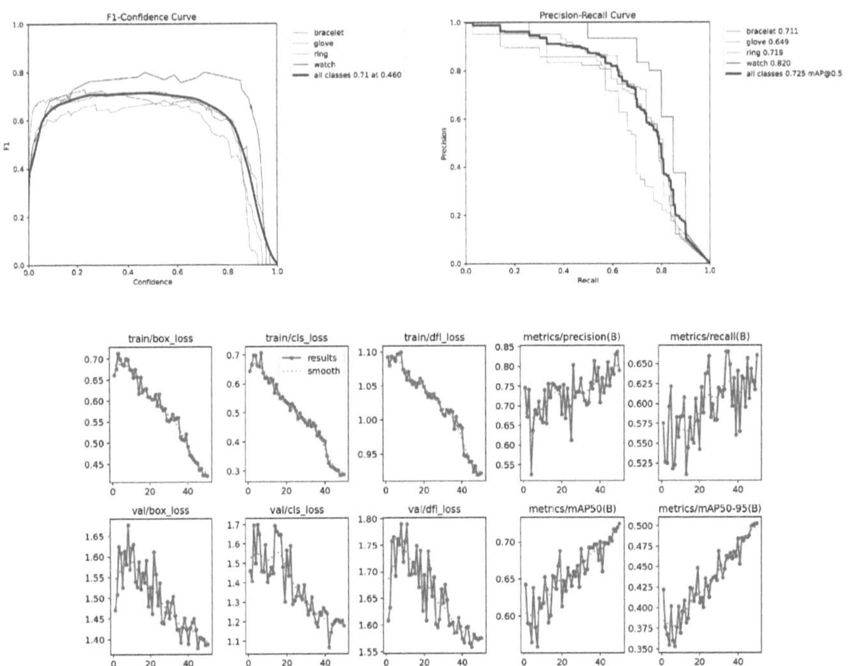

Fig. 7. Evaluation metrics for the inference model.

6   Future Work

The current implementation of the proposed system has been designed primarily in the context of neonatal intensive care units (NICUs), where the risk of infection transmission is extremely high and hand hygiene is of critical importance. While the architecture is modular and generalizable, further validation is required in other clinical environments, including emergency departments, surgical units, and long-term care facilities.

One significant limitation is the limited availability of real-world clinical deployment data. Although preliminary testing has been conducted in controlled environments, and some early-stage deployment data is being collected, a comprehensive evaluation of the system's impact on hand hygiene compliance and infection rates in active hospital settings is still ongoing. Given the novelty of the proposed approach, meaningful longitudinal data will require time and broader institutional adoption. Future work will include extended pilot deployments and outcome-based studies to assess behavioral change, improved adherence, and potential reductions in hospital-acquired infections (HAIs).

At present, the detection logic focuses primarily on hand hygiene events before and after patient contact, as well as interactions within the patient proximity zone. However, the system does not fully address aseptic procedures, such as hand disinfection before clean or sterile tasks (e.g., catheter insertion), nor the specific post-exposure hand hygiene following contact with biological fluids. Extending coverage to the full set of WHO's "5 Moments for Hand Hygiene" will be an important enhancement.

The current dataset, while functional, could benefit from expansion. Increasing the volume and diversity of annotated images—especially those related to glove use, accessory detection, and nuanced handwashing steps—will help improve model accuracy, generalizability, and mAP performance metrics.

Hygiene reminders and digital certificates could also be issued through mobile applications for visitors and family members, improving awareness and compliance. Finally, blockchain logging may be extended to supply chain monitoring, enabling the system to alert staff when sanitizing products are low or missing from key zones.

7   Conclusion

This study introduced a blockchain-based framework that integrates computer vision to monitor hand hygiene. The implementation of a specially optimized YOLOv8 architecture enabled precise, real-time identification of critical compliance factors including sanitization procedures, proper glove utilization, and unauthorized accessory wear. Complementing this, the Hyperledger Fabric blockchain established a tamper-proof repository for compliance records, guaranteeing unprecedented levels of data transparency and verifiable traceability.

Our laboratory testing revealed the system's superior performance compared to conventional manual observation approaches, delivering both enhanced detection accuracy and immediate intervention capabilities. The solution not only elevated compliance rates but also introduced a non-intrusive, real-time feedback mechanism that seamlessly integrated with existing clinical operations. The blockchain component provided transparency, traceability and accountability to hygienization procedures compliance records, resolving the longstanding conflict between individual privacy and institutional accountability.

These findings validate the transformative potential of converging AI with distributed ledger technology in healthcare settings. The framework establishes a new paradigm for compliance systems by unifying real-time behavioral analysis with immutable documentation, thereby addressing both immediate infection prevention needs and long-term quality assurance requirements. This dual-capability approach represents a significant advancement in intelligent healthcare monitoring systems.

References

1. Abbas, A., Alroobaea, R., Krichen, M., Rubaiee, S., Vimal, S., Almansour, F.M.: Blockchain-assisted secured data management framework for health information analysis based on internet of medical things. Pers. Ubiquitous Comput. **28** (2024). https://doi.org/10.1007/s00779-021-01583-8

2. Alrebish, S.A., Yusufoglu, H.S., Alotibi, R.F., Abdulkhalik, N.S., Ahmed, N.J., Khan, A.H.: Epidemiology of healthcare-associated infections and adherence to the HAI prevention strategies. Healthcare **11** (2023). https://doi.org/10.3390/healthcare11010063

3. Arip, A.A.S., Sazali, N., Kadirgama, K., Jamaludin, A.S., Turan, F.M., Razak, N.A.: Object detection for safety attire using yolo (you only look once). J. Adv. Res. Appl. Mech. **113** (2024). https://doi.org/10.37934/aram.113.1.3751

4. Arul, R., Al-Otaibi, Y.D., Alnumay, W.S., Tariq, U., Shoaib, U., Piran, M.D.: Multi-modal secure healthcare data dissemination framework using blockchain in IoMT. Pers. Ubiquitous Comput. **28** (2024). https://doi.org/10.1007/s00779-021-01527-2

5. Arunakumar, S.P.K., et al.: Improving 'hand-hygiene compliance' among the health care personnel in the special newborn care unit. Indian J. Pediatr. **91** (2024). https://doi.org/10.1007/s12098-022-04466-9

6. Balasubramanian, S., Shukla, V., Islam, N., Manghat, S.: Construction industry 4.0 and sustainability: an enabling framework. IEEE Trans. Eng. Manag. **71** (2024). https://doi.org/10.1109/TEM.2021.3110427

7. Choi, T.M., Shi, X.: On-demand ride-hailing service platforms with hired drivers during coronavirus (covid-19) outbreak: can blockchain help? IEEE Trans. Eng. Manag. **71** (2024). https://doi.org/10.1109/TEM.2021.3131044

8. Şirin Gündüz, M., Işık, G.: A new yolo-based method for real-time crowd detection from video and performance analysis of yolo models. J. Real-Time Image Process. **20** (2023). https://doi.org/10.1007/s11554-023-01276-w

9. Iversen, A.M., Hansen, M.B., Kristensen, B., Ellermann-Eriksen, S.: Clinical evaluation of an electronic hand hygiene monitoring system. Am. J. Infect. Control **51** (2023). https://doi.org/10.1016/j.ajic.2022.06.017

10. Li, N., Li, T., Venkatasubramanian, S.: t-closeness: privacy beyond k-anonymity and l-diversity. In: 2007 IEEE 23rd International Conference on Data Engineering, pp. 106–115. IEEE (2007)

11. Mani, V., Manickam, P., Alotaibi, Y., Alghamdi, S., Khalaf, O.I.: Hyperledger healthchain: patient-centric IPFS-based storage of health records. Electronics **10** (2021). https://doi.org/10.3390/electronics10233003

12. Mohammadi, F., Panou, A., Ntantogian, C., Karapistoli, E., Panaousis, E., Xenakis, C.: Curex: secure and private health data exchange. In: Proceedings - 2019 IEEE/WIC/ACM International Conference on Web Intelligence Workshops, WI 2019 Companion (2019). https://doi.org/10.1145/3358695.3361753

13. Ndzimakhwe, M., Telukdarie, A., Munien, I., Vermeulen, A., Chude-Okonkwo, U.K., Philbin, S.P.: A framework for user-focused electronic health record system leveraging hyperledger fabric. Information **14** (2023). https://doi.org/10.3390/info14010051

14. Omori, K., et al.: Virtual reality as a learning tool for improving infection control procedures. Am. J. Infect. Control **51** (2023). https://doi.org/10.1016/j.ajic.2022.05.023

15. Ortiz, M.B., Karapetrovic, S.: Developing internet of things-related ISO 10001 hand hygiene privacy codes in healthcare. TQM J. **35** (2023). https://doi.org/10.1108/TQM-03-2022-0081

16. Ozturk, T., Talo, M., Yildirim, E.A., Baloglu, U.B., Yildirim, O., Acharya, U.R.: Automated detection of covid-19 cases using deep neural networks with X-ray images. Comput. Biol. Med. **121** (2020). https://doi.org/10.1016/j.compbiomed.2020.103792

17. Quach, L.D., Quoc, K.N., Quynh, A.N., Ngoc, H.T., Thai-Nghe, N.: Tomato health monitoring system: tomato classification, detection, and counting system based on yolov8 model with explainable mobilenet models using grad-cam++. IEEE Access **12** (2024). https://doi.org/10.1109/ACCESS.2024.3351805
18. Rubeis, G.: Ethical implications of blockchain technology in biomedical research. Ethik in der Medizin (2024). https://doi.org/10.1007/s00481-024-00805-w
19. Saranya, R., Murugan, A.: A systematic review of enabling blockchain in healthcare system: analysis, current status, challenges and future direction. Mater. Today Proc. **80** (2023). https://doi.org/10.1016/j.matpr.2021.07.105
20. Thantharate, P., Thantharate, A.: Zerotrustblock: enhancing security, privacy, and interoperability of sensitive data through zerotrust permissioned blockchain. Big Data Cogn. Comput. **7** (2023). https://doi.org/10.3390/bdcc7040165
21. Tomar, A., Gupta, N., Rani, D., Tripathi, S.: Blockchain-assisted authenticated key agreement scheme for IoT-based healthcare system. Internet Things **23** (2023). https://doi.org/10.1016/j.iot.2023.100849
22. Vasishta, M.V.A., Palanisamy, B., Sural, S.: Decentralized authorization using hyperledger fabric. In: Proceedings - 2022 IEEE International Conference on Blockchain, Blockchain 2022 (2022). https://doi.org/10.1109/Blockchain55522.2022.00040
23. Yanhui, L., et al.: Research on identity authentication system of internet of things based on blockchain technology. J. King Saud Univ. Comput. Inf. Sci. **34** (2022). https://doi.org/10.1016/j.jksuci.2022.10.027

Smart Contract Verification

A Framework for Supporting Decentralised Applications Analysis

Flavio Corradini, Lorenzo Luzi, Fausto Marcantoni, Alessandro Marcelletti[(✉)],
Andrea Morichetta, and Barbara Re

University of Camerino, Camerino, Italy
{flavio.corradini,fausto.marcantoni,alessand.marcelletti,
andrea.morichetta,barbara.re}@unicam.it, lorenzo.luzi@studenti.unicam.it

Abstract. Blockchain technology has enabled the development of decentralised applications, which rely on smart contracts to implement their core logic. A critical phase in the development of such applications is the verification and analysis of the underlying smart contracts. The execution of these contracts can lead to unexpected behaviours caused by vulnerabilities or logical flaws. While various techniques have been established to analyse security aspects and prevent such issues, less attention has been given to execution data. This data is produced during the actual execution of smart contracts and exposes how these applications behave in practice. By analysing this data, domain experts can access novel perspectives of the application and uncover meaningful insights or patterns. In this work, we present a framework designed to support the analysis of decentralised applications. It provides functionalities to analyse and visualise execution data of smart contracts. The framework was implemented as a web-based application and evaluated by analysing its performance over synthetic logs.

Keywords: DApps · Analysis · Visualisation · Architecture · Graph

1 Introduction

The adoption of blockchain has led to the development of Decentralised Applications (DApps) across several domains like finance, Internet of Things, and retail [25]. The immutability and transparency provided by the blockchain, together with its consensus mechanism, have enabled the development of trustworthy applications, removing the need for a central authority. Crucial is the role of smart contracts, programs deployed and executed in the blockchain that encode DApps' business logic, constraints, and activities [20]. Various approaches have been adopted to ensure the correct behaviour of DApps and to prevent vulnerabilities or unintended outcomes in smart contracts.

In particular, various techniques have been developed to analyse DApps and provide support during their development [14,22]. Among the various techniques,

W. Knottenbelt et al. (Eds.): Blocktea 2025, LNICST 669, pp. 197–213, 2026.
https://doi.org/10.1007/978-3-032-12335-0_12

symbolic execution, formal verification, fuzzing, and static analysis have been proposed.

These approaches focus on verifying the implementation of smart contracts by analysing data obtained before their deployment, such as source code or bytecode.

In contrast, little attention has been given to execution data, derived from the actual outcome of deployed smart contracts. Indeed, smart contract execution generates on-chain data (e.g., transactions, events) that can be particularly meaningful during analysis and monitoring activities [6,7]. This kind of data represents, for instance, how users interact within the blockchain, how tokens are moved, or recurring executed operations. Such data represents the actual behaviour of a DApp and its components, permitting the uncovering of the operational logic and interactions [11,12]. Furthermore, the analysis of this data can reveal unexpected behaviours, patterns, as well as detect logical flaws, arising from incorrect assumptions, unhandled conditions, or unintended interactions between different contract functions [2]. Such aspects are not always detectable before smart contract deployment, and, although correctly implemented at a technical level, produce unintended output. Checking for code errors or vulnerabilities is therefore not sufficient, and additional tools considering execution data are necessary [4,5,10]. For instance, runtime analysis may uncover market manipulation tactics such as sandwich attacks [21], or identify unexpected transaction patterns that indicate abuse or logic misinterpretation not caught during testing. In addition to analysis tools, domain knowledge plays a crucial role in recognising relevant situations starting from data. The use of domain knowledge applies to different stages of an analysis, such as identifying data relevant for business objectives or interpreting obtained results [16]. In this way, it is possible to further support DApps development, enabling the analysis of novel multiple perspectives. To this end, visualisation techniques are particularly valuable, as they provide a clear and intuitive understanding of the complex interactions among smart contracts, users, and other components. [9,19]. Specifically, graph-based representations can effectively depict different kinds of data and their relationships, facilitating exploratory analysis to identify relevant insights that otherwise may remain hidden in raw execution data [17].

In this work, we propose a framework supporting the analysis of DApps leveraging data generated through the execution of smart contracts. The framework offers functionalities for the visualisation and analysis of various types of data, along with their relationships and insights into the executed operations. This is achieved through a chart-based dashboard that facilitates the analysis of different smart contracts, and a customisable graph-based visualisation for representing blockchain data and relationships. These functionalities are built upon the data extraction methodology proposed in [5], which enables the collection of meaningful logs from executed smart contracts. In particular, we focus on Ethereum Virtual Machine (EVM)-based applications and data, fostering the extraction and analysis from different networks, without being limited to a single one. Thanks to the variety of considered data and analytical views, the framework provides a comprehensive exploration of multiple perspectives of a DApp. As a result, it assists domain experts, such as business stakeholders or developers, in conducting in-depth analyses. The framework was implemented as an open-source online web-based application, guiding the user during the analysis without requiring advanced technical skills. To evaluate the feasibility of the proposed implementation, we analysed its performance over logs of scaling dimensions, measuring the latency during the different functionalities.

The remainder of the paper is structured as follows. Section 2 introduces the types of data considered for building the analyses supported by the framework. Section 3 provides an overview of the state of the art in blockchain analysis tools. Section 4 describes the architecture of the framework and the functionalities it offers. Section 5 presents the implemented web application and its main features, while Sect. 6 evaluates its performance. Finally, Sect. 7 concludes the paper and outlines directions for future work.

2 Background

In this section, we present the main types of data produced by smart contract execution that are used by the framework.

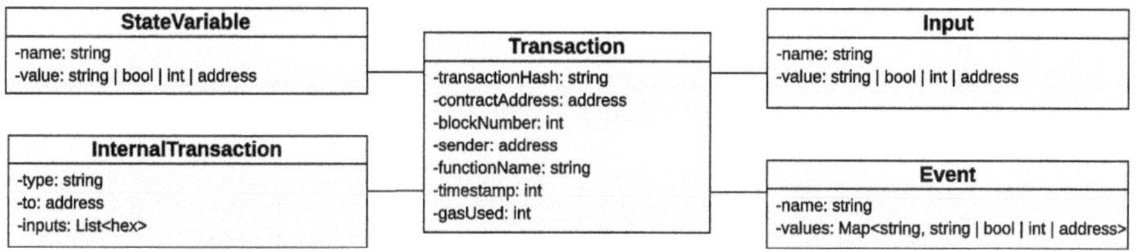

Fig. 1. Execution data of a smart contract.

In EVM-based platforms, smart contracts encode the core features of DApps, permitting their execution after deployment. Users can interact with the deployed smart contract to trigger the execution of certain activities, resulting in a transaction and further kinds of data [4,5]. **Transactions** are cryptographically signed instructions that are sent by users and finalized in the blockchain to invoke a **smart contract function**. After a transaction is validated and executed by the network, it is inserted into a block, propagated across the network, and appended to the blockchain. A transaction contains several data like its **hash**, the **block number** in which it was included, its **timestamp**, the **sender** address creating the transaction, and the **gas used**. A transaction can also include **events** emitted during the execution of a smart contract and containing additional log to notify external applications. Events may include both indexed and non-indexed parameters. Indexed parameters are stored in the event's topics and are primarily used for efficient filtering and search, while non-indexed parameters are stored in the event's data field. In our framework, we extract all event parameters, including their indexed status, as part of the raw data. However, in the graph visualisation, we display only the parameter names and values for clarity and usability. When different smart contracts interact, they produce **internal transactions**, typically stored off-chain, not being part of the blockchain. Each smart contract has a key-value storage area, persistent between function calls and transactions. **State variables** are defined in the smart contract and represent those variables permanently maintained in the storage over the blockchain and updated by smart contract functions.

3   State of the Art

The analysis of DApps and their underlying smart contracts has gained increasing attention over the years, leading to the development of various approaches that offer different types of analyses and supporting tools. In this section, we review relevant works that provide analysis capabilities and tools focused on blockchain execution data. The work in [8] analyses Ethereum transaction data to study the structural and statistical properties of the transaction network using network science theory. In particular, they consider data like the address of the sender, the address of the recipient, and the units of transferred cryptocurrency. This data is used to build a graph and measure its statistical properties to provide physical insights into the transaction relations.

The work in [3] provides an investigation of Ethereum via graph analysis. The authors construct three types of graphs: the money flow graph, the smart contract creation graph, and the smart contract invocation graph. These graphs derive from transaction data that include sender and recipient addresses, the amount of Ether transferred, transaction type, and success status, bytecode, gas usage, and input data. They apply several network metrics, with the main analysis purpose related to attack forensics, anomaly detection, and deanonymisation. Graph visualisation is also employed in [18], which focuses on network visualisation combined with mathematical and statistical modelling for graph analysis. However, no ready-to-use tool is provided; instead, only prioritised datasets are made available. A framework for the user-centric visualisation of blockchain transactions is proposed in [13]. Their work considered a generalised graph-based approach for blockchain transactions based on the Bitcoin and Ethereum networks. The framework has different layers that take the transaction data and transform it into a user-centric visualisation. Tracing illicit financial flows is a critical aspect of blockchain transaction analysis. The work in [23] introduces TRacer, a tool designed to trace transactions by constructing a graph that captures complex DeFi semantics. The authors propose a ranking algorithm to prioritize relevant paths and extract concise subgraphs. Their focus is on combating blockchain fraud, supporting forensic analysis, and assisting in the recovery of stolen funds. Another significant area within the Ethereum blockchain is NFT trading. [15] studies the growth rate and the evolutionary nature of the NFT network and tries to understand the ecosystem. The authors investigate the

NFT transaction graphs and analyse the different global network properties, such as reciprocity, assortativity, core decomposition, and clustering coefficient. Similarly, [1] provides an analysis in the NFT context. Here, an interactive visual analytics system is proposed, named NFTeller. Their system analyses data from NFT marketplaces, including social media signals, transaction data, and visual features. By incorporating five coordinated views, NFTeller enables a dual-centric analysis, offering insights into both NFT collection projects and whale account behaviours. Unlike the previous work, this study [24] focuses on IoT-generated operational data generated from a cattle farming supply chain. In this case, real-time smart contract visualisation is achieved by proposing a dashboard highlighting the token lifecycle events and activity logs.

Table 1. Comparison of the state of the art analysis approaches

Paper	Tool Provided	Analysis Type	Data Considered
[8]	✗	Complex network analysis	Transactions, accounts
[3]	✗	Graph analysis	Transaction data
[18]	✗	Graph analysis	Transaction data
[13]	✓	Graph-based user-centric visualisation	Transaction data
[23]	✓	Graph-based transaction tracing analysis	Transaction data
[15]	✗	Graph analysis	Transactions data
[1]	✓	Dual-centric visual analytics of NFT transactions	Transaction data
[24]	✓	Events lifecycle, activity timelines, operational analytics	Events
This work	✓	Network graph visualisation, data analysis	Transactions, state variables, internal transactions, events and inputs

A comparison of the analysis approaches is provided in Table 1, indicating whether they offer (i) a supporting tool for analysis, the kind of (ii) analysis conducted, and the type of (iii) data considered. When comparing the various approaches, existing works assist blockchain experts through data analytics and visualisations. However, these solutions often present limitations in terms of analysis scope, tool flexibility, and the variety of data they can handle.

In most cases, the analysis outcomes rely only on datasets, while few open-source **tools** are available, but with little to no integration across different types of logs and data. Furthermore, these tools are frequently designed for a fixed type of analysis or tied to specific algorithms (e.g., for graph construction), offering limited customisation. Indeed, in terms of **analysis type**, while some approaches support general monitoring of DApp execution data and related statistics, most of them are designed for security assessments. This leads to the application and development of specific techniques, such as vulnerability detection, complex network analysis, or custom visualisations. In contrast, our approach offers a general-purpose dashboard suitable for a variety of analysis objectives. The graph visualisation functionality supports custom selection of nodes and edges, without being tied to specific algorithms. This flexibility enables a broader range of uses, adaptable to different needs. Regarding the **data considered**, existing solutions typically focus on simple data types such as transactions and events, or they target specific entities represented by accounts and their token transfers. This highlights the need for novel approaches that support the analysis and visualisation of more complex and heterogeneous data types.

There is, therefore, a lack of structured proposals aimed at supporting comprehensive analysis and visualisation for blockchain domain experts without being limited to predefined objectives. This gap becomes even more apparent when considering the analysis of complex execution data, which can offer richer insights into the behaviour of DApps and their underlying smart contracts. With our work, we aim to address this gap by providing an open-source framework designed to support the analysis of DApps from multiple perspectives, leveraging a wide range of data produced by smart contract execution. Rather than focusing on a specific analysis objective or implementing particular algorithms, the framework serves as a flexible support tool for domain experts, facilitating the exploration and understanding of DApps and their underlying smart contracts.

4   The Framework Architecture

In this section, we describe the proposed framework, focusing on its architecture and functionalities. Figure 2 illustrates the various components of the framework, highlighting in yellow the extended ones. The architecture builds upon the extraction methodology and related architecture proposed in [5], to which we have added new components dedicated to analysis. The newly introduced components focus on analysis and visualisation, each implemented as a dedicated frontend module and integrated with the data processing service. The analysis module offers insights by presenting metrics and statistics across different smart contracts, while the visualisation module enables a graph-based representation of smart contract execution data and their relationships. The data processing service connects to a database that stores logs, which are extracted using existing modules. In the following, we first provide an overview of the existing modules and then focus on the newly introduced ones.

The data considered is obtained by the extraction methodology in [5]. To extract and decode execution data, the methodology relies on the contract's Application Binary Interface (ABI). The ABI is obtained either from the manually uploaded source code or automatically via blockchain explorer APIs (e.g., Etherscan).

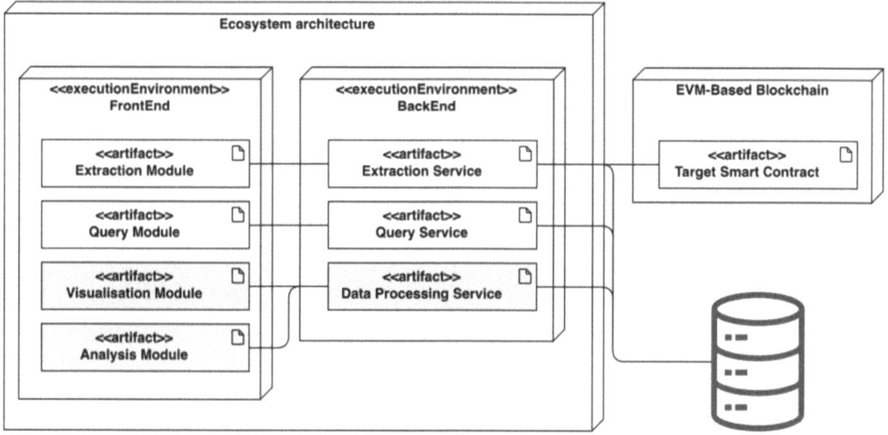

Fig. 2. Component diagram of the framework architecture. The diagram shows the modular structure of the framework, distinguishing between existing (white) components and newly added (yellow) components

Extraction and Query Modules. These components offer a range of functionalities aimed at extracting data related to smart contract execution. The process begins with the definition of configuration parameters, such as the target network (e.g., Ethereum, Polygon), block range, and transaction filters (e.g., gas usage, sender addresses). The smart contract code is then automatically retrieved, and relevant transactions are collected and filtered according to the specified configuration. Leveraging data from the compiled smart contract, the execution data is decoded and stored, structured according to the model shown in Fig. 1. A comprehensive log is generated, and all extracted data is saved in a local database, which is accessible to the user via query interfaces. This setup not only enables faster data retrieval but also allows for the formulation of complex queries and aggregations through the use of a standard DBMS.

Analysis Module. This component offers users the ability to access various insights into the smart contracts under analysis. Specifically, it is implemented as a chart-based dashboard that retrieves and displays data from the stored logs of multiple smart contracts. Users can select the contract of interest and obtain a comprehensive overview of its associated information, enabling immediate comparisons across different contracts.

Users can also define additional parameters to refine the analysis, such as selecting a specific transaction interval based on timestamps or block ranges. Table 2 outlines the different types of data considered within the module, organized into thematic sections. Each section includes both a chart and a corresponding table to present statistical information in a clear and accessible format.

Visualisation Module. In this module, the extracted log is visualised as an undirected graph. This choice is motivated by several factors. First, graph-based

Table 2. Execution data considered in the analysis module and how they are depicted in the analysis module

Section	Chart content	Table content
Gas Used	Total percentage of gas consumed by each function	Smart contract information, function name, total gas consumed by each function
Function	Occurrence of executed function by each function	Smart contract information, function name, occurrences of executed function
Sender	✗	Sender address, occurrences of transaction performed, average gas used
Time	Time interval of sent transaction	✗
Input	Occurrences of each input variable	Smart contract information, input name, input type, occurrences of each input variable
Event	Occurrences of each emitted event	Smart contract information, event name, occurrences of each emitted event
Internal transaction	Occurrences of each internal transaction	Smart contract information, internal call type, occurrences of each internal transaction
Storage state	Occurrences of each updated state variable	Smart contract information, variable name, occurrences of each update state variable

visualisation enhances data interpretability, enabling users to better understand complex data structures and the relationships among them. Second, it aligns naturally with the structure of blockchain systems. Blockchain transactions often involve multiple data types and exhibit many-to-many relationships, making graph representations particularly well-suited for capturing these intricate interaction networks [17–19]. To construct the graph, users define the edge configuration by selecting the node types of interest. Nodes are generated by extracting the corresponding data fields from the transaction log, while edges are created when the selected fields co-occur within the same transaction. If the same pair of nodes and their relation appear in multiple transactions, the edge weight is incremented to reflect the frequency of their connection. A detailed explanation of node and edge creation is provided in Sect. 5. Furthermore, the module includes filtering capabilities to highlight specific nodes or edges, along with a panel that displays detailed information about the transaction associated with a selected node.

5   Implemented Framework

This section shows the implemented framework, which is provided as a web-based application divided into a frontend and a backend, with the latter implemented

Fig. 3. Extraction page, functionalities and example of extracted log

as a server connected to a database. The application is accessible online[1]. The backend handles the overall logic and manages the communication with the frontend and the database. It is built using the ExpressJS framework[2] with the NodeJS[3] runtime environment. For data storage, the framework uses MongoDB[4], a NoSQL database that stores the data in JSON-like format. The frontend comprises several technologies for the various modules, each developed as a separate page. The main user interface is built with the React library[5]. The visualisation module integrates SigmaJS[6] to support graph rendering, while the analysis module is developed using the Material UI library[7]. In the following, we show the existing pages, moving then to the visualisation and analysis ones, illustrating their features and functionalities.

Extraction and Query Pages. The extraction and query pages enable users to extract and query execution data, as described in Sect. 4. Here we provide a brief overview of the extraction page, while for a detailed illustration, we direct the reader to [5]. Figure 3 shows the extraction page. This contains several features to extract execution data from an identified smart contract and access other pages. The various panels (i-iv) allow the configuration of the parameters necessary for selecting the target smart contract and triggering the extraction. After extracting

---

[1] https://github.com/AlessandroMarcellettiUnicam1/DApp_analysis_ecosystem.
[2] https://expressjs.com/.
[3] https://nodejs.org/en.
[4] https://www.mongodb.com/.
[5] https://react.dev/.
[6] https://www.sigmajs.org/.
[7] https://mui.com/material-ui/.

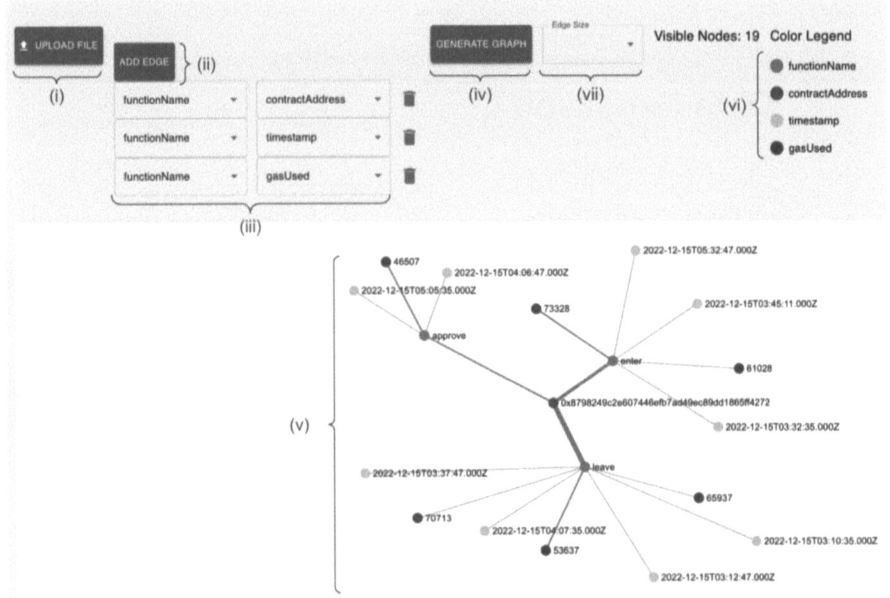

Fig. 4. Graph visualisation page with its panels and functionalities

data, the right-side panel (v) displays a preview of the obtained log, which can be downloaded in JSON or CSV. Finally, the remaining buttons provide access to the other pages (vi).

Visualisation Page. Figure 4 shows the page and its main panels, providing the functionalities for creating and interacting with the graph. The *Upload file* button (i) allows loading a JSON log file containing transactions and related data to use to generate the graph. Once uploaded, the application queries and extracts the keys in the log automatically, making them available as potential nodes of the graph. These nodes can then be selected by users for the creation of the edges to visualise. Notice, while the input log is thought to have a structure like the one presented in Fig. 1, this is not strict, and other kinds of logs can be uploaded. Once the log is processed, the graph can be defined using the *Add edge* button (ii). This creates two separate selection boxes: one for the source node of the edge and one for the target node (iii). The user can select the desired node types for both ends of the edge. After defining all the required edges, the user can click the *generate graph* to produce the final visualisation (iv). In the dedicated panel (v), the graph is visualised having distinct colours, randomly assigned, for the various kinds of nodes (vi). The application processes the entire log by iterating over each transaction to create nodes and edges based on the selected source and target fields, using their values as unique node identifiers. Each node in the graph has a unique ID. When multiple connections occur between the same pair of nodes across different transactions, instead of creating

```
˅ { 11 items 📋
  "functionName": string "approve"
  "transactionHash": string "0x33d6849f7af893becdf14c225e76d7bfc3aa805b924ffa5523a0c95b718be847"
  "blockNumber": int 16187604
  "contractAddress": string "0x8798249c2e607446efb7ad49ec89..."
  "sender": string "0x74f85fe5538dbfcf3b46399e121c..."
  "gasUsed": int 46507
  "timestamp": string "2022-12-15T04:06:47.000Z"
  ˅ "inputs": [ 2 items
    ˅ 0: { 3 items
        "inputName": string "spender"
        "type": string "address"
        "inputValue": string "8798249c2E607446EfB7Ad49eC89dD..."
      }
    ˅ 1: { 3 items
        "inputName": string "amount"
        "type": string "uint256"
        "inputValue": int 1.157920892373162e+77
      }
    ]
  "storageState": [] 0 items
  "internalTxs": [] 0 items
  ˅ "events": [ 1 item 📋
    ˅ 0: { 2 items 📋
        "eventName": string "Approval" 📋
        ˅ "eventValues": { 7 items
            "0": string "0x74f85Fe5538DbfCF3B46399E121c..."
            "1": string "0x8798249c2E607446EfB7Ad49eC89..."
            "2": int 1.157920892373162e+77
            "__length__": int 3
            "owner": string "0x74f85Fe5538DbfCF3B46399E121c..."
            "spender": string "0x8798249c2E607446EfB7Ad49eC89..."
            "value": int 1.157920892373162e+77
          }
      }
```

Fig. 5. Panel with transaction details for selected node. The JSON represents the data extracted from a transaction based on the structure of Fig. 1

multiple edges, the application aggregates these into a single edge with a weight indicating the frequency of that connection. The edge thickness or size in the graph visualisation is scaled proportionally to the weight, with a scaling function applied to prevent excessively large edge sizes.

Because the node selections are based on keys from the input JSON log, there are two possible cases when extracting node information. In the case of a simple key, where the value is a primitive type (such as a string or number), the node is created directly from that key-value pair. In contrast, if the key corresponds to a complex object (i.e., the value is itself a nested JSON object), the application attempts to create the node using that entire object as its data. However, if this complex key is empty or does not contain valid data, no node will be created for that entry. This flexible approach allows the system to handle a variety of input log structures while maintaining meaningful graph representations. To have a clearer view of the nodes and their edges, the application includes filter functionalities based on the size of the edge (vii). The drop-down menu contains all the sizes of the edges inside the graph. When the user selects a specific edge, the application automatically hides all the edges and related nodes that do not meet the selected criteria, in order to highlight the desired edges. The sizes of the edges listed in the drop-down menu reflect the real values, not the scaled ones

Fig. 6. Panel for data filtering based on time interval, block range, and smart contract identifier

mentioned earlier. Additionally, by clicking on a node, the corresponding transaction with all its data is shown, as visible in Fig. 5. This is done by extracting the transaction from the log in which the clicked node is contained.

Analysis Page. The analysis page is implemented as a dashboard displaying relevant insights and statistics about the logs of different smart contracts. Figure 6 shows the dashboard with its filters and the various sections described in Table 2. The dashboard allows users to select, among the smart contracts in the database, those to analyse. It is also possible to define a timestamp interval and block range to further filter the transactions for analysis. Based on the selected filters, the various sections of the dashboard are populated and made accessible through the different tabs shown in Fig. 6. As an example of an implemented tab, we consider the **Storage state** tab shown in Fig. 7. This tab includes all the state variables updated during the execution of the transactions in the log. Specifically, the bar chart displays the variables and their frequency within the log, while the accompanying table shows the smart contract reference, the variable name, and the exact number of occurrences.

6   Evaluation

To provide an evaluation of the framework, we analyse its performance under different conditions. In particular, we tested the rendering performance of the graph visualisation module and the dashboard generation in the analysis module.

Visualisation Module Performance. The visualisation module was tested on a commonly used machine without a dedicated GPU, simulating the environment of an average user. The machine used for the experiments was equipped with an Apple M1 processor and 8 GB of RAM. The tests were conducted using a log

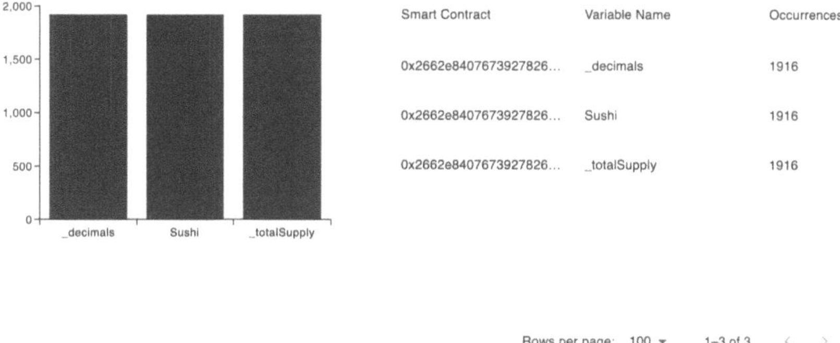

Fig. 7. Panel for visualising storage state variables and their occurrences

with synthetic data. The decision to use synthetic data was motivated by the
ability to precisely control the volume, distribution, and type of data. Instead,
real data can be more inconsistent as extracted logs contain transactions varying
in the amount and type of related information. This allowed for more systematic and reproducible performance testing. To evaluate the performance of graph
generation, we measured the latency involved in generating graphs with up to
100,000 nodes. The nodes were divided into frames of 2,500 to manage resource
allocation better and the rendering workload. To maintain a controlled testing
environment, the number of edges was scaled linearly, assigning a single edge
to each pair of nodes with a weight of one. This configuration ensured consistent performance benchmarking under predictable conditions. The results of the
experiments are reported in Fig. 8. Some considerations can be made from this
chart. The chart initially exhibits a linear increase in latency corresponding to
the growing number of nodes, with minimal latency observed for smaller graphs.
Specifically, for graph sizes up to 35,000 nodes and 17,500 edges, the generation
time consistently remained below 1 s. Beyond this threshold, latency increases
progressively, reaching approximately 10 s for graphs comprising 100,000 nodes
and 50,000 edges. Notably, once the initial rendering is completed, the graph
can be interactively explored and filtered without incurring additional computational overhead or latency. Future work will focus on optimising the graph
generation pipeline to further reduce latency, particularly for large-scale graphs.

Analysis Module. For the analysis module, we evaluated the system's performance in creating and populating the dashboard as the number of transactions
scaled. To this end, we used synthetic logs with an increasing number of trans-

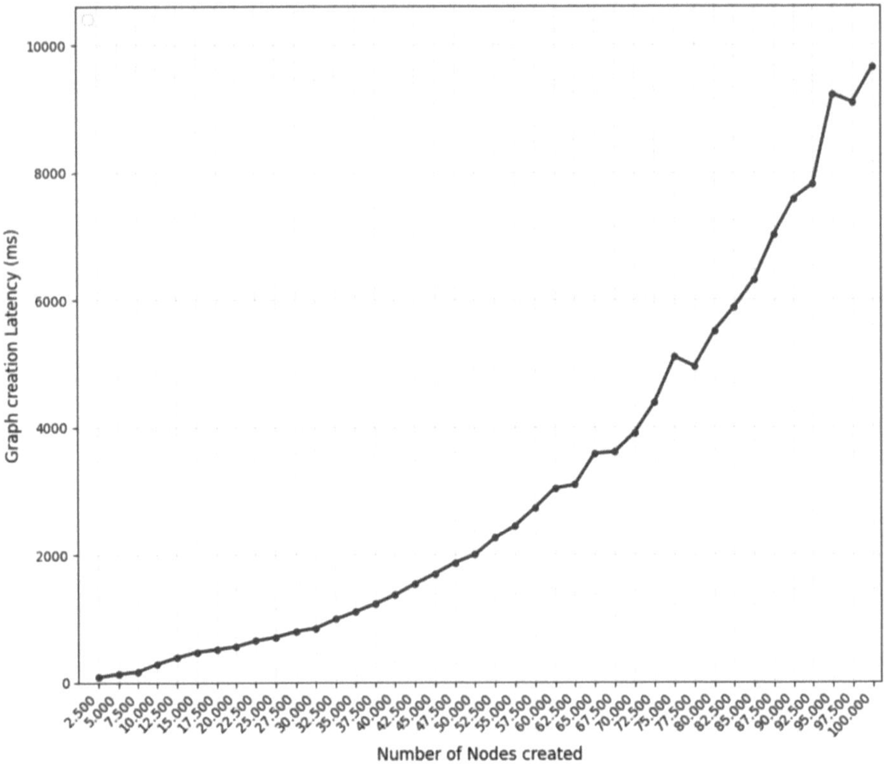

Fig. 8. Performance of graph creation with a growing number of transactions

actions, up to a maximum of 100,000, identified as the upper limit that could be handled without any functional issues. As in the previous evaluation, we adopted a stepwise progression of 2,500 transactions. Since the computation begins as soon as the framework is executed, we measured the total latency for populating the complete dashboard rather than isolating individual panel timings. Figure 9 illustrates the latency results. For logs up to 100,000 transactions, the latency remains below 500 ms. Once the initial log upload and dashboard population are completed, subsequent navigation across panels incurs no additional latency, as all components have been preloaded. Additionally, the dashboard's filtering functionality allows users to limit the number of transactions being analysed in real time, which can further reduce perceived latency. Future work will focus on optimising performance for handling larger log files and minimising the associated latency.

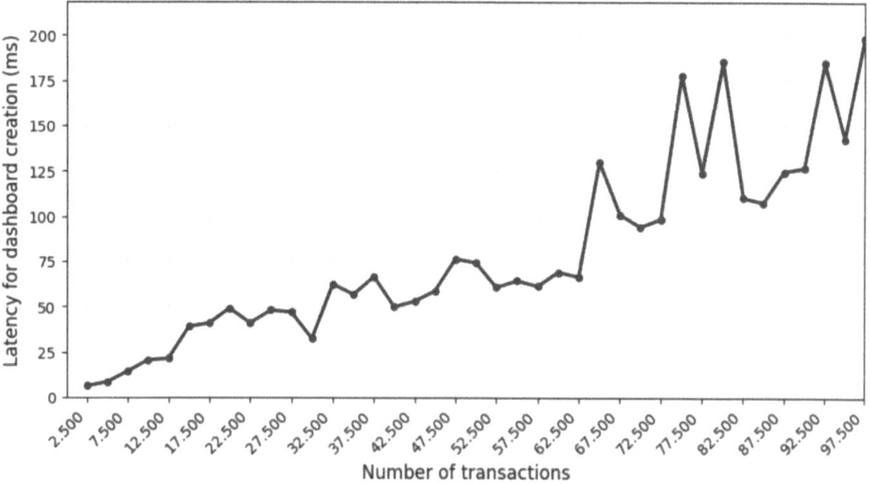

Fig. 9. Performance of dashboard population with a growing number of transactions

7   Conclusions

The advent of blockchain and its inherent characteristics has enabled the development of DApps, where logic is executed without third parties. Smart contracts encode and execute business logic, serving as core components of DApps. Ensuring their correctness is therefore fundamental. During development, vulnerabilities and errors can lead to security issues, making prevention essential. Over the years, several approaches have been adopted to verify smart contract code and detect bugs at design time, such as testing, static analysis, and dynamic analysis. While security analysis is crucial, considering execution data can offer new insights. This data captures runtime behaviour, including contract interactions, token transfers, and account activities. Analysing it allows domain experts to identify patterns, trends, or anomalies not evident through code analysis alone. In this work, we present a framework designed to analyse decentralised applications, focusing on smart contract execution data. The system includes data analysis and graph visualisation modules and is implemented as an open-source, web-based application with guided, user-friendly features. Its performance was evaluated using synthetic logs.

In future work, we plan to enhance the graph functionalities by enabling custom node aggregation or clustering and by improving overall performance. We also aim to integrate more advanced dashboard interactions, allowing for deeper data exploration and additional metrics. Finally, we intend to explore novel approaches for analysing DApp behaviour, such as applying process mining techniques to study smart contract execution patterns.

Acknowledgment. This work was partially supported by project SERICS (PE00000014) under the MUR National Recovery and Resilience Plan funded by the European Union - NextGenerationEU.

References

1. Cao, Y., et al.: Nfteller: dual centric visual analytics of NFT transactions. In: International Conference on Big Data and Smart Computing, pp. 293–294. IEEE (2023)
2. Chen, J., Xia, X., Lo, D., Grundy, J., Luo, X., Chen, T.: Defining smart contract defects on ethereum. IEEE Trans. Software Eng. **48**(1), 327–345 (2022)
3. Chen, T., et al.: Understanding ethereum via graph analysis. ACM Trans. Internet Technol. **20**(2), 1–32 (2020)
4. Corradini, F., Marcelletti, A., Morichetta, A., Re, B.: A data extraction methodology for ethereum smart contracts. In: 2024 IEEE International Conference on Pervasive Computing and Communications Workshops and other Affiliated Events (PerCom Workshops), pp. 524–529. IEEE (2024)
5. Corradini, F., Marcelletti, A., Morichetta, A., Re, B.: A methodology for extracting and decoding smart contracts data. Comput. Commun. 108204 (2025)
6. Di Ciccio, C., Meroni, G., Plebani, P.: Business process monitoring on blockchains: potentials and challenges. In: Enterprise, Business-Process and Information Systems Modeling. LNBIP, vol. 387, pp. 36–51. Springer (2020)
7. Di Ciccio, C., Meroni, G., Plebani, P.: On the adoption of blockchain for business process monitoring. Softw. Syst. Model. **21**(3), 915–937 (2022). https://doi.org/10.1007/S10270-021-00959-X
8. Guo, D., Dong, J., Wang, K.: Graph structure and statistical properties of ethereum transaction relationships. Inf. Sci. **492**, 58–71 (2019)
9. Härer, F., Fill, H.G.: A comparison of approaches for visualizing blockchains and smart contracts. Jusletter IT (2019)
10. Hobeck, R., Berti, A., Weber, I., van der Aalst, W.: Object-centric process mining for blockchain applications: extracting and representing ethereum execution data in OCEL 2.0. Enterp. Model. Inf. Syst. Architect. (EMISAJ) **20** (2025)
11. Hobeck, R., Klinkmüller, C., Bandara, H.D., Weber, I., van der Aalst, W.: On the suitability of process mining for enhancing transparency of blockchain applications. Bus. Inf. Syst. Eng. 1–20 (2024)
12. Ibba, G., et al.: Mindthedapp: a toolchain for complex network-driven structural analysis of ethereum-based decentralized applications. IEEE Access **12**, 28382–28394 (2024). https://doi.org/10.1109/ACCESS.2024.3366069
13. Jeyakumar, S.T., Ko, R., Muthukkumarasamy, V.: A framework for user-centric visualisation of blockchain transactions in critical infrastructure. Association for Computing Machinery, New York, NY, USA (2023)
14. Jiao, T., Xu, Z., Qi, M., Wen, S., Xiang, Y., Nan, G.: A survey of ethereum smart contract security: attacks and detection. Distrib. Ledger Technol. Res. Pract. **3**(3), 1–28 (2024)
15. Khati, P.: Measurement, analysis, and insight of NFTS transaction networks. arXiv preprint arXiv:2211.15600 (2022)
16. Kopanas, I., Avouris, N.M., Daskalaki, S.: The role of domain knowledge in a large scale data mining project. In: Vlahavas, I.P., Spyropoulos, C.D. (eds.) SETN 2002. LNCS (LNAI), vol. 2308, pp. 288–299. Springer, Heidelberg (2002). https://doi.org/10.1007/3-540-46014-4_26

17. Song, J., Zhang, P., Qu, Q., Bai, Y., Gu, Y., Yu, G.: Why blockchain needs graph: a survey on studies, scenarios, and solutions. J. Parallel Distrib. Comput. **180**, 104730 (2023)
18. Tharani, J.S., Charles, E.Y.A., Hóu, Z., Palaniswami, M., Muthukkumarasamy, V.: Graph based visualisation techniques for analysis of blockchain transactions. In: Conference on Local Computer Networks, pp. 427–430. IEEE (2021)
19. Tovanich, N., Heulot, N., Fekete, J.D., Isenberg, P.: Visualization of blockchain data: a systematic review. IEEE Trans. Visual Comput. Graphics **27**(7), 3135–3152 (2019)
20. Viriyasitavat, W., Da Xu, L., Niyato, D., Bi, Z., Hoonsopon, D.: Applications of blockchain in business processes: a comprehensive review. IEEE Access **10**, 118900–118925 (2022)
21. Wang, Y., Zuest, P., Yao, Y., Lu, Z., Wattenhofer, R.: Impact and user perception of sandwich attacks in the defi ecosystem (2022). https://doi.org/10.1145/3491102.3517585
22. Wu, G., Wang, H., Lai, X., Wang, M., He, D., Chan, S.: A comprehensive survey of smart contract security: state of the art and research directions. J. Netw. Comput. Appl. 103882 (2024)
23. Wu, Z., Liu, J., Wu, J., Zheng, Z., Chen, T.: Tracer: scalable graph-based transaction tracing for account-based blockchain trading systems. IEEE Trans. Inf. Forensics Secur. **18**, 2609–2621 (2023)
24. Yap, S.K., Dong, Z., Toohey, M., Lee, Y.C., Zomaya, A.Y.: Smart contract data monitoring and visualization. In: IEEE International Conference on Blockchain and Cryptocurrency, pp. 1–8. IEEE (2023)
25. Zheng, P., Jiang, Z., Wu, J., Zheng, Z.: Blockchain-based decentralized application: a survey. IEEE Open J. Comput. Soc. **4**, 121–133 (2023)

Unmasking Fraud in DeFi: Behavioral and Statistical Insights into Scam Token Detection

Mahdiyeh Barzegar[1], Hamid Reza Barzegar[1], Nabil El Ioini[2], and Claus Pahl[1(✉)]

[1] Free University of Bozen-Bolzano, Bolzano, Italy
{mahdiyeh.barzegar,hamid.barzegar,claus.pahl}@unibz.it
[2] University of Nottingham Malaysia, Selangor, Malaysia
ioini.nabil@nottingham.edu.my

Abstract. Decentralized Finance (DeFi) has revolutionized financial transactions, enabling peer-to-peer exchanges without intermediaries. However, its rapid growth has also fueled the rise of Scam tokens—fraudulent cryptocurrencies designed to deceive investors. These scams, including rug pulls, Ponzi schemes, and phishing attacks, exploit the decentralized nature of blockchains to evade oversight. This paper systematically analyzes scam token behaviors, differentiating them from Legitimate tokens using financial metrics, transaction patterns, and smart contract functionalities. Leveraging on-chain data and statistical methods, we identify key fraud indicators to enhance detection mechanisms. Our findings offer valuable insights for investors, researchers, and regulators, improving security in DeFi markets. Additionally, we propose strategies to strengthen scam detection and mitigate financial risks, fostering a safer and more transparent blockchain ecosystem.

Keywords: Decentralized Finance · Scam tokens · Blockchain Security · Fraud Detection · Smart Contracts

1 Introduction

The rise of decentralized finance (DeFi) has revolutionized financial transactions by eliminating intermediaries. While DeFi fosters financial inclusion and innovation, it also facilitates the proliferation of Scam tokens, which exploit investors through Ponzi schemes, rug pulls, and phishing scams [1,3,4].

Rug pulls, among the most notorious scams, involve developers attracting investments before withdrawing liquidity, leaving investors with worthless tokens [1,7]. Ponzi schemes promise high returns by redistributing funds from new investors, creating a false sense of profitability [3]. Phishing scams, meanwhile, manipulate blockchain transparency to deceive users into transferring funds to malicious addresses [4].

© ICST Institute for Computer Sciences, Social Informatics and Telecommunications Engineering 2026
Published by Springer Nature Switzerland AG 2026. All Rights Reserved
W. Knottenbelt et al. (Eds.): Blocktea 2025, LNICST 669, pp. 214–225, 2026.
https://doi.org/10.1007/978-3-032-12335-0_13

Despite these risks, many legitimate DeFi projects provide valuable services, backed by transparent teams, community engagement, and rigorous audits [2]. Distinguishing between legitimate and fraudulent tokens is essential for DeFi security and trust.

This study analyzes scam token behavior, comparing their statistical characteristics with Legitimate tokens on Uniswap V3. To achieve this, we investigate the following research questions:

- **RQ1:** What key financial, transactional, and temporal features differentiate Scam tokens from Legitimate tokens in DeFi?
- **RQ2:** How can transaction and market behavior patterns be utilized for scam token detection?
- **RQ3:** What role do smart contract functionalities play in identifying fraudulent token activities?

By answering these questions, this research contributes to enhancing fraud detection mechanisms and improving security within the DeFi landscape.

2   Literature Review

The detection of Scam tokens on blockchain platforms has gained increasing attention in academia as these scams continue to rise. This literature review synthesizes key findings from studies analyzing scam token behaviors and detection methodologies.

A major research focus is phishing scams in the Ethereum ecosystem. Chen and Fu highlighted their alarming financial impact, stressing the need for robust detection mechanisms [4]. Zhang and Chen proposed a multi-channel graph classification approach, leveraging blockchain transaction transparency to identify fraud [13].

Beyond phishing, studies address Ponzi schemes and other fraudulent token behaviors. Chen et al. developed a framework for detecting smart Ponzi schemes by analyzing transaction patterns and contract behaviors [3]. Agarwal et al. documented rug pulls in DeFi, where developers abandon projects after raising funds, leaving investors with worthless tokens [1]. Sharma et al. further analyzed fraudulent NFT rug pulls, identifying key structural and behavioral scam properties [9].

Xia et al. examined Scam tokens on Uniswap using a guilt-by-association heuristic and machine learning to flag fraudulent tokens based on transaction data [10]. Xiong et al. explored graph neural networks for phishing detection, showing that traditional methods are insufficient for blockchain-based scams [12].

Overall, the literature underscores the complexity of scam detection, requiring empirical analysis, machine learning, and smart contract understanding. These studies provide a foundation for improving detection methods and increasing investor awareness in a fraud-prone cryptocurrency market.

3   Methodology

This research follows a structured methodology with three key stages to analyze behavioral differences between scam and Legitimate tokens on Uniswap V3:

1. **Data Retrieval and Selection**: Blockchain data is collected from trusted sources like Etherscan and Infura.io, covering transactional activities, token attributes, and liquidity pool interactions to capture token behavior on Uniswap V3.
2. **Data Labeling and Heuristic Propagation**: Tokens are classified as scam, legitimate, or unknown based on predefined criteria. Heuristic-based label propagation, informed by prior research, analyzes relationships among tokens, liquidity pools, and creator addresses.
3. **Feature Extraction and Analysis**: Key behavioral attributes—trading volume fluctuations, transaction frequency, liquidity withdrawals, and smart contract functionalities—are extracted. Statistical tests, including Welch's t-test, identify significant differences between scam and Legitimate tokens.

This methodology enables a rigorous, data-driven comparison of scam and Legitimate tokens, enhancing scam detection in decentralized exchanges.

3.1   Data Retrieval and Selection

To build a comprehensive dataset, we leveraged multiple blockchain sources, including Etherscan and Infura.io, for transaction, token, and pool-level data. Etherscan provides access to Ethereum contract interactions and token transfers, essential for tracking Uniswap V3 activity [5]. Infura.io offers an API-based gateway for efficient Ethereum transaction extraction without running a full node [6].

Integrating these sources, we compiled a structured dataset covering tokens, pools, and transactions, ensuring both real-time and historical data. The dataset is stored in PostgreSQL for efficient querying and analysis[1].

3.2   Data Labeling and Heuristic-Based Propagation

Data Labeling. To differentiate between scam and Legitimate tokens, we applied a structured labeling strategy:

- **Legitimate tokens**: Tokens that appeared in the top 1,000 listings from both Etherscan and CoinMarketCap, which are actively traded on Uniswap V3. These tokens have high market trust and liquidity.
- **Scam tokens**: Tokens listed in Etherscan's scam reports, which are flagged due to fraudulent behavior, such as rug pulls, phishing attempts, and malicious smart contract functionalities.

---

[1] The dataset used in this study is available at https://github.com/MahdiyehBarzegar/UniswapV3/blob/main/dataset_uniswap_v3.csv.

– **Unknown Tokens**: Tokens that did not fall into either category, including lesser-known tokens with limited trading history or uncertain trustworthiness.

By categorizing tokens into these three groups, we created a labeled dataset that forms the foundation for comparative behavioral analysis.

Rule-Based Label Propagation. Following initial labeling, we applied rule-based label propagation to extend scam token classifications using heuristics from prior studies. This ensures that related entities (e.g., token creators and associated pools) are also flagged. Table 1 outlines the applied heuristics.

Table 1. Literature-Based Heuristics for Identifying Scam tokens

Heuristic	Description	Source
Token Similarity	Flags tokens mimicking well-known assets	[11]
Guilt-by-Association	Labels tokens linked to known scams	[7]
Liquidity Analysis	Detects rug pulls via liquidity withdrawal patterns	[8]
Malicious Contracts	Flags contracts enabling unilateral fund withdrawals	[8]
Fraud Pattern Matching	Identifies scams using past fraudulent token behaviors	[8]
Community Reports	Considers scam reports from users	[8]

Using this approach, Scam tokens were not only identified through direct reports but also inferred based on behavioral patterns and associations.

3.3 Feature Extraction and Comparative Analysis

To distinguish scam from Legitimate tokens, we extracted features across four categories: financial metrics, transaction-based features, temporal activity, and market dynamics. These features reveal behavioral differences in a decentralized exchange environment.

1. **Financial Metrics**: Scam tokens often have low total value locked (TVL), sudden volume spikes, and sharp price fluctuations, while Legitimate tokens show higher median trading volumes and fees, indicating sustained market participation. Extracted features include total supply, trading volume (ETH/USD), TVL (USD), fees (USD), and price volatility.
2. **Transaction-Based Features**: These capture on-chain activity, revealing how tokens interact with Uniswap liquidity pools. Scam tokens display short bursts of activity followed by inactivity, whereas Legitimate tokens engage consistently. Key features include transaction count (`txcount`), mint, burn, swap transaction counts, pool count, and swap sender count.

3. **Temporal Activity**: This evaluates a token's lifespan in trading and liquidity operations. Scam tokens are short-lived, often disappearing after rug pulls or manipulation events. Selected features include the duration from the first to the last transactions, minting, burning, and swapping.
4. **Market Dynamics**: Scam tokens often exhibit pump-and-dump cycles, characterized by a rapid price increase followed by a sharp decline, typically signaling manipulative trading. In contrast, Legitimate tokens show more stable and sustained engagement. Extracted features in this category include price manipulation indicators, address diversity (i.e., the number of unique interacting addresses), and swap behavior trends such as burstiness and irregular trading patterns.

3.4   Welch's t-Test for Scam Detection

To determine significant differences between scam and Legitimate tokens, we apply Welch's t-test to financial metrics, transaction patterns, temporal behaviors, and market dynamics. Welch's t-test is chosen over Student's t-test as it accounts for unequal variances and sample sizes, crucial for analyzing skewed financial data. To mitigate false positives, we apply the Bonferroni correction.

Null Hypothesis (H_0): No significant difference exists between scam and Legitimate tokens across financial, transactional, temporal, and market features.

Alternative Hypothesis (H_1): At least one feature differs significantly, indicating distinct behavioral patterns.

Welch's t-test results highlight key differentiating features. A low p-value ($<$ 0.05, Bonferroni-adjusted) confirms statistical significance, aiding fraud detection and improving classification models for identifying malicious tokens in decentralized exchanges.

4   Results

In this section, we present and analyze the obtained results.

4.1   Dataset and Data Collection

We collected a comprehensive dataset of tokens listed on Uniswap V3, as detailed in Sect. 3.1. Using Subquery tools, we extracted real-time and historical data on tokens, liquidity pools, and transactions, including mints, burns, and swaps, structuring it in a PostgreSQL database for efficient management and analysis. Covering all tokens listed up to June 30, 2024, the dataset captures detailed token, pool, and transaction data, along with daily and hourly trading activity (first 48 h) to analyze early-stage behaviors. The statistical properties are summarized in Table 2. To enhance reliability, we focused on well-characterized tokens classified as legitimate or scam, reducing noise and improving precision. The final dataset comprises 1028 Scam tokens and 814 Legitimate tokens, all from Uniswap V3.

Table 2. Statistical Properties of the Uniswap V3 and Collected Datasets

Property	Count	Features
Uniswap V3 Dataset		
Tokens	17,059	15
Pools	20,955	28
Mints	223,061	18
Burns	226,420	17
Swaps	938,435	17
Market daily	908,281	14
Market hourly	286,818	14
Collected Dataset Statistics		
CoinMarketCap	10,114	-
Etherscan	1,200	-
Scams	1,028	-

4.2 Financial Metrics Analysis

Financial metrics provide insights into liquidity, trading activity, and price movements. Key indicators include `total supply`, `volume`, `volume usd`, `fees usd`, `total value locked`, and `price`. Legitimate tokens typically exhibit higher medians and more varied distributions for `volumeusd` and `feesusd`, indicating market stability and investor confidence. In contrast, Scam tokens often cluster near zero, reflecting low activity and poor liquidity. The distribution of these metrics is visualized in Fig. 1a.

4.3 Transaction-Based Features Analysis

Transaction-based features analyze how tokens interact with liquidity pools. Indicators such as `tx count`, `pool count`, `mint count`, `burn count`, and `swap count` help in distinguishing Scam tokens from legitimate ones. Legitimate tokens generally have more pools, higher transaction counts, and sustained engagement over time. Scam tokens tend to have fewer pools, lower transaction counts, and shorter engagement durations, suggesting limited or manipulated activity. The distribution of these metrics is visualized in Fig. 1b.

4.4 Market Dynamics Analysis

Market dynamics focus on detecting fraudulent activities such as pump-and-dump schemes and centralized control of tokens. Key features include `pump dump`, `mint address`, `burn address`, and `swap address`. Legitimate tokens show decentralized engagement, while Scam tokens often display limited interaction diversity and sharp liquidity withdrawals. These insights are crucial for identifying fraudulent token behaviors and improving market security. These differences are highlighted in Fig. 1c.

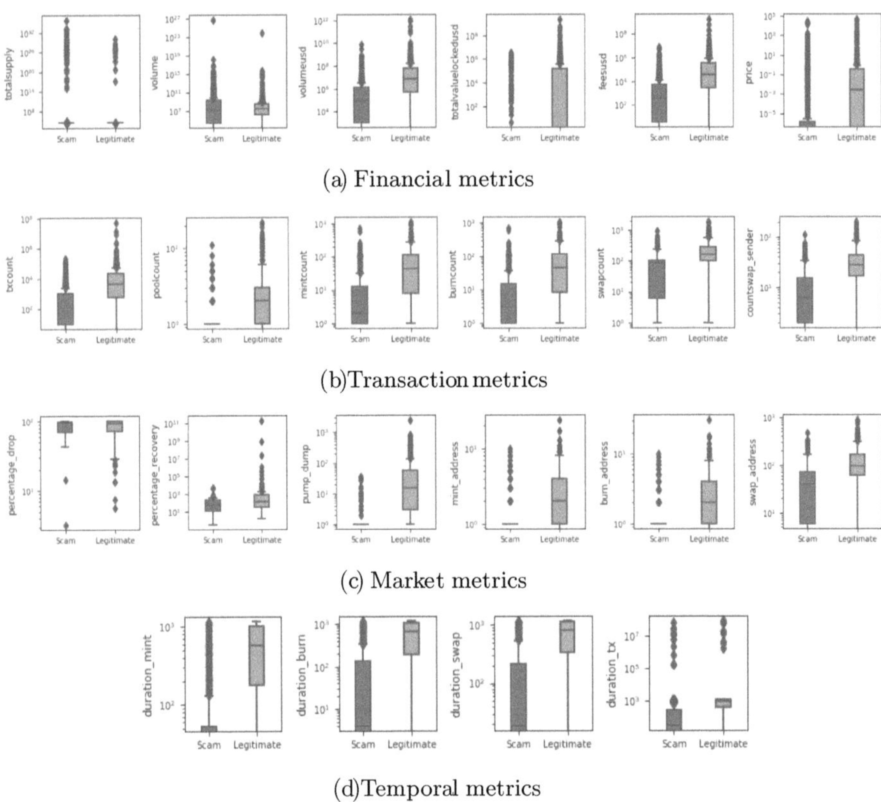

(a) Financial metrics

(b) Transaction metrics

(c) Market metrics

(d) Temporal metrics

Fig. 1. Feature distributions across different metric categories.

4.5 Temporal Activity Analysis

Temporal analysis examines transaction durations, including key events (`first mint`, `last burn`, `first swap`, `last swap`) and activity durations (`duration mint`, `duration burn`, `duration swap`, `duration tx`). Legitimate tokens generally sustain longer transaction durations, while Scam tokens exhibit shorter intervals, reinforcing transient and deceptive behavior (Fig. 1d).

Transaction timelines further highlight these patterns (Fig. 2). Reliable tokens maintain prolonged, steady activity, whereas scams display brief, irregular intervals, indicating manipulative strategies.

- **Minting:** Reliable tokens ensure sustained liquidity, whereas scams show brief, sporadic minting, hinting at manipulation.
- **Burning:** Reliable tokens maintain controlled burns, while scams concentrate burns before inactivity, suggesting liquidity withdrawal.
- **Swapping:** Reliable tokens engage in steady trading, while scams cluster swaps, often inflating volume artificially.

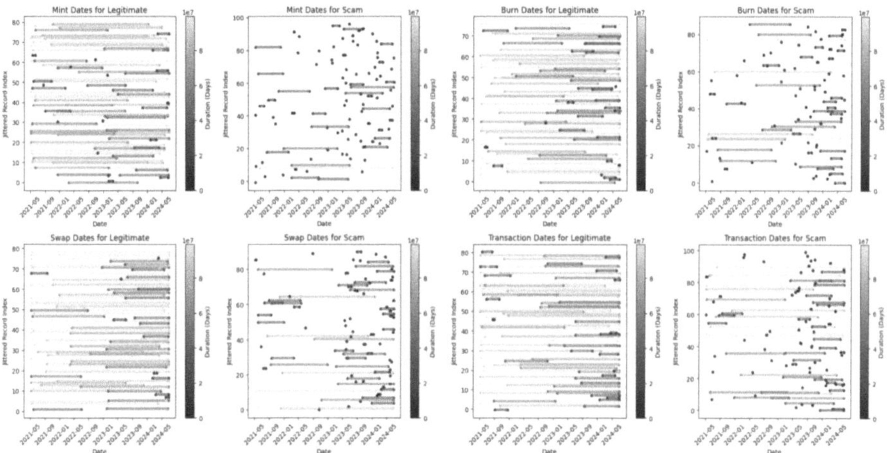

Fig. 2. Comparative Analysis of Transaction Duration for Legitimate vs. Scam tokens

– **Transaction Timeline:** Reliable tokens show continuous activity, while scams have isolated, erratic transactions.

These insights improve fraud detection by identifying erratic behavioral patterns, enhancing token reliability assessment and DeFi security.

4.6   Correlation Analysis Between Metrics

To analyze feature relationships in legitimate and Scam tokens, we computed Pearson correlation matrices (Figs. 3a and 3b). Positive correlations (red) indicate direct relationships, while negative correlations (blue) suggest inverse dependencies.

Legitimate tokens exhibit strong correlations among financial metrics (`total supply`, `volume`, `total value locked usd`) and transaction-based features (`tx count`, `swap count`), reflecting stable market behavior. In contrast, Scam tokens show weaker, erratic correlations, particularly in temporal activity (`duration swap-now`, `duration tx-now`), and stronger dependencies between fraud indicators (`percentage-drop`, `pump-dump`) and trading volume. These patterns highlight distinct behavioral differences between scams and Legitimate tokens.

4.7   T-Test Analysis

We applied Welch's t-test to evaluate the statistical differences between scam and Legitimate tokens across financial, transaction-based, temporal, and market dynamics features. This test assesses whether the mean values of these features differ significantly between the two groups.

Our findings indicate that transaction-based, temporal, and market behavior features show strong statistical differences, while financial metrics exhibit no significant variation. Specifically:

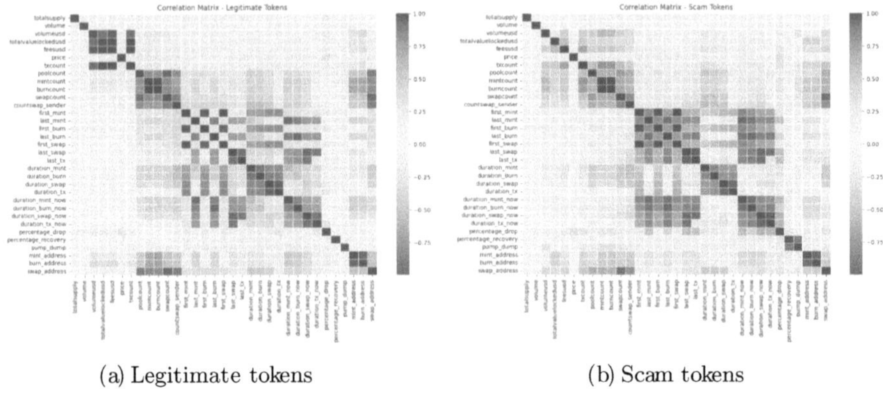

(a) Legitimate tokens

(b) Scam tokens

Fig. 3. Comparison of correlation matrices for legitimate and Scam tokens (Color figure online)

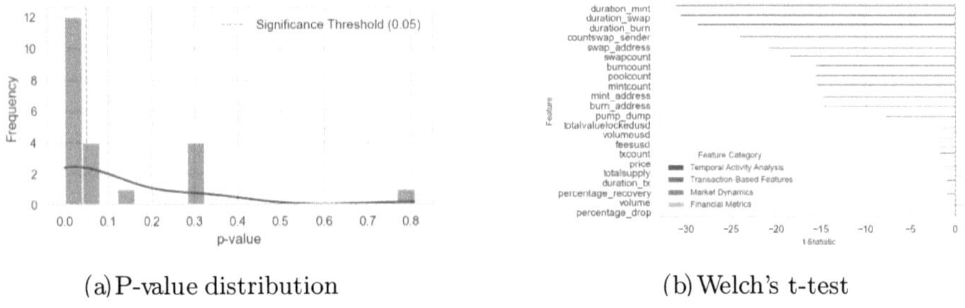

(a) P-value distribution

(b) Welch's t-test

Fig. 4. Welch's t-test analysis of scam vs. Legitimate tokens.

- **Transaction-Based Features:** Scam tokens operate in fewer liquidity pools and exhibit irregular transaction patterns, as reflected in significantly lower *pool count, mint count, burn count, and swap count.*
- **Temporal Activity:** Scam tokens have shorter *minting, burning, and swapping durations*, reinforcing their transient nature and association with rapid fraudulent activity.
- **Market Dynamics:** Scam tokens display higher *centralization in mint, burn, and swap addresses*, indicating control by a small number of entities. Additionally, *pump-and-dump activity* is significantly more prevalent.

Conversely, financial metrics such as *total supply, volume, and price* show no significant differences, suggesting that Scam tokens may attempt to mimic legitimate market behavior in terms of liquidity and valuation.

Table 3 presents the t-test results, summarizing the t-statistic, p-value, and significance for each feature.

To further assess the statistical significance of these features, we analyzed the p-value distribution from Welch's t-tests. Figure 4a illustrates the proportion of

Table 3. Welch's t-Test Results for Scam vs. Legitimate tokens

Financial Metrics

Feature	t-stat	p-value	Sig.
Total Supply	1.011	3.12×10^{-1}	No
Volume	0.998	3.18×10^{-1}	No
Volume USD	-1.818	6.95×10^{-2}	No
TVL USD	-1.828	6.79×10^{-2}	No
Fees USD	-1.805	7.15×10^{-2}	No
Price	-1.462	1.44×10^{-1}	No

Transaction-Based Features

Feature	t-stat	p-value	Sig.
TX Count	-1.773	7.65×10^{-2}	No
Pool Count	-15.623	3.41×10^{-49}	Yes
Mint Count	-15.484	1.21×10^{-48}	Yes
Burn Count	-15.646	1.66×10^{-49}	Yes
Swap Count	-18.469	9.54×10^{-66}	Yes
Swap Sender	-24.143	4.01×10^{-103}	Yes

Market Dynamics

Feature	t-stat	p-value	Sig.
Drop%	-0.244	8.08×10^{-1}	No
Recovery%	-1.004	3.17×10^{-1}	No
Pump-Dump	-7.766	6.11×10^{-14}	Yes
Mint Address	-14.859	2.04×10^{-45}	Yes
Burn Address	-14.755	6.37×10^{-45}	Yes
Swap Address	-20.882	1.44×10^{-81}	Yes

Temporal Activity Analysis

Feature	t-stat	p-value	Sig.
Duration Mint	-31.271	4.33×10^{-154}	Yes
Duration Burn	-28.751	1.67×10^{-138}	Yes
Duration Swap	-30.677	1.56×10^{-158}	Yes
Duration TX	-1.008	3.13×10^{-1}	No

features with p-values below 0.05, reinforcing that transaction-based, temporal, and market metrics are the most distinguishing characteristics.

Figure 4b presents the t-statistics of various features, highlighting key behavioral differences. Features with highly negative t-statistics, such as *duration mint*, *duration swap*, and *count swap sender*, suggest that Scam tokens tend to have significantly shorter lifespans and more centralized transactions. Conversely, financial metrics exhibit t-statistics close to zero, confirming their limited effectiveness in scam detection.

These findings emphasize the role of transactional and temporal features in scam token detection, supporting the hypothesis that Scam tokens differ significantly in liquidity and lifespan patterns.

5 Discussion

This study provides valuable insights into distinguishing Scam tokens from legitimate ones in DeFi. By analyzing transaction patterns, financial metrics, temporal activity, market dynamics, and feature correlations, we address key questions in DeFi fraud detection.

5.1 Key Features Differentiating Scam and Legitimate Tokens (RQ1)

Scam tokens exhibit distinct financial, transactional, and temporal characteristics. They have lower trading volumes (`volume usd`), transaction fees (`fees usd), and liquidity pool participation (`pool count`), reflecting weak market engagement. High price volatility, artificial liquidity inflations, and centralized control with limited address diversity further indicate manipulative behaviors. Additionally, Scam tokens have significantly shorter lifespans, often disappearing after rapid minting and burning cycles, a hallmark of exit scams.

5.2   Transaction and Market Behavior in Scam Detection (RQ2)

Transaction patterns and market behaviors provide critical signals for scam detection. Legitimate tokens show strong correlations between financial and transactional metrics (`volume usd`, `fees usd`, `tx count`), indicating stable market presence. In contrast, Scam tokens correlate with price manipulation indicators (`pump dump`, `percentage drop`, `percentage recovery`) and often operate within small, controlled networks, with transactions concentrated among a few wallets. These factors highlight fraudulent activity and support automated scam detection models.

5.3   Smart Contract Functionalities in Scam Identification (RQ3)

Smart contracts play a key role in identifying fraudulent tokens. Many scams use deceptive mechanisms such as restricting sales, imposing excessive transfer fees, or stealth minting to manipulate supply and liquidity. Rug-pull scams frequently integrate hidden functions that allow developers to drain liquidity, leaving investors with worthless tokens. Identifying these exploitative contract traits is crucial for early fraud detection and prevention.

These insights contribute to enhancing scam detection through statistical analysis, transaction monitoring, and smart contract auditing, strengthening security within DeFi ecosystems.

6   Conclusion

This study analyzed Scam and Legitimate tokens on Uniswap V3, revealing distinct behavioral patterns across financial, transactional, temporal, and market dynamics. Legitimate tokens tend to show higher trading volumes, sustained activity, and strong liquidity-trading correlations. In contrast, Scam tokens often exhibit irregular trading, inflated prices, centralized control, and manipulative behaviors such as pump-and-dump schemes.

Rather than employing a machine learning model, we conducted statistical analysis to evaluate the discriminative power of extracted features. This approach provides clearer insights into underlying behavioral differences and lays a foundation for future feature engineering in automated fraud detection systems.

Although limited to Uniswap V3 and historical data, our findings offer actionable indicators for assessing token legitimacy and improving DeFi security. Future work should expand to other platforms, incorporate smart contract audits, and prioritize real-time detection using streaming data, early behavioral signals, and predictive modeling to flag suspicious tokens as they emerge.

References

1. Agarwal, S., Siu, G., Ordekian, M., Hutchings, A., Mariconti, E., Vasek, M.: Short paper: DeFi deception—uncovering the prevalence of rugpulls in cryptocurrency projects (2023). https://doi.org/10.1007/978-3-031-47754-6_21
2. Bartoletti, M., Lande, S., Loddo, A., Pompianu, L., Serusi, S.: Cryptocurrency scams: analysis and perspectives. IEEE Access **9**, 148353–148373 (2021). https://doi.org/10.1109/access.2021.3123894
3. Chen, W., et al.: Sadponzi: detecting and characterizing ponzi schemes in ethereum smart contracts. Proc. ACM Measur. Anal. Comput. Syst. **5**(2), 1–30 (2021). https://doi.org/10.1145/3460093
4. Chen, Y., Fu, Z.: Phishing scam detection on ethereum via mining trading information. J. Cyber Secur. **4**(3), 189–200 (2022). https://doi.org/10.32604/jcs.2022.038401
5. Etherscan: Uniswap v3: Router | 0xe592427a0aece92de3edee1f18e0157c05861564 (address) (2023). https://etherscan.io
6. Infura: Infura documentation (2023). https://infura.io/docs
7. Mazorra, B., Adan, V., Daza, V.: Do not rug on me: leveraging machine learning techniques for automated scam detection. Mathematics **10**(6), 949 (2022). https://doi.org/10.3390/math10060949
8. Nguyen, M.H., Huynh, P.D., Dau, S.H., Li, X.: Rug-pull malicious token detection on blockchain using supervised learning with feature engineering. In: 2023 Australasian Computer Science Week (ACSW 2023), p. 10. ACM, Melbourne, VIC, Australia (2023). https://doi.org/10.1145/3579375.3579385
9. Sharma, T., Agarwal, R., Shukla, S.: Understanding rug pulls: an in-depth behavioral analysis of fraudulent NFT creators. ACM Trans. Web **18**(1), 1–39 (2023). https://doi.org/10.1145/3623376
10. Xia, P., et al.: Trade or trick? Detecting and characterizing scam tokens on uniswap decentralized exchange. arXiv preprint (2021). https://doi.org/10.48550/arxiv.2109.00229
11. Xia, P., et al.: Trade or trick? detecting and characterizing scam tokens on uniswap decentralized exchange. Proc. ACM Measur. Anal. Comput. Syst. **5**(3), 1–26 (2021)
12. Xiong, A., et al.: Ethereum phishing detection based on graph neural networks. IET Blockchain **4**(3), 226–234 (2023). https://doi.org/10.1049/blc2.12031
13. Zhang, D., Chen, J.: Blockchain phishing scam detection via multi-channel graph classification. arXiv preprint (2021). https://doi.org/10.48550/arxiv.2108.08456

An Overview of Termination in the Ethereum Blockchain

Luca Olivieri[1]([✉]) [iD], Luca Pasetto[2] [iD], Luca Negrini[1] [iD], and Pietro Ferrara[1] [iD]

[1] Ca' Foscari University of Venice, Venice, Italy
{luca.olivieri,luca.negrini,pietro.ferrara}@unive.it
[2] University of Luxembourg, Esch-sur-Alzette, Luxembourg
luca.pasetto@uni.lu

Abstract. The emergence of the Ethereum blockchain and the rise of Turing-complete smart contracts have led to the creation of new solutions for ensuring different kinds of termination. Indeed, non-termination of a smart-contract execution within the blockchain network may have critical consequences, ranging from slow performance to a complete denial of service in the worst scenarios. Furthermore, smart contracts lack a global access-control mechanism and may be executed indefinitely over time, even after they have exhausted their purposes. Therefore, this requires, in some cases, developing solutions implementing *"soft"* and *"hard"* terminations—such as pausable, interruptions, and *kill-switch* mechanisms—as well as providing *safe* termination guarantees. In addition, termination is even more crucial when we consider legal aspects of smart contracts, including compliance with laws and regulations, such as the smart contract requirements proposed by the *European Union Data Act*.

In this paper, we explore several mechanisms to ensure various kinds of termination in Ethereum, the most widely used blockchain. Moreover, we investigate similar mechanisms for traditional programming languages that can be applied to smart contracts in the blockchain context. The primary purpose of this study is to fill the gap caused by the lack of standards for these mechanisms and the emerging solutions typically proposed by practitioners.

Keywords: Smart contract · blockchain · distributed ledger technology · termination · kill switch · interruption · alt · pause · stop · revert · upgradable · undo · rollback · restore · design pattern · legal contracts · EU Data Act

1 Introduction

The blockchain is a distributed ledger that is shared among a decentralized peer-to-peer network, where decisions are made through a consensus mechanism and transactions containing data are recorded and grouped into immutable blocks within the ledger. In 2008, Bitcoin [5,46] introduced the first killer application implementing a protocol based on the blockchain to exchange economic assets

W. Knottenbelt et al. (Eds.): Blocktea 2025, LNICST 669, pp. 226–248, 2026.
https://doi.org/10.1007/978-3-032-12335-0_14

without third-party intermediaries and in a pseudo-anonymous way. Later, in 2014, the Ethereum [6,65] platform proposed a similar protocol but including the deployment and execution of Turing-complete smart contracts within the blockchain thanks to the Ethereum Virtual Machine (EVM), a decentralized computing virtualized environment for code execution. In particular, Ethereum smart contracts are stateful computer programs written in a Turing-complete low-level language called EVM bytecode. Compilers from high-level languages such as Solidity generate it. Then, bytecode instructions (aka EVM opcodes) are deployed through a transaction into the blockchain, where they are immutably stored. The code execution of smart contracts within the blockchain occurs through transactions that contain execution proposals and are subsequently carried out by the EVM. This new type of blockchain has contributed to the wide diffusion of decentralized applications (DApps), i.e., blockchain-based applications implemented through smart contracts, and has attracted the attention of enterprises, academia, and governments.

Termination of smart contracts is a complex and essential aspect of blockchain systems, carrying different meanings and implications depending on the context, whether technical or legal. From a computer-science perspective, termination refers to the property of a program or code execution halting after a finite number of steps. Ensuring termination is vital to prevent infinite or unbounded computations. On a blockchain, if a piece of code executed by a node fails to terminate, it can cause resource exhaustion, degrade node performance, and increase latency. When such behavior spreads across multiple nodes, it can lead to a denial-of-service (DoS) scenario, potentially disrupting the blockchain's operation or interfering with consensus protocols, which often depend on majority agreement among nodes. In addition, ensuring *safe* termination means that a program not only terminates but does not cause unexpected, malicious, or adverse behavior, such as leaving the system in an inconsistent, vulnerable, or corrupted state.

In a broader legal or operational context, termination can also refer to the intentional disabling or suspension of a smart contract's ability to process its functionalities, either temporarily or permanently. Since smart contracts on public, permissionless blockchains like Ethereum are typically immutable and always accessible, this form of termination plays a critical role in risk management. It enables developers or stakeholders to halt contract execution in response to unauthorized activity, fraudulent use, or the discovery of critical vulnerabilities. Such mechanisms are essential for protecting users, preserving trust, and preventing the continued exploitation of faulty or maliciously crafted contracts. Recently, these aspects have also been accentuated by the final text approval of the European Union Data Act [30] regulation, which mandates essential requirements for data-sharing agreements based on smart contracts, including a *"kill switch"* clause for safe termination and interruption:

to ensure that a mechanism exists to terminate the continued execution of transactions and that the smart contract includes internal functions which can reset or instruct the contract to stop or interrupt the operation, in particular, to avoid future accidental executions (art. 36, par. 1, EU Data Act [30])

According to EU Crypto Initiative [38], these behaviors can be classified into two different types of termination: *soft termination* and *hard termination*. Soft termination occurs when a program is temporarily paused/interrupted, i.e., an access-control mechanism remains active, and it may be triggered in order to restart the core program operations. Instead, hard termination occurs when the pausing becomes irreversible, and this de facto "terminates" the program because core operations can no longer be performed. Despite the several critical implications of termination, there is currently a lack of comprehensive information on the topic and how to effectively implement termination in blockchain systems. Specifically, there are no established standards to guide best practices, scientific literature on the topic is limited, and most solutions are provided by practitioners who tailor them to specific use cases without verification or broad applicability.

The goal of this paper is to offer a comprehensive understanding of termination mechanisms within the Ethereum ecosystem. In this regard, the paper clarifies the different types of termination, provides examples and code snippets of the current state-of-the-art and state-of-practice, and discusses verification solutions to formally ensure termination occurs correctly.

The key contributions of this paper are the following:

- a comprehensive summary of the different kinds of termination in Ethereum;
- an investigation of the possible solutions to ensure termination and interruptions of code executions;
- an investigation of rollback techniques to restore previous smart-contract states;
- an investigation of techniques to mitigate the consumption of gas and funds incurred for termination due to failures, errors, or unsafe states; and
- an investigation of verification techniques to formally guarantee the termination of smart-contract executions.

Paper Structure. Section 2 examines the mechanisms adopted by the blockchain to force program termination through the gas mechanism. Section 3 discusses soft and hard terminations, proposing solutions to achieve them at the smart-contract level, along with related pitfalls. Section 4 investigates safe-termination mechanisms. Section 5 discusses related work, and Sect. 6 concludes the paper.

2   Mechanisms for Program Termination

In the blockchain context, ensuring program termination of smart contracts is crucial to prevent issues like infinite code execution that could lead to resource exhaustion and denial of service. However, determining whether a non-trivial program can terminate for each input is undecidable (the well-known *halting problem* [60]).

The solutions to enforce program termination vary, ranging from time to instruction-count limits. However, among them, the most famous is the *gas mechanism* proposed by Ethereum [6,65]. When a smart contract is executed, it also sets an amount of gas that it *"burns"* during its execution. If the gas is depleted before the execution is completed, then the contract execution is halted, leading to a transaction failure, and any changes made during the execution are rolled back. Gas units are purchased with cryptocurrency to avoid the abuse of the network. In addition, a maximum limit for consumable gas is set by the Ethereum protocol to avoid large executions by wealthy users that could congest the network. Therefore, the gas system ensures that a program's execution ends regardless of the input. Furthermore, thanks to the rollback in case of failed transactions due to running out of gas, this termination can also be considered safe because it restores a previous state without corrupting or modifying the smart-contract state.

2.1 Pitfalls and Security Implications of Gas Mechanism

Although the gas mechanism is a powerful solution, it also introduces potential security risks, known as out-of-gas vulnerabilities [4,35], which in 2018 affected Ethereum contracts with a combined value of over \$2.8 billion [35]. In these cases, the attack surface includes the maximum gas limit per transaction and components that can be dynamically increased over time, such as collections and arrays. For instance, if a large number of elements are generated, an array might become so long that its manipulation exceeds the maximum gas (metering of code execution) allowed for Ethereum transactions, potentially leading to a denial-of-service of functionalities involving that data structure [25,26].

3   Mechanisms for Soft and Hard Termination

As reported in Sect. 1, the concepts of soft and hard terminations for smart contracts originate mainly from domains outside traditional computer science. Furthermore, Ethereum's gas mechanism is designed to enforce economic bounds and ensure program termination, and for this reason is not suitable for these purposes.

Soft termination may evoke the notion of a *"pause"* in traditional software systems, i.e., the act of suspending the rescheduling of a process or task and putting it into an idle state, eventually resuming it once an explicit or implicit event is triggered. However, this analogy cannot fully fit the behaviors of Ethereum smart contracts, because there is no way to truly pause a contract. The code of a smart contract becomes immutable (that is, it cannot be later modified) and it is publicly accessible and available after its deployment in the Ethereum blockchain. This means any Ethereum user can send a transaction request for the smart contract to execute, because there is no global block on contract access. Hence, in this specific context, we can define the notion of *"pause"* as a way implemented in the internal logic of the contract, preferably governed by some form of access control, for making the program exit (i.e., some code not being executed) under certain circumstances. In other words, this form of pause allows the contract to bypass or disable certain execution paths, thanks to the mutability of the contract's state, which can be used to control execution flow. Similarly, hard termination can be achieved by permanently setting the state to disable any contract's functionality. Additionally, hard termination can also be achieved by a specific native Ethereum instruction to delete contracts.

Below, we discuss the different ways to implement and achieve soft and hard terminations in Ethereum smart contracts. Additionally, we also focus on the security implications and concerns of different approaches.

3.1   Termination Through Conditional Statements

```
1   contract  Pausable {
2
3     address  public  adminAddress;
4
5     constructor() {
6       // store  the  address  of  the  contract  deployer
7       adminAddress =  msg.sender;
8     }
9
10    bool public  pause;
11
12
13    function  transfer( address  receiver,  uint256  amount) external  {
14
15      // pause  check
16      require (pause == false,   "The transfer  is  paused");
17
18      // logic  for  the  token  transfer
19      require (balances[ msg.sender] >= amount,  "Not enough tokens");
20      balances[ msg.sender] -= amount;
21      balances[receiver] += amount;
22    }
23
24    function  setPause( bool _pause) public  {
25      require (msg.sender == adminAddress,  "Invalid  sender");
26      pause = _pause;
27    }
28  }
```

Fig. 1. Pausable implementation based on a boolean flag, which temporarily inhibits the execution of the core token transfer instructions.

As suggested by Wohrer et al. [64], a simple way to implement soft termination into an Ethereum smart contract is by using conditional statements and Boolean guards acting like a switch button to inhibit parts of the code, effectively pausing it. Figure 1 shows a code snippet written in Solidity implementing a simple pausable mechanism. The global variable `pause` declared at line 10 manages the pause capabilities. It can be set by the `setPause` method, and it is exploited within the `transfer` method to drop the code execution, thus inhibiting the transfer of tokens. Specifically, if `pause` is `false`, the `require` statement at line 16 does not have any effect on the execution flow. Otherwise, if `pause` is `true`, the `require` statement at line 16 halts the execution returning the message `"The transfer function is paused"` in the transaction response. Note that the `require` statement at line 25 ensures that only the admin user can activate the pause.

Similarly, it is also possible to implement hard termination of the transfer functionality simply by implementing `pause` as a *write-once* variable. To do this, we simply need to implement the same contract in Fig. 1 by replacing the `setPause` method with the `terminate` method proposed in Fig. 2. In particular, in this way, it is no longer possible to change the value of `pause` arbitrarily since the `setPause` method is missing. When the contract is deployed for the first time, the value of `pause` will be the default one, i.e., `false`. The only way to change it is through `terminate`, which, after the first execution, leads to an irreversible contract state because it sets `pause` to `true`, and the value of `pause` cannot be changed anymore.

```
1 function terminate() public {
2
3    require(msg.sender == adminAddress, "Invalid sender");
4
5    require(pause == false, "Value has already been set");
6    pause = true;
7 }
```

Fig. 2. Write-once mechanism which forces the contract to be permanently paused.

For the sake of simplicity, Figs. 1 and 2 assume that the user who deploys the contract is the admin user. The assignment is implemented in the constructor at line 7, and the value of admin's address is stored in field `adminAddress` at line 3. Note that the visibility of `adminAddress` is `public`, meaning it can be read externally outside the contract (e.g., through web APIs such as web3.js or by other contracts), but can only be modified from inside the contract unless there is an explicit setter function provided. Then, in the case of Fig. 1, it can be set only by invoking the constructor. In state-of-the-art implementations, the most popular pausable contracts, such as those proposed by OpenZeppelin [53,55], implement more sophisticated access control layers to handle who and how a user or the contract can pause operations. Instead, our contract focuses on the termination problem, and more sophisticated access control mechanisms can be added without modifying the termination functionalities.

3.2   Termination Through Cross-Contract Invocations

In Ethereum, it is possible to execute cross-contract invocations between smart contracts already deployed in the blockchain. This means that a smart contract can invoke a function in another deployed smart contract through the `CALL`, `STATICCALL`, and `DELEGATECALL` opcodes. Cross-contract invocations can be exploited to communicate with other contracts for data exchange (e.g. values, assets, and cryptocurrencies), to build libraries of shared code that multiple contracts can access, to overcome limitations related to contract size [17], and to circumvent code immutability through proxy upgrade patterns [45] to include new features and patches in DApps. They can also implement soft and hard termination mechanisms. For instance, the proxy upgrade pattern [45] allows the building of a DApp based on multiple smart contracts where it is possible to upgrade the application logic while maintaining the same contract address. Then, in the settings of soft and hard terminations, it is possible to implement a "switch" to inhibit parts of code by changing the target of cross-contract invocations.

Considering the simplified version of a proxy upgrade pattern scenario in Fig. 3, where the code proxy contract with address `0xa...` is reported in Fig. 4 and the logic contracts with addresses `0xb...` and `0xc...` are reported in Fig. 5a and Fig. 5b, respectively. The proxy upgrade pattern can be viewed as a *template* [32] design pattern where a *proxy contract* acts as a *template* providing *hook functions* that perform cross-contract invocations to other deployed contracts containing the application logic. In Fig. 4, the hook function is `foo` at line 20, while the concrete functions that implement the application logic are the `foo` functions at lines 10 and 4 in Fig. 5a and Fig. 5b, respectively. In these cases, the cross-contract invocations are parametric. The parameter values are stored in the contract state, and they can typically be modified by user input. This proxy maintains the contract state, and it can be updated to point to a new implementation, allowing the underlying application logic to be upgraded without changing the proxy contract's address. In this way, it is possible to inhibit functionalities by redirecting cross-contract invocation to a no-op function of the same or another logic contract. In Fig. 4, the cross-contract invocations are executed by the `delegatecall` at line 25 which calls a hardcoded function defined as `"foo(uint256)"` from a contract that is specified by the address coming from in the global variable `logicContract`, which can be changed over the time by the admin user using the method `upgrade` at line 13. Note that, it is a delegate call because it allows the proxy to execute the logic contract's code in its own context. In the settings of Fig. 3, we have the concrete application logic at the address `0xb...`, i.e. the `foo` method of Fig. 5a that increase a counter, while the `foo` method of Fig. 5b at the address `0xc...` correspond to the no-op. Then, it is possible to turn on and off the application logic, switching the addresses `0xb...` and `0xc...` respectively by playing with the `upgrade` method of Fig. 4.

Compared with the termination through conditional statements only, the solution with cross-contract invocations is generally economically more expensive because it requires one to consume a greater amount of gas to deploy multiple smart contracts. Indeed, as currently reported by the fee schedule in the Yellow Paper of Ethereum [65, Appendix G], the cost paid for each contract-creating transaction is at least 32000 units of gas against the few dozen units consumed by each basic EVM opcode that makes up the conditional statements. Moreover, the implementation of upgradable contracts is error-prone due to non-trivial security implications such as correct management checks, restrictions, or versioning [42]. According to Huang et al. [37], it is also necessary to consider transparency mechanisms because a contract may be quietly upgraded, when the functionality of the contract has changed, without the user being aware that the contract has

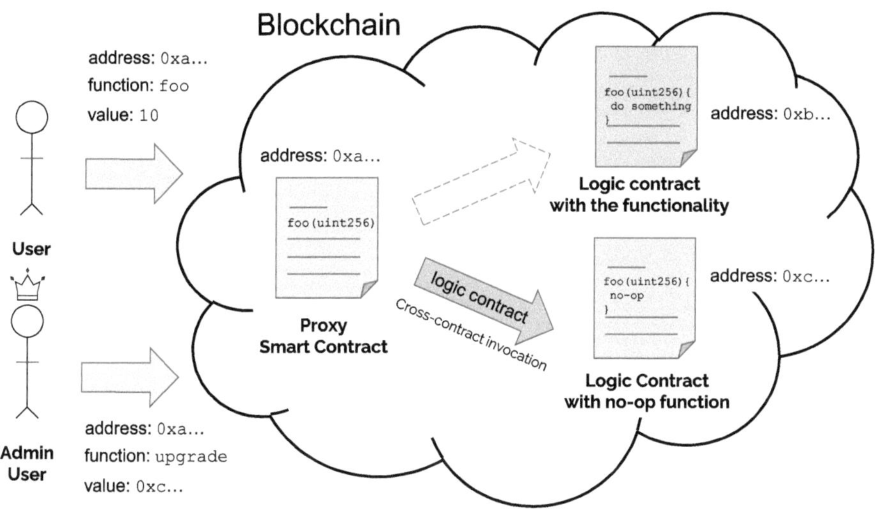

Fig. 3. Termination scenario with upgrade pattern

been upgraded, which may lead to financial losses for the users. Furthermore, in the worst-case scenario, if the contract runs a malicious update, there are greater risks of a user becoming a victim. However, termination through cross-contractual invocations allows the evolution of the DApp, with the possibility of implementing new switches over time, allowing for greater possibility of future extensions.

3.3 An Instruction for the Self-destruction

As mentioned previously, the code of smart contracts is immutable and cannot be changed. However, the EVM opcode SELFDESTRUCT (previously called SUICIDE [7]) with its execution allows one to *"delete"* a contract and send any contract funds to a specified address [6], ensuring hard termination.

In practice, during a smart contract deployment in Ethereum, the code is uniquely associated to a special type of account called *smart contract account*, which will be controlled by the code rather than private keys as it happens instead for user accounts. In this way, the code can be identified in the network thanks to the account address. The semantics of SELFDESTRUCT removes the code and its internal state (storage) from the contract address, leaving a blank account. Furthermore, if a transaction with an execution proposal is sent to an empty account, no code execution results, since there is no longer any code to execute there. However, note that the SELFDESTRUCT only affects the state of the account. Therefore, it does not remove the transactions' history of the contract prior to the SELFDESTRUCT execution since the blockchain itself is immutable. Furthermore, it is also important to note that SELFDESTRUCT must be present in the contract code and be executed to have its effect. Indeed, if the contract code

```
 1  contract Proxy {
 2
 3    address public adminAddress;
 4
 5    constructor() {
 6      // store the address of the contract deployer
 7      adminAddress = msg.sender;
 8    }
 9
10    address public logicContract;
11
12    // set of the logic contract after deployment
13    function upgrade(address _newlogicContract) public {
14      require(msg.sender == adminAddress, "Invalid sender");
15
16      logicContract = _newlogicContract;
17    }
18
19    // hook function
20    foo(uint256 _value) external payable {
21      address logic = logicContract;
22      require(logic != address(0), "Logic contract not set");
23
24      //  cross-contract invocation
25      (bool success, bytes memory data) = logic.delegatecall(abi.encodeWithSignature("foo(
             uint256)", _value));
26      require(success, "Delegatecall failed");
27    }
28  }
```

Fig. 4. Proxy contract based on external calls that allows the admin to change the target contract containing the application logic.

```
 1  contract Logic1 {
 2    address constant public proxyAddress = 0
          xa...;
 3
 4    uint256 public counter;
 5
 6    constructor() {
 7      counter = 0;
 8    }
 9
10    function foo(uint256 _value) public {
11      // drop execution if the sender is not
            the proxy
12      require(msg.sender == proxyAddress, "
            Invalid sender");
13      // application logic
14      counter = counter + _value;
15    }
16  }
```

```
 1  contract Logic2 {
 2    address constant public proxyAddress = 0
          xa...;
 3
 4    function foo(uint256 _value) public {
 5      // drop execution if the sender is not
            the proxy
 6      require(msg.sender == proxyAddress, "
            Invalid sender");
 7
 8      // no-op
 9      require(false, "This function is
            disabled")
10    }
11  }
```

(a) Enabled function   (b) Disabled function

Fig. 5. Target contracts which enable and disable the application logic of proxy contract.

does not have a SELFDESTRUCT opcode (not included by default) or this is not reachable during the execution, the smart contract cannot be deleted.

The SELFDESTRUCT instruction has always been highly debated in the Ethereum community due to security and trust concerns. According to Chen et al. [20], SELFDESTRUCT, this is a double-edged sword for developers. On the one hand, it enables contract owners to have the ability to reduce financial loss when emergency situations happen or when the code has ceased to serve its purposes. On the other hand, this function is also harmful because it opens attack vectors for malicious users. Moreover, according to Buterin [18], SELFDESTRUCT is the only EVM opcode that breaks important invariants: (i) it causes an unbounded number of state objects to be altered in a single block, (ii) it cause the code of a contract to change, and (iii) it can change other accounts' balances without their consent. For these reasons, in 2022, the EVM opcode SELFDESTRUCT has been proposed for the deprecation [29], and over time, several alternatives have been proposed for its replacement or to change its semantics (e.g., [8,9,12]).

3.4 Pitfalls and Security Implications of Hard Termination

According to Ezeozue [39], changes and actions to SELFDESTRUCT may reduces certain attack vectors, but significant risks persist. For instance, EIP-6780 [9] in 2023 modified SELFDESTRUCT semantics to only clear contract code and storage if executed in the same transaction as contract creation. However, this creates compatibility issues in terms of blockchain interoperability. Indeed, some major EVM-compatible blockchains (e.g. Binance Smart Chain (BSC) and certain Polygon chains) have not yet enforced EIP-6780 restrictions, leaving SELFDESTRUCT fully functional. Furthermore, this still leaves unresolved issues related to proxy, implementations [27,39], such as front-run initialization transactions to execute SELFDESTRUCT before proper setup is completed.

Regarding hard termination vulnerabilities, they are mainly caused by insufficient and/or improperly implemented access control, which can unexpectedly allow users to access hard termination functions [59]. According to Ressi et al. [59], those related to SELFDESTRUCT can be referred in different ways in literature. The terms *Guard Suicide* [19], *Unprotected Suicide* [36,44], *Suicidal Contract* [47], *Destroyable contracts* [15] or simply *Suicide* [31] identify cases where an attacker deliberately destroys smart contracts, and eventually performing an token transfers to specific smart contracts that were not supposed to receive them, i.e. those containing a SELFDESTRUCT. Specifically, according to Brent et al. [14], they can be classified in two different types: (i) *accessible self-destruct*s that can allow any user to trigger the contract destruction and (ii) *tainted self-destruct*s where an attacker can also control/become the receiver address of the funds returned by the contract destruction. Furthermore, the notion of *accessible self-destruct* can be also generalized in *accessible hard termination* including also all operations, not only SELFDESTRUCT operations, that leads to a permanent and irreverable paused state.

4 Safe Termination

The term *safe termination* can have different meanings depending on the context in which it is used, and can be understood both in terms of preventing errors or failures and as protection against malicious actors.

In the blockchain context, a contract can be terminated due to an unexpected error, data corruption, or malicious activity by an administrator. In these cases, termination should guarantee that the contract remains in a safe state where no data is corrupted and malicious activities are prevented. For example, this could involve denying transactions that could lead to an insecure termination, restoring a previously safe state, and, if possible, returning any spent funds or gas.

In general, this is often unfeasible because it would require rolling back transactions already stored immutably on the blockchain. In fact, data changes at the blockchain level are extremely rare events in permissionless blockchains, since the absence of a central entity requires that the majority of the blockchain network, often made up of several thousand peers, must agree. Furthermore, this could lead to a *hard fork* in which the blockchain is split in two, and some nodes choose the restored version while others keep the original one without rollback. For instance, a hard fork due to a transaction rollback in the Ethereum blockchain occurred because of the *DAO attack*, which affected the majority of peers and users, causing economic damage exceeding $50 million [57].

Although transactions are immutable within the blockchain and cannot be modified, it is still possible to modify the state of smart contracts and mitigate gas consumption in the event of errors or failures. In the rest of this section, we discuss revert and undo mechanisms that can partially address state-restore issues, as well as methods to mitigate gas consumption using specific Ethereum instructions at the smart-contract level.

4.1 Restore Through Snapshots

Although rolling back transactions already stored in the blockchain is almost impracticable, this does not exclude the possibility of acting on the smart contract state to totally or partially restore a previously safe state.

In current practice, some Ethereum smart contracts for tokens implement mechanisms to collect snapshots of their states over time [54]. According to Crosara et al. [25,26], the main purpose of snapshots is to provide an immutable view of the ledger that a client can query without the risk that it changes during the query, which would result in a race condition. Furthermore, they are useful for investigating the consequences of an attack, for creating forks of the token and for implementing mechanisms based on token balances such as weighted voting. In practice, these contracts implement a mapping between addresses and snapshot structures containing the values to be remembered.

Similarly, it is possible to design a solution that exploits a snapshot-like structure to collect a smart contract state and then restore its information over time. In traditional software programming, the *memento* [32,58] design pattern is particularly involved in scenarios where one needs to implement undo or rollback functionalities. It can be used to capture and store the current state of an object so that it can be restored later without breaking the encapsulation.

Considering the rollback scenario based on the memento pattern proposed in Fig. 6, the code of the originator contract is reported in Fig. 7, the code of the caretaker in Fig. 8, and the code of memento instances in Fig. 9.

The purpose of the originator contract is to handle application logic of the state that one wants to save and restore. For simplicity, in Fig. 7, the state is just an integer value collected in the variable `state` at line 7, and the application

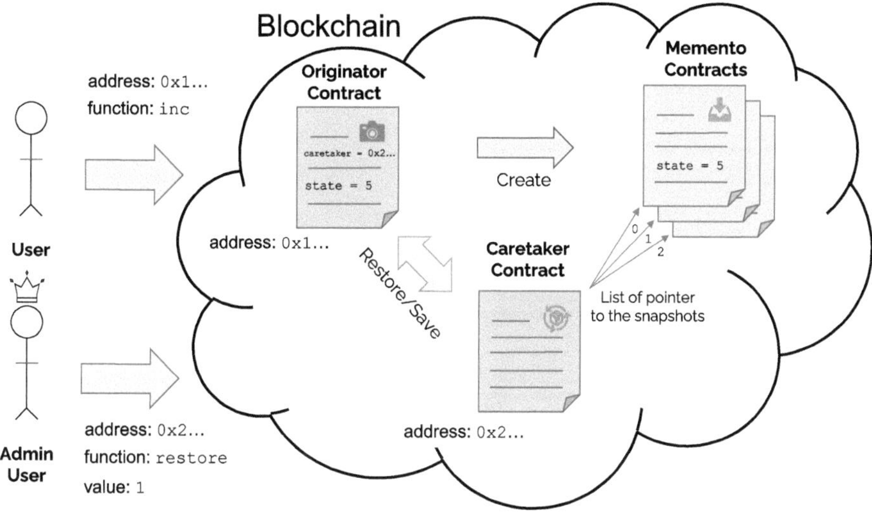

Fig. 6. Rollback scenario with memento pattern

logic is the increment function `inc` at lines 14–16 that can be called by to change the variable `state`. The operations of save and restore are instead delegated to the caretaker.

As reported in Fig. 8 at lines 11–14, an originator contract is created, and an admin is set when a caretaker contract is deployed. In this way, an admin can save the states of originator by calling the function `saveState`. This function at line 18 asks the originator to create a snapshot of its state (Fig. 7 at lines 18–21), i.e., a memento contract. It then collects the snapshot in an array at line 19. These collected states can be restored by the admin calling the function `restoreState` that at line 25 asks the originator to replace the current state value with that of the selected snapshot (Fig. 7 at lines 23–26).

As shown in Fig. 9, the memento contract collects just the values of the originator contract at lines 4–6 in variable `state`, and it provides the function `getState` at lines 8–10 to return to the saved state.

Alternatively, it is possible to manage snapshots not as contracts but as structures within the Caretaker contract using the `struct` data type and declaring custom fields. However, the advantage of contracts is that they can also embed code and utility functions.

The main limitation of this approach is that it is not possible to fully restore all the values of a contract state from a previous snapshot. When a transfer token or funds are involved, the moved tokens and funds cannot be forced back to their owners because transfers are irreversible actions without a fork.

```solidity
1  import "./Memento.sol"
2
3  contract Originator {
4
5    address public caretakerAddress;
6
7    uint256 public state;
8
9    constructor(address _caretakerAddress) {
10     caretakerAddress = _caretakerAddress;
11     state = 0;
12   }
13
14   function inc() public {
15     state = state + 1;
16   }
17
18   function createMemento() public view returns (Memento) {
19     require(msg.sender == caretakerAddress, "Invalid caretaker address");
20     return new Memento(state);
21   }
22
23   function restoreMemento(Memento memento) public {
24     require(msg.sender == caretakerAddress, "Invalid caretaker address");
25     state = memento.getState();
26   }
27 }
```

Fig. 7. Originator contract which contains the application state and allows the caretaker to save it or restore a previous one.

```solidity
1  import "./Originator.sol";
2  import "./Memento.sol";
3
4  contract Caretaker {
5
6    address public adminAddress;
7
8    Originator private originator;
9    Memento[] private mementos;
10
11   constructor() {
12     adminAddress = msg.sender;
13     originator = new Originator(address(this));
14   }
15
16   function saveState() public {
17     require(msg.sender == adminAddress, "Invalid admin address");
18     Memento memento = originator.createMemento();
19     mementos.push(memento);
20   }
21
22   function restoreState(uint256 index) public {
23     require(msg.sender == adminAddress, "Invalid admin address");
24     require(index < mementos.length, "Invalid index");
25     originator.restoreMemento(mementos[index]);
26   }
27 }
```

Fig. 8. Caretaker contract that orchestrates the originator contract and all its snapshots stored as memento contracts.

```solidity
1  contract Memento {
2    uint256 private state;
3
4    constructor(uint256 _state) {
5      state = _state;
6    }
7
8    function getState() public view returns (uint256) {
9      return state;
10   }
11 }
```

Fig. 9. Memento contract that captures a snapshot of the originator's state at a specific point in time.

4.2   Lock of Resources

While it is not possible to roll back a token transfer without performing a fork, techniques to mitigate such behavior can still be applied. Lockup mechanisms in smart contracts refer to features that restrict the movement or transfer of resources, assets, or tokens for a specified period. These mechanisms are commonly used in decentralized finance (DeFi) protocols and cross-chain token transfer protocols to enhance security, prevent premature selling, and align incentives among participants.

In the context of safe termination, a lockup mechanism can allow a fund transfer to be postponed and kept pending for a specified period. This provides an opportunity for an admin user to intervene in case of anomalies and return the resources to the original owner before contract termination.

Figure 10 implements a smart contract with temporized lockup logic to handle fund transfers in Solidity. The idea is that a sender user can submit transfer proposals to the contract calling the function `transferProposal` at lines 19–35, specifying the recipient and the duration of the time window in which the admin can roll back the transaction. Then, the time window is computed at line 23, and transaction information, including the value to transfer, is collected and locked in a map at lines 25–32. At this point, the recipient can claim the fund transfer from the sender if the time window has expired by calling the function `claimTransfer` at lines 37–47, which will retrieve the transfer information from the map containing the transfer proposals and will perform the transfer if the proposal has not been reversed previously during the time window.

The revert can be performed only by the admin user calling the function `revertTransfer` at lines 49–62 that gets the transfer proposal and send back the funds to the sender at line 61 if the time windows are still valid at line 58.

For simplicity, the code does not allow you to notify the administrator via code. However, it can be implemented by enriching the program with *events* and using the `emit` instruction to notify the admin client.

The main drawbacks of this solution are reduced decentralization, potential for abuse, and increased operational complexity. Additionally, the transfer would still be carried out if the administrators were not notified in time during the time window or were unable to carry out the operations.

4.3   Reverting Transactions and Fee Recovery

In Ethereum, transaction failures during smart-contract execution are mainly due to running out of gas or executing an invalid instruction. In these cases, a reversal of the operations occurs, and all the transaction gas is consumed. Once this happens, the gas is deducted from the sender's balance and is paid to network peers involved in processing the transactions. Moreover, the revert of EVM execution means that all changes, including log information, are lost and there is no way to convey a reason for aborting an EVM execution.

To avoid this scenario, it is possible to add to a smart contract the REVERT [13] opcode that provides a way to stop execution and revert state changes,

```solidity
1  contract TemporizedFundTransfer {
2
3    address public adminAddress;
4
5    struct Transfer {
6      address sender;    address recipient;
7      uint256 amount;    uint256 releaseTime;
8      bool claimed;      bool reverted;
9    }
10
11   uint256 transferId;
12   mapping(uint256 => Transfer) public transfers;
13
14   constructor() {
15     adminAddress = msg.sender;
16     transferId = 0;
17   }
18
19   function transferProposal(address recipient, uint256 duration) external payable {
20     require(msg.value > 0, "Must send some funds");
21     require(recipient != address(0), "Invalid recipient");
22
23     uint256 releaseTime = block.timestamp + duration;
24
25     transfers[transferId] = Transfer({
26       sender: msg.sender,
27       recipient: recipient,
28       amount: msg.value,
29       releaseTime: releaseTime,
30       claimed: false,
31       reverted: false
32     });
33
34     transferId = transferId + 1;
35   }
36
37   function claimTransfer(uint256 transferId) external {
38     Transfer storage transfer = transfers[transferId];
39
40     require(msg.sender == transfer.recipient, "Invalid recipient address");
41     require(block.timestamp >= transfer.releaseTime, "Transfer is still locked");
42     require(!transfer.reverted, "Transfer already reverted");
43
44     require(!transfer.claimed, "Transfer already claimed");
45     transfer.claimed = true;
46     payable(transfer.recipient).transfer(transfer.amount);
47   }
48
49   function revertTransfer(uint256 transferId) external {
50
51     // drop execution if the sender is not the admin
52     require(msg.sender == adminAddress, "Invalid sender");
53
54     Transfer storage transfer = transfers[transferId];
55
56     require(!transfer.claimed, "Transfer already claimed");
57     require(!transfer.reverted, "Transfer already reverted");
58     require(block.timestamp < transfer.releaseTime, "Lockup period has ended");
59
60     transfer.reverted = true;
61     payable(transfer.sender).transfer(transfer.amount);
62   }
63 }
```

Fig. 10. Temporized transfer lockup mechanism with a revert capability.

consuming only the gas used up to that point, preventing all the transaction gas from being consumed. Additionally, the REVERT instruction also provides a pointer to a memory section, which can be interpreted as an error code or message.

Note that transaction fees will still be burned, and no log information will be saved if the contract code does not include a REVERT instruction (which is not included by default), the instruction is unreachable during execution, or the cases mentioned above occur before REVERT is executed.

The REVERT instruction is typically used for error handling, assertions, and custom revert reasons based on the application logic.

Specifically, in Solidity, there are few high level instructions that include `REVERT` for these purposes. For instance, `require()` validates conditions and refunds unused gas upon failure. While, `revert()` provides a flexible alternative to `require()` encouraging the use of custom errors over string messages and improving gas efficiency and code clarity [63]. By contrast, `assert()` checks invariants but does not refund unused gas, because its compilation omits `REVERT`. For this reason, developers typically advise against overusing `assert()` to prevent excessive gas usage.

5   Related Work

Despite the importance of topics related to termination, the current literature in the blockchain context offers only limited results, with few studies providing detailed examinations. Compared to this article, related work tends to focus narrowly on specific aspects of termination, often presenting only partial overviews and omitting implementation details, or failing to address the associated issues and pitfalls comprehensively.

For the sake of readability, the literature can be divided into two strands: (i) verification methods for proving and ensuring termination and (ii) the implications of termination in the legal sphere.

5.1   Literature About Termination Verification

Ensuring smart contract termination is necessary in several contexts. However, the only way to prove that a program terminates is through formal methods.

In general, program termination analysis has benefited from many research advances, and several tools have emerged over the years [16,22,28,34,40]. According to Courant and Urban [23], traditional methods for proving program termination rely on the synthesis of a ranking function, a well-founded metric that strictly decreases during program execution, which quantifies the remaining distance to termination. Moreover, it is also possible to exploit abstract interpretation [56] to approximate the most precise ranking function [23,24,62].

On the other hand, for the blockchain context, Le et al. [41] describe a preliminary study for a static lazy approach to proving conditional termination and non-termination of a smart contract by determining the input conditions under which the contract terminates or not and whether the contract is qualified (i.e., eventually terminating) to run on the blockchain. In particular, they consider non-termination due to infinite loops in smart contracts of blockchain without a gas mechanism, such as Hyperledger Fabric. In contrast, they consider termination failure due to insufficient gas for blockchains with a gas mechanism, such as Ethereum. In this approach, when a smart contract is submitted to the blockchain, the system first automatically calculates logical formulas that determine the preconditions of the contract's inputs and the chain states under which its execution terminates or not. These formulas are verifiable and then recorded into the blockchain as metadata of the contract. Later, when a transaction invokes the contract, the system will check if the current blockchain state and the contract's input satisfy any recorded termination precondition. If this is the case, then the contract is executed. Otherwise, the transaction is aborted. However, according to Olivieri et al. [51,52], the assumption of applying the verification directly on the blockchain may have non-trivial impacts on the system, such as slowdowns or performance drops.

However, unlike traditional software, according to Genet et al. [33], reasoning about the gas mechanism in blockchain software could make program termination of contracts easier to prove, i.e., proving that *"it is impossible to construct an infinite loop that does not consume any gas"*. However, the official definition of gas usage makes the proof of this property complex due to the decidedly non-trivial semantics of contract calls and the fact that cash-in of call cost is delayed until after the return in both regular and exceptional cases. Furthermore, it is also necessary that the gas model and the implementation are sound, i.e., during the execution, the gas must be burned correctly to avoid a greater waste of resources or, in the worst case, non-termination issues. More technically, Genet et al. [33] propose a formal and general proof of termination of smart contracts based on a measure of EVM call stacks. They proved that no program can execute indefinitely without consuming gas in the EVM execution model by leveraging the Isabelle/HOL proof assistant to mechanize the proof. The model is sound by leveraging safe over-approximates of the EVM semantics with minimal assumptions on the concrete gas costs due to the fact that the costs has already changed several times during the life of the EVM.

There are also studies to verify the detection of unexpected terminations due to out-of-gas issues related to the gas limit caps in the smart contract execution. Grech et al. [35] present a tool to detect gas-focused vulnerabilities in Ethereum smart contracts automatically. It performs a static analysis that combines abstract-interpretation-based low-level analysis for decompilation of EVM bytecode, and declarative program analysis techniques for higher-level analysis. The main limitation of the tool is that it provides a *soundy* implementation, i.e., it does not provide a guarantee of identifying all gas vulnerabilities, nor that the reported vulnerability is a real bug. The reasons for this implementation choice are due to the need to scale to a very large number of contracts. A sound gas analyzer is instead proposed by Albert et al. [4]. It automatically infers upper bounds on the gas consumption for each public function of Ethereum smart contracts by relying on existing cost analysis techniques [2,3]. Then, the tool allows one to identify functions with a constant memory gas consumption and functions with a memory gas bound that is not constant, which could lead to out-of-gas vulnerabilities.

Soft and hard termination, on the other hand, require verifying the code of smart contracts. However, according to Olivieri et al. [51], this kind of verification is challenging due to cross-component interactions of multiple contracts and the need for formalization of the properties to be proven. Indeed, in DApps based on multiple contracts, it may require that multiple parts of code are inhibited and in specific orders to prevent the individual components from being used alone and improperly. Furthermore, the verification becomes much more complex if one also want to consider cross-chain and multi-chain scenarios [48].

Moreover, current smart contract verification tools are not primarily focused on ensuring soft and hard termination. However, this challenge might be addressed similarly to how the liquidity property is verified [11]. According to Bartoletti et al. [10], ensuring the liquidity property means that from *"every reachable state a user can execute a sequence of transactions to withdraw a given amount of crypto-assets"*, reducing the verification problem to symbolic model checking.

In a similar manner, soft and hard termination can be framed as ensuring that, from every reachable state, an admin user can execute a sequence of transactions to terminate the contract. This would reduce the verification problem to model checking [21].

Regarding the detection of vulnerabilities related to hard termination, several works [15,19,31,47] rely on static and dynamic symbolic execution techniques to assess the feasibility of execution paths that include SELFDESTRUCT operations without proper guarding conditions, commonly referred to as *accessible self-destruct* [14]. However, these approaches do not analyze the target address of the SELFDESTRUCT instruction, and thus cannot detect cases where the target is tainted by user input, known as *tainted self-destruct* [14]. While, Brent et al. [14] applies an information flow analysis tracking tainted data to detect both these types of issues. Ressi et al. [59] investigate detection via machine learning techniques, and Hu et al. [36] apply knowledge-graphs checks. Instead, Mavridou et al. [44] propose a framework for the secure generation of smart contracts using formal methods, ensuring that SELFDESTRUCT operations are properly guarded by construction.

5.2 Literature About Termination in the Legal Sphere

Regarding the intersection of computer science and legal aspects, Marino et al. [43] describe how to design alter and undo features based on legal definitions, such as *"Termination by Right"*, *"Rescission by Agreement"*, and *"Rescission by Court"*. They also develop prototypes of Ethereum smart contracts written in Solidity that implement and align with these definitions. In these prototypes, the termination mechanisms are implemented using conditional statements. Olivieri et al. [49,50] investigate the compliance of blockchain-based smart contracts with the European Union Data Act. Among various compliance issues, they also address termination problems, emphasizing a lack of standards beyond just the "kill switch" clause. However, they do not propose any code implementations in this context.

Instead, Seneviratne [61] provides a study fully focused on the "kill switch" mechanism reported in the European Union Data Act. Compared to our work, it does not go into deep details related to the Ethereum blockchain and does not include technical code details about the smart contracts. However, it provides a high-level overview regarding the mechanisms for smart contract termination across several major blockchains and distributed ledgers (e.g., Ethereum, Cardano, Hyperledger Fabric, IOTA, . . .). Abdrashitov et al. [1] discuss the normative regulation and practical aspects of smart contract termination in the investment context, specifically focusing on Russian legislation. They define smart contract termination as the legal termination of an agreement and highlight the inadequacy of Russian regulations, which currently makes it impossible to fully apply the smart contracts to the traditional civil law rules.

6   Conclusion

In this paper, we investigated the termination of smart contract execution on the Ethereum blockchain platform. In general, program termination is ensured by the gas mechanism, which halts smart-contract execution when the gas associated with a transaction runs out due to the execution of smart contract instructions.

Regarding soft and hard termination, solutions can be developed and implemented in the code of smart contracts. These solutions can include kill switches ranging from simple conditional statements to more complex designs inspired by traditional design patterns. However, such solutions generally require access-control policies to enable or disable the kill-switch functionality. This reliance on admin users necessitates trusting a third party, which may not serve users' interests or could arbitrarily block valid transfers. Moreover, this runs counter to the "permissionless" principle, which aims to eliminate third-party intermediaries. Additionally, verification techniques must be applied to ensure the correctness of access-control implementations and the proper activation of soft and hard termination mechanisms.

Finally, achieving safe termination in the blockchain context is challenging because rolling back approved transactions typically requires proposing a fork and securing the consensus of the majority of the blockchain network. However, some program behaviors can be mitigated at the code level to reduce costs in the event of failures, restore snapshots of specific smart-contract states, and add timed lock-up mechanisms for fund transfers.

Acknowledgements. Work partially supported by SERICS (PE00000014 - CUP H73C2200089001), iNEST (ECS00000043 – CUP H43C22000540006) projects funded by PNRR NextGeneration EU, and by the Luxembourg National Research Fund (FNR) (INTER/DFG/23/17415164/LODEX).

References

1. Abdrashitov, V.M., Davudov, D.A., Kolosov, N.F., Slezhenkov, V.V.: Risks of Smart Contracts Termination in the Investment Sphere, pp. 291–298. Springer, Cham (2024). https://doi.org/10.1007/978-3-031-51536-1_27
2. Albert, E., et al.: Object-sensitive cost analysis for concurrent objects. Softw. Test. Verif. Reliab. **25**(3), 218–271 (2015). https://doi.org/10.1002/stvr.1569

3. Albert, E., Arenas, P., Genaim, S., Puebla, G., Zanardini, D.: Cost analysis of object-oriented bytecode programs. Theor. Comput. Sci. **413**(1), 142–159 (2012). https://doi.org/10.1016/j.tcs.2011.07.009, quantitative Aspects of Programming Languages (QAPL 2010)
4. Albert, E., Correas, J., Gordillo, P., Román-Díez, G., Rubio, A.: Don't run on fumes–parametric gas bounds for smart contracts. J. Syst. Softw. **176**, 110923 (2021). https://doi.org/10.1016/j.jss.2021.110923
5. Antonopoulos, A.M.: Mastering Bitcoin: Programming the Open Blockchain, 2nd edn. O'Reilly, Sebastopol (2017)
6. Antonopoulos, A.M., Wood, G.: Mastering Ethereum: Building Smart Contracts and Dapps. O'Reilly, Sebastopol (2018)
7. Ballet, G., Buterin, V., Feist, D.: EIP-6: Renaming SUICIDE opcode (2015), ethereum Improvement Proposals, no. 6, November 2015. https://eips.ethereum.org/EIPS/eip-6. Accessed Aug 2024
8. Ballet, G., Buterin, V., Feist, D.: EIP-4758: Deactivate SELFDESTRUCT [DRAFT] (2022), ethereum Improvement Proposals, no. 4758, February 2022. https://eips.ethereum.org/EIPS/eip-4758. Accessed Aug 2024
9. Ballet, G., Buterin, V., Feist, D.: EIP-6780: SELFDESTRUCT only in same transaction (2022). https://eips.ethereum.org/EIPS/eip-6780. Accessed Aug 2024
10. Bartoletti, M., Ferrando, A., Lipparini, E., Malvone, V.: Solvent: liquidity verification of smart contracts. arXiv preprint arXiv:2404.17864 (2024)
11. Bartoletti, M., Zunino, R.: Verifying liquidity of bitcoin contracts. In: Nielson, F., Sands, D. (eds.) Principles of Security and Trust, pp. 222–247. Springer, Cham (2019)
12. Beregszaszi, A.: EIP-6046: Replace SELFDESTRUCT with DEACTIVATE [DRAFT] (2022), ethereum Improvement Proposals, no. 6046, November 2022. https://eips.ethereum.org/EIPS/eip-6046. Accessed Aug 2024
13. Beregszaszi, A., Mushegian, N.: EIP-140: REVERT instruction (2017), ethereum Improvement Proposals, no. 140, February 2017. https://eips.ethereum.org/EIPS/eip-140. Accessed Aug 2024
14. Brent, L., Grech, N., Lagouvardos, S., Scholz, B., Smaragdakis, Y.: Ethainter: a smart contract security analyzer for composite vulnerabilities. In: Proceedings of the 41st ACM SIGPLAN Conference on Programming Language Design and Implementation, PLDI 2020, pp. 454–469. Association for Computing Machinery, New York (2020). https://doi.org/10.1145/3385412.3385990
15. Brent, L., et al.: Vandal: a scalable security analysis framework for smart contracts. arXiv preprint arXiv:1809.03981 (2018)
16. Brockschmidt, M., Cook, B., Fuhs, C.: Better termination proving through cooperation. In: Sharygina, N., Veith, H. (eds.) Computer Aided Verification, pp. 413–429. Springer, Heidelberg (2013)
17. Buterin, V.: EIP-170: Contract code size limit (2016), ethereum Improvement Proposals, no. 170, November 2016. https://eips.ethereum.org/EIPS/eip-170. Accessed Aug 2024
18. Buterin, V.: Pragmatic destruction of SELFDESTRUCT (2024). https://hackmd.io/@vbuterin/selfdestruct#Pragmatic-destruction-of-SELFDESTRUCT. Accessed Aug 2024
19. Chang, J., Gao, B., Xiao, H., Sun, J., Cai, Y., Yang, Z.: sCompile: critical path identification and analysis for smart contracts. In: Ait-Ameur, Y., Qin, S. (eds.) ICFEM 2019. LNCS, vol. 11852, pp. 286–304. Springer, Cham (2019). https://doi.org/10.1007/978-3-030-32409-4_18

20. Chen, J., Xia, X., Lo, D., Grundy, J.: Why do smart contracts self-destruct? Investigating the selfdestruct function on ethereum. ACM Trans. Softw. Eng. Methodol. **31**(2) (2021). https://doi.org/10.1145/3488245
21. Clarke, E.M.: Model checking. In: Ramesh, S., Sivakumar, G. (eds.) FSTTCS 1997. LNCS, vol. 1346, pp. 54–56. Springer, Heidelberg (1997). https://doi.org/10.1007/BFb0058022
22. Cook, B., Podelski, A., Rybalchenko, A.: Terminator: beyond safety. In: Ball, T., Jones, R.B. (eds.) Computer Aided Verification, pp. 415–418. Springer, Heidelberg (2006)
23. Courant, N., Urban, C.: Precise widening operators for proving termination by abstract interpretation. In: Legay, A., Margaria, T. (eds.) Tools and Algorithms for the Construction and Analysis of Systems, pp. 136–152. Springer, Heidelberg (2017)
24. Cousot, P., Cousot, R.: An abstract interpretation framework for termination. In: Proceedings of the 39th Annual ACM SIGPLAN-SIGACT Symposium on Principles of Programming Languages, POPL 2012, pp. 245–258. Association for Computing Machinery, New York (2012). https://doi.org/10.1145/2103656.2103687
25. Crosara, M., Olivieri, L., Spoto, F., Tagliaferro, F.: Re-engineering ERC-20 smart contracts with efficient snapshots for the java virtual machine. In: 2021 Third International Conference on Blockchain Computing and Applications (BCCA), pp. 187–194 (2021). https://doi.org/10.1109/BCCA53669.2021.9657047
26. Crosara, M., Olivieri, L., Spoto, F., Tagliaferro, F.: Fungible and non-fungible tokens with snapshots in java. Cluster Comput. **26**(5), 2701–2718 (2023). https://doi.org/10.1007/s10586-022-03756-3
27. David, E.C.: The Hidden Dangers of Using Selfdestruct in Upgradable Smart Contracts (2025). https://coinsbench.com/the-hidden-dangers-of-using-selfdestruct-in-upgradable-smart-contracts--832466bf6b95. Accessed July 2025
28. D'Silva, V., Urban, C.: Conflict-driven conditional termination. In: Kroening, D., Păsăreanu, C.S. (eds.) Computer Aided Verification, pp. 271–286. Springer, Cham (2015)
29. Entriken, W.: EIP-6049: Deprecate selfdestruct (2022), ethereum Improvement Proposals, no. 6049, November 2022. https://eips.ethereum.org/EIPS/eip-6046. Accessed Aug 2024
30. European Parliament and the Council: Regulation (EU) 2023/2854 of the European Parliament and of the Council of 13 December 2023 on harmonised rules on fair access to and use of data and amending Regulation (EU) 2017/2394 and Directive (EU) 2020/1828 (Data Act) (2023), document 32023R2854. PE/49/2023/REV/1 OJ L, 2023/2854, 22.12.2023, ELI: http://data.europa.eu/eli/reg/2023/2854/oj
31. Fu, M., Wu, L., Hong, Z., Zhu, F., Sun, H., Feng, W.: A critical-path-coverage-based vulnerability detection method for smart contracts. IEEE Access **7**, 147327–147344 (2019). https://doi.org/10.1109/ACCESS.2019.2947146
32. Gamma, E., Helm, R., Johnson, R., Vlissides, J.: Design Patterns: Elements of Reusable Object-Oriented Software. Addison-Wesley, United States (1994)
33. Genet., T., Jensen., T., Sauvage., J.: Termination of ethereum's smart contracts. In: Proceedings of the 17th International Joint Conference on e-Business and Telecommunications - SECRYPT, pp. 39–51. INSTICC, SciTePress (2020). https://doi.org/10.5220/0009564100390051
34. Giesl, J., Schneider-Kamp, P., Thiemann, R.: Aprove 1.2: automatic termination proofs in the dependency pair framework. In: Furbach, U., Shankar, N. (eds.) Automated Reasoning, pp. 281–286. Springer, Heidelberg (2006)

35. Grech, N., Kong, M., Jurisevic, A., Brent, L., Scholz, B., Smaragdakis, Y.: Madmax: surviving out-of-gas conditions in ethereum smart contracts. Proc. ACM Program. Lang. **2**(OOPSLA) (2018). https://doi.org/10.1145/3276486
36. Hu, T., Li, B., Pan, Z., Qian, C.: Detect defects of solidity smart contract based on the knowledge graph. IEEE Trans. Reliab. **73**(1), 186–202 (2024). https://doi.org/10.1109/TR.2023.3233999
37. Huang, Y., et al.: The sword of damocles: upgradeable smart contract in ethereum. In: Proceedings of the 32nd IEEE/ACM International Conference on Program Comprehension, ICPC 2024, pp. 333–345. Association for Computing Machinery, New York (2024). https://doi.org/10.1145/3643916.3644426
38. EU Crypto Initiative: Europe's Data Act: Implications for the Future of Innovation in Europe (2024). https://eu.ci/the-data-act-implications-for-the-future-of-smart-contracts-in-europe-annex/. Accessed Aug 2024
39. Kwesili, O.: The Incompatibility of Self-Destruct Mechanisms in Upgradeable Smart Contract Architectures (2025). https://coinsbench.com/the-incompatibility-of-self-destruct-mechanisms-in-upgradeable-smart--contract-architectures-979f846f9265. Accessed July 2025
40. Le, T.C., Qin, S., Chin, W.N.: Termination and non-termination specification inference. In: Proceedings of the 36th ACM SIGPLAN Conference on Programming Language Design and Implementation, PLDI 2015, pp. 489–498. Association for Computing Machinery, New York (2015). https://doi.org/10.1145/2737924.2737993
41. Le, T.C., Xu, L., Chen, L., Shi, W.: Proving conditional termination for smart contracts. In: Proceedings of the 2nd ACM Workshop on Blockchains, Cryptocurrencies, and Contracts, BCC 2018, pp. 57–59. Association for Computing Machinery, New York (2018). https://doi.org/10.1145/3205230.3205239
42. Li, X., Yang, J., Chen, J., Tang, Y., Gao, X.: Characterizing ethereum upgradable smart contracts and their security implications. In: Proceedings of the ACM on Web Conference 2024, WWW 2024, pp. 1847–1858. Association for Computing Machinery, New York (2024). https://doi.org/10.1145/3589334.3645640
43. Marino, B., Juels, A.: Setting standards for altering and undoing smart contracts. In: Alferes, J.J., Bertossi, L., Governatori, G., Fodor, P., Roman, D. (eds.) Rule Technologies. Research, Tools, and Applications, pp. 151–166. Springer, Cham (2016)
44. Mavridou, A., Laszka, A., Stachtiari, E., Dubey, A.: VeriSolid: correct-by-design smart contracts for ethereum. In: Goldberg, I., Moore, T. (eds.) FC 2019. LNCS, vol. 11598, pp. 446–465. Springer, Cham (2019). https://doi.org/10.1007/978-3-030-32101-7_27
45. Mudge, N.: ERC-2535: Diamonds, multi-facet proxy (2020), ethereum Improvement Proposals, no. 2535, February 2020. https://eips.ethereum.org/EIPS/eip-2535. Accessed Aug 2024
46. Nakamoto, S.: Bitcoin: A Peer-to-Peer Electronic Cash System (2008). https://bitcoin.org/bitcoin.pdf. Accessed June 2023
47. Nikolić, I., Kolluri, A., Sergey, I., Saxena, P., Hobor, A.: Finding the greedy, prodigal, and suicidal contracts at scale. In: Proceedings of the 34th Annual Computer Security Applications Conference, ACSAC 2018, pp. 653–663. Association for Computing Machinery, New York (2018). https://doi.org/10.1145/3274694.3274743
48. Olivieri, L., Mukherjee, A., Chaki, N., Cortesi, A.: Cross-chain Smart Contracts and dApps Verification by Static Analysis: Limits and Challenges, vol. 3962 (2025). https://ceur-ws.org/Vol-3962/paper16.pdf

49. Olivieri, L., Pasetto, L.: Towards compliance of smart contracts with the european union data act. In: CEUR Workshop Proceedings, vol. 3629, pp. 61–66 (2024). https://ceur-ws.org/Vol-3629
50. Olivieri, L., Pasetto, L., Negrini, L., Ferrara, P.: European union data act and blockchain technology: challenges and new directions. In: CEUR Workshop Proceedings, vol. 3791. CEUR-WS (2024). https://ceur-ws.org/Vol-3791/paper30.pdf
51. Olivieri, L., Spoto, F.: Software verification challenges in the blockchain ecosystem. Int. J. Softw. Tools Technol. Transfer (2024). https://doi.org/10.1007/s10009-024-00758-x
52. Olivieri, L., Spoto, F., Tagliaferro, F.: On-chain smart contract verification over tendermint. In: Bernhard, M., et al. (eds.) FC 2021. LNCS, vol. 12676, pp. 333–347. Springer, Heidelberg (2021). https://doi.org/10.1007/978-3-662-63958-0_28
53. OpenZeppelin: Erc-20 pausable (2024). https://docs.openzeppelin.com/contracts/4.x/api/token/erc20#ERC20Pausable. Accessed Aug 2024
54. OpenZeppelin: Erc-20 snapshot (2024). https://docs.openzeppelin.com/contracts/4.x/api/token/erc20#ERC20Snapshot. Accessed Aug 2024
55. OpenZeppelin: Erc-721 pausable (2024). https://docs.openzeppelin.com/contracts/4.x/api/token/erc721#ERC721Pausable. Accessed Aug 2024
56. Patrick, C.: Principles of Abstract Interpretation. MIT Press Academic, Cambridge (2021)
57. Popper, N.: A Hacking of More Than $50 Million Dashes Hopes in the World of Virtual Currency. The New York Times (2016)
58. Rajasekar, V., Sondhi, S., Saad, S., Mohammed, S.: Emerging design patterns for blockchain applications. In: ICSOFT, pp. 242–249 (2020)
59. Ressi, D., Spanò, A., Benetollo, L., Piazza, C., Bugliesi, M., Rossi, S.: Vulnerability detection in ethereum smart contracts via machine learning: a qualitative analysis. arXiv preprint arXiv:2407.18639 (2024)
60. Rice, H.G.: Classes of recursively enumerable sets and their decision problems. Trans. Am. Math. Soc. **74**, 358–366 (1953). https://doi.org/10.1090/s0002-9947-1953-0053041-6
61. Seneviratne, O.: The feasibility of a smart contract "kill switch". In: 2024 6th International Conference on Blockchain Computing and Applications (BCCA), pp. 473–480 (2024). https://doi.org/10.1109/BCCA62388.2024.10844477
62. Urban, C., Miné, A.: A decision tree abstract domain for proving conditional termination. In: Müller-Olm, M., Seidl, H. (eds.) Static Analysis, pp. 302–318. Springer, Cham (2014)
63. Wasiu, A.: Mastering Solidity: require and Custom Errors in Ethereum Contracts (2023). https://medium.com/coinmonks/mastering-solidity-require-and-custom-errors-in-ethereum-contracts--b491565f1592. Accessed May 2025
64. Wohrer, M., Zdun, U.: Smart contracts: security patterns in the ethereum ecosystem and solidity. In: 2018 International Workshop on Blockchain Oriented Software Engineering (IWBOSE), pp. 2–8 (2018). https://doi.org/10.1109/IWBOSE.2018.8327565
65. Wood, G., et al.: Ethereum: a secure decentralised generalised transaction ledger. Ethereum Project Yellow Paper **151**(2014), 1–32 (2014)

Author Index

If you have any concerns about our products,
you can contact us on
ProductSafety@springernature.com

In case Publisher is established outside the EU,
the EU authorized representative is:
Springer Nature Customer Service Center GmbH
Europaplatz 3, 69115 Heidelberg, Germany

Printed by Libri Plureos GmbH
in Hamburg, Germany